INNOVATION IN PRIMARY EDUCATION

*A study of recent developments in
primary education in England and the U.S.A.*

INNOVATION IN PRIMARY EDUCATION

A study of recent developments in
primary education in England and the U.S.A.

G. W. Bassett
*Professor of Education, University of
Queensland, Australia*

WILEY - INTERSCIENCE
a division of John Wiley & Sons Ltd
London . New York . Sydney . Toronto

372.241
B 319

Library of Congress catalog card No. 78-102687
SBN 471 05554 9

Reproduced photolitho in Great Britain by
J. W. Arrowsmith Ltd., Bristol 3

PREFACE

A spirit of change and innovation pervades educational activities in many sections of the world. This spirit is in part dissatisfaction: dissatisfaction with schools geared to the needs of only some of the pupils enrolled; dissatisfaction with the narrow focus of many schools; dissatisfaction with the irrelevance of much of the curriculum. But it is the positive side of this spirit of change that has made the past dozen years so interesting from an educational point of view. A few thoughtful innovators and thousands of creative teachers, often far apart geographically, seem almost to be joined in a common quest for schooling that is meaningful and satisfying to each individual. And a trans-Atlantic, trans-Pacific dialogue is emerging.

In his new book, Professor Bassett contributes significantly to this dialogue. He focuses on both the substance and the context of recent developments in primary (or elementary) education in England and the United States of America. Although he clearly addresses an Australian audience, his observations and analyses are relevant to a much broader one. They are particularly salient for educators and lay citizens in England and the United States. Often it is the perceptive visitor to our shores who turns the most revealing light on our fads and fancies, excesses and liabilities, assets and accomplishments.

Out of the many features of this book which might be discussed here, I have chosen four. The first is the comprehensiveness of the descriptive analyses. Professor Bassett moves comfortably from theoretical and conceptual roots to classroom practices, from empirical research to implications for teaching, and from the purity of models to the accommodations of actual school practice. All of this is done simply, deceptively simply. No doubt some readers will be quite unaware of the garbage which he has dropped quietly into the wastebasket in order to get to the lean meat of educational innovations in the two countries he describes. The result is perhaps the most comprehensive account currently available of *both* the newer practices which are changing the observable character of primary schooling in these two countries *and* the ideas to which these practices owe at least some allegiance.

A second notable feature of the book, alluded to above, is the extent to which this observable character of innovation is placed in larger perspective. Two kinds of perspective are dealt with consistently. One is the relationship of practice to theory and research; the other is the relationship of one practice to others. Thus, for example, in discussing the nongraded school, Professor Bassett describes not only the practice of nongrading and the concepts underlying it but also the features which differentiate nongraded from graded schools.

v

Consequently, we do not see innovations in isolation from everything except their own conceptual baggage. We see the possible relationships among new practices and ideas in curriculum, school organization, and instruction. In view of the fact that no single innovation is powerful enough to effect the needed changes in education, the provision of this twofold perspective is exceedingly important.

The third feature worthy of note is perhaps the most unusual in a volume of this kind. Few visitors to another land have the temerity to analyse contextual forces affecting education. It is much safer to stick with description. Those who stray most confidently beyond the borders of description usually depart before the comfort of initial certainty is upset by further observation. I cannot speak for the English setting, but I am enormously impressed with Professor Bassett's analysis of factors and agents in the innovative process here in the United States. He provided me with a third eye, so to speak, for viewing daily experience. I have a hunch as to why he, in contrast to many who have tried and failed, was so successful in this regard. But, before developing this hunch a little, let me turn to the fourth feature I have chosen to discuss.

For want of a better term, I call this 'balance', but the word is quite inadequate to convey what I have in mind. We are prone in education, as in other fields, to dismiss quickly what does not resolve a great many issues or, by contrast, to claim too much, depending upon our predilections. Professor Bassett, like the rest of us, has his biases and they come through from time to time – often in the form of wry humour. In the large, however, he holds them in abeyance, seeking instead to weigh the innovations he discusses against the counterweight of research findings, logic, historical perspective, and the demands of teaching and learning. The satisfying result is a balanced picture of dedicated effort to improve primary education in England and the United States. Through the whole runs optimism, tempered by realistic understanding of and respect for the difficulties involved in effecting broad-scale educational reform.

The book presents a bonus which should be appreciated particularly by students of education seeking to identify with the current educational ferment. It draws upon an enormous list of seminal books and reports in both countries, some of which are not readily accessible, especially in other countries. Few references of significance are omitted. The most important ones recur.

That all of this comes off so well cannot be explained solely by the fact that the author is an able, experienced educator. There are at least three additional explanations. First, he has visited these shores before and, through reading, has kept abreast of developments long enough to maintain a sense of continuity. Second, he stayed long enough to check and recheck his impressions, to intensify his reading, and to compare what he read with what he saw. Third – and perhaps most important – he was no passive observer; he was involved. In the United States, for example, he sat in with teachers and principals, tested his impressions with them, and even made his services available to them as consultant, speaker, and discussant.

One aspect of this involvement should be taken very seriously by others who would seek to come to intimate terms with another educational system. If possible, one should become virtually a part of some on-going educational enterprise characterized by dialogue, decisions, and action in the areas of one's interest. For five months, Professor Bassett was scholar-in-residence of the Research and Development Division, Institute for Development of Educational Activities, Inc. (supported by the Charles F. Kettering Foundation). In this capacity, he attended our staff meetings, weighed our issues, presented his views, participated in our field programme, shared our successes and failures, favoured us with his humour and wisdom. He was one of us. I am sure that this had much to do with the sharp authenticity of the views that follow.

It was a pleasure to have Dr. and Mrs. Bassett with us. It is a privilege, now, to write this foreword to his fine volume — and to forward, I hope, the trans-Pacific, trans-Atlantic dialogue about innovation in primary education.

John I. Goodland,
Director, Research and Development Division,
I/D/E/A, Inc., and Dean, Graduate School of Education,
University of California, Los Angeles.

CONTENTS

Contents

PART III THE PROCESS OF INNOVATION

Introduction

The major changes that have occurred in education in most western countries in the middle decades of the 20th century have been concerned with the secondary and higher levels. The 19th century saw the establishment of universal elementary education; the 20th century is seeing the growing acceptance of the idea of universal secondary education, and the extension of opportunities for university and other forms of higher education.

This growth has been beset with many problems. The social and political changes which have brought about this increased demand for education have outpaced the knowledge and imagination of educators to meet it. Problems of vocational specialization, of general education, of curriculum development to cope with new knowledge and new objectives, and of examinations and selection have been insistent and perplexing.

One result of this ferment in secondary education has been to direct new attention to the stage preceding it, and it is likely that innovation in primary education will also become a prominent feature of the educational revolution of the 20th century.

It has become increasingly obvious that success at the secondary level is dependent on the child's earlier schooling. Bloom, from his research,[1] has stressed the importance of the introductory period. After surveying the data on the development of general learning as based on overall achievement indices (achievement test batteries, reading comprehension, and teachers' marks) or based on general vocabulary development, he concludes as follows:

'We are inclined to believe that this is the most important growing period for academic achievement, and that all subsequent learning in the school is affected, and in large part determined, by what the child has learned by the age of nine.'

This is particularly true of the objectives that derive from the challenge of new scientific knowledge, and the emphasis on mastery of this knowledge in a way that encourages productive thinking rather than rote recall. It is also true of the emphasis on favourable attitudes towards learning, and the acceptance of personal responsibility for pursuing it. Attitudes to school are firmly, if not irrevocably, formed during the primary years.

It is obvious also that the progress of children who are gifted or culturally deprived, or otherwise exceptional, will depend greatly on their early identification, and on appropriate early provision for them.

Traditionally the primary school has placed most emphasis on establishing foundation habits in the simple skills of learning, and on giving the pupil a store of basic factual knowledge; and it has often pursued these goals in a fairly rigid, if kindly, disciplinary setting.

Modernizing the primary school is likely to involve many changes. Improving its efficiency by making the teaching more suited to the needs of each of the pupils, and to their speed of learning, could affect it at virtually every point — its organization, curriculum, teaching methods, techniques of assessment and reporting, building and equipment, and parental and community relations with the school.

The task of curriculum development will require the effective relating of the best available knowledge about children's learning, the nature of the subject, and the use of materials to assist learning; and, most difficult of all, it will require an imaginative break with familiar ways of thinking about the primary school curriculum.

There will need to be acceptance of new media, of old media made more useful by technological changes which improve their efficiency, reduce their size, and lower their cost, and of improved methods of teacher education with adequate provision (and incentive) for continuing professional development.

All these measures will have to be taken in ways that are appropriate to the country concerned. It has often been pointed out that a social institution is a product of unique cultural and historical influences, and that because of this it cannot be transplanted successfully to a different setting. This is as true of the primary school as of any other institution.

Yet, to any country interested in innovation a knowledge of practice elsewhere can provide a stimulus and a guide. Familiarity, habituation, acceptance — these are the usual gyroscopic forces that keep an institution stable, and that tend to make self-renewal mainly a process of self-perpetuation. To be aware of different assumptions and practices elsewhere certainly does not ensure that innovation at home will occur, but at least it makes it more likely. If we can see the need for change, then it is of value to know what is happening elsewhere, and how these changes are being brought about. It is in this belief that this book has been written.

In the two countries chosen for study, England and the U.S.A., primary education is undergoing major change, and, even though practices and ideas from them cannot be slavishly copied, much can be learnt from them. Each in its own way serves to make a re-examination of one's own objectives and methods valuable.

The two countries are dissimilar in their approach to innovation in primary education, and this also is valuable for comparative purposes.

The focus of attention in England is the school itself, where teachers and headmasters are trying by experimental practice to see how individual learning and productive thinking may be encouraged. To this movement the influence of a well-established and virile infant-school tradition is contributing, as are the recently founded Schools Council and the curriculum projects sponsored by the Nuffield Foundation, but the strategic area is in the classrooms of the more adventurous schools, and the leaders of change are the teachers themselves.

In the U.S.A. too, elementary education is receiving great attention. Curriculum projects are legion, and research into teaching methods, learning, new media, school organization, and teacher education has expanded enormously. A spate of Federal legislation, unprecedented in American history, has concentrated attention on both new and old problems, and has given educationists both a mandate and the necessary financial assistance to tackle them with vigour. The slow learner, the gifted, and the culturally impoverished have all come under close scrutiny, and new ideas for dealing with them have been advanced.

Technological developments have turned educational effort into new paths, and have opened up prospects, seductive to some, of virtually replacing teachers by programmed machines.

In all this activity the dominant figures appear to be the politicians, the professors, the research and curriculum specialists, the engineers, and the publishers, rather than the teachers. The forces working towards change come for the most part from outside the schools. One of the major contrasts between the two countries appears to be in the role of the teachers as agents for change.

An obvious difficulty in any statement about new practices is to use the term 'innovation' in a consistent way. Humpty Dumpty, it will be recalled, said that when he used words they meant what he wanted them to mean, even if he had to pay them extra. An anonymous American writer,[2] in an article with the intriguing title 'How to become an instant innovator', makes this sardonic comment:

> 'Most instant innovation practices utilize the basic operational principle of label-switching, . . . the practice of pinning an innovative title onto a conventional practice. Administrators who have become

adept at educational label-switching find that grants from foundations and state departments are easier to get; and that their reputations as forward-thinking administrators are enhanced.'

In view of a comment like this one has to be careful in using the word 'innovation' at all, and some attempt at an elaboration of the meaning of the term is needed.

First, there are educational ideas or practices that are new in the sense that they were not previously known. There are few of these. Most educational ideas have existed in some form or other even though new terms are used. Sir James Pitman's augmented alphabet* comes close to being new in this first sense.

Second, there are adaptations, extensions, or modifications of earlier ideas that are currently affecting practice. These are common forms of innovation.

Third, there are revivals of former practices. These revivals may occur for a number of reasons.

(i) There may be a renewed emphasis on objectives to which these practices relate.

(ii) There may be changed conditions which give promise that ideas that were previously unsuccessful may now succeed. For example, classes may now be smaller; there may be more and better teaching material; there may now be auxiliary teaching staff.

(iii) There may be a changed attitude on the part of teachers or administrators towards the ideas.

Fourth, there are new situations in the sense that the elements combine in new ways. For example, earlier teaching methods may have failed because of an unsuitable examining system, and unsuitable physical facilities. Now they succeed because the examining system and the physical facilities are designed to support the methods. This is a most significant form of innovation. Change occurs because of a better mobilization of influences.

Finally, the obvious comment must be made that there are new things in the sense that someone has not heard of them, or has not understood them, or seen their importance. A major part of the effort of any country to improve its education system must always be directed towards making promising ideas and practices more widely prevail.

It may be assumed to be self-evident that the purpose of innovation is to secure the achievement of some objective, yet it seems necessary to keep labouring the obvious to combat the support of innovation for its own sake. The point is amusingly made in the following quotation:[3]

---

* Known as initial teaching alphabet, i.t.a. This is discussed in Part I.

'For years the professional journals and the popular press have been bemoaning the fact that it takes 50 years for new knowledge in the form of an idea or a technique to become an accepted part of everyday classroom practice. This has prompted many persons to place increased emphasis on the study of change in education. The unfortunate consequence of this condition is that there is a growing army of persons who have made change and innovation the sacred cow, and they generally do not understand that a strategy for change follows the careful development of objectives. Those who overlook this principle find themselves in the position of the airplane pilot who announced to the passengers, "We are lost, folks, but we are making good time." '

To understand better the innovations that are occurring in England and America, it is necessary to know the educational objectives that underlie them, even though it is recognized that aims and practices are not always rationally related. This examination of aims is attempted in Part I of the book. A description of the actual changes is given in Part II, and an analysis of the role of the various institutions and groups in bringing the changes about is undertaken in Part III.

REFERENCES

1. B. S. Bloom, *Stability and Change in Human Characteristics*, Wiley, New York, 1964.
2. E. R. H., *Nation's Schools*, April 1967.
3. Ole Sand and Donald A. Myers, 'Creating a Productive Dialogue: Research, Discussion and Rationale', in *Rational Planning in Curriculum and Instruction,* National Education Association Center for the Study of Instruction, 1967, pp. 57–58.

Part I

THE BASIS FOR INNOVATION:
EDUCATIONAL OBJECTIVES

Chapter 1

The Nature of Educational Objectives

Discussion about objectives often becomes vague or confused because of the different forms in which they are stated. The educational theorist talking about education being for complete living (in Spencer's terms), and the teacher talking about his objective in a lesson to clarify the concept of congruence of triangles, are scarcely using the same universe of discourse; yet both are talking about objectives. We need to be able to recognize the form in which each is expressed, and, if it is a valid form in each case, to be able to trace the connexion from one to the other.

To clarify the distinction between different forms in which expressions of aims are cast, we should recognize that they may express broad social purposes – such as securing equality of opportunity for all citizens, or raising the technological efficiency of the nation – or they may express the practical steps necessary to achieve these social purposes. These practical steps may be distinguished according to whether they occur at the level of the system, or at that of the institutions comprising the system. Practices at the level of the system are largely administrative, those at the level of the institution are concerned with teaching and organizing. Thus, it is envisaged that social aims lead to political and administrative action, and this in turn leads to action at the level of particular institutions.

To state the relation between aims and practice in this way implies that educational practice, whether it be administrative or teaching, can be considered only as a means to some remote end, and not as having more immediate objectives appropriate to itself. It is this implication that has confused teachers who, wishing to justify their procedures, have had to relate even the minutiae of school practice to remote and general statements about the aims of education. They have not found this easy to do, and many have been sceptical about the value to practising teachers of discourses about aims.

A more adequate appraisal of the relation between general educational aims and practice recognizes objectives at different levels, related to one another, but expressed in terms appropriate to the level concerned. At the level of the system,

7

procedures are moderated by political theory and expediency, and by administrative theory and practice. At the level of the school, procedures are moderated by theories of action based on organization theory, psychology, sociology, and other bodies of knowledge. Each of these disciplines has objects and methods of its own. Accordingly the practice of education, whether at the level of administration or of teaching, has objectives which arise from its relation to theories of administration and teaching, as well as objectives which derive from the wider aims of education.

Thus we can state that educational objectives may exist at three levels which correspond with the levels already distinguished. We shall call these

(i) the societal level,

(ii) the system, or strategic level, and

(iii) the institutional, or tactical level.

(The terms 'strategic' and 'tactical' are usually applied to military science, and may seem unsuitable to use in connexion with education. Brickell,[1] however, disarmingly defines strategy as a 'high-level, long-range plan for reaching a broad objective', and this fits closely the meaning attached to it here.)

Some elaboration of these terms may make their meaning in this context more definite.

The societal level. Aims at this level are expressed in philosophical terms (including those of social philosophy and religion), and are explained and supported by argument according to the degree of sophistication reached and expressed about social values in the society concerned.

Many distinguished scholars, from Plato to Dewey, Buber, and others in our day, have discussed educational aims, and the number of definitions is legion. They usually express some view of life and human destiny, of society and the individual, of initiation into tradition, social utiltiy, vocational efficiency, social intelligence, civic responsibility, personal development, and so on.

Within countries attempts are made to state national philosophies which have distinctively shaped educational policies and practices. This is often difficult because of the lack of explicitness in the value systems which underlie a country's institutions, and which unite its groups. But, for the educationist, what is implicit must be made explicit, difficult as it is to interpret social purposes and aspirations. Inescapably the school has to undertake initiation in some form or other.

The system level. Aims at this level are expressed through legislation (since political action is one of the important ways in which social aims are made effective in practice), and through policy statements and action by administrators. They relate to the arrangements necessary to create and maintain the system, and are subject to such considerations as the legislative responsibility of the government concerned, the priority of action in relation to other governmental programmes, the political views of the government, the administrative structure of the authority involved, financial considerations, professional or public criticism, and a host of others. The complex of ideas and pressures in which planning and action occur at this level affects not only the steps taken towards the objective, but also the form in which the objective is stated. Not uncommonly, because of the 'realities' of politics, finance, regulations, precedents, and the like, some of the grandiloquence of aims at the societal level is missing.

The institutional level. Objectives at this level are expressed in methodological terms, and are inextricably linked with relevant knowledge in such fields as psychology, sociology, logic, and the study of organizations and of the structure of knowledge in the various forms.

Examples of such objectives are as follows: individualizing teaching, cultivating attitudes of various kinds, helping children to understand the concept of similarity in mathematics, developing a liking for reading, writing fluently, speaking pleasantly, accurately, and effectively, encouraging children to think analytically. The list is endless, depending on the degree of specificity used.

It is within this tactical domain that so much of educational research has been concentrated, and so much technical progress has been made in education.

Once the place of a subject in a curriculum and the general purpose it serves are established, a great many tactical objectives can be formulated which arise out of the nature of the subject and the nature of the learner. These are the objectives with which the ordinary teacher feels most at home. When the enthusiastic teacher talks about objectives, it is usually to objectives at this level that he refers. It hardly occurs to him to go outside it.

The fact that there are educational objectives of three kinds, or that are appropriate at three levels, has an important bearing on innovation.

We may stress first that educational objectives need to be stated in detail at *all three levels'*, so that there will be clear and consistent direction given to action, and equally clear and consistent criteria for judging the success of the action taken.

How well this can be done at the societal level depends on the clarity and definiteness with which a society accepts common purposes, and expresses them in a way that commands assent. Societies which are totalitarian in outlook, and in which belief is constrained and perhaps coerced by authority, often have clearly stated and straightforward educational aims. These are usually based on some interpretation of efficiency, and are buttressed by a simple view of loyalty to the state.

In open societies the concept of society itself as a substantive entity is vague, and is seen as a psycho-sociological phenomenon of interaction between individuals and groups. This interaction results in some sharing of values, but also in some alienation. Alienation may take different forms — toleration or respect for differences, competitiveness, separation, even conflict. Group interests often gain expression as educational aims, and, if these interests are sufficiently divergent, may result in separate educational institutions being established. Thus there may exist within the same society, whose unity at the political level is acknowledged, different institutions expressing religious, racial, class, and language differences.

In a free society there is usually a major group of shared values concerning the idea of social freedom itself. These beliefs, which can transcend race, class, and other differences, are probably the most powerful factors in creating unity within the diversity that a free society permits. Educational aims which express this idea of social freedom, and which include the knowledge, skills, and beliefs on which it rests, are of major importance for a democracy. They are more fundamental than the aims which arise within a society because it is democratic.

Educational aims which express democratic values are not easy to translate into practical programmes. It is usually easier to express in practical terms such utilitarian values as vocational efficiency and economic development than liberal and humanistic values, personal development, intellectuality, freedom, and responsibility.

At the present time in the countries being considered in this book, the major pressures towards change in the school are coming from social changes. Technological, demographic, economic, and cultural changes are creating the need for substantial adaptations in the school. There is a great need to assess educational aims clearly in terms of social values, and to put the social changes in correct perspective. We are frequently reminded that so much of the current ferment in the U.S.A. towards educational improvement has occurred 'since Sputnik'; and in other countries technological phenomena of this kind are also given as the reason for change. But it does not seem credible that any highly developed country with a considerable history, and which has been heir to western values, would attribute its present educational effort to an event of this kind, no matter how remarkable it was technologically. To attempt to express innovative pressures too much in terms of it could throw the social picture out of focus, and distort educational aims.

There is a great need today for educationists with a sense of history, and with philosophical and sociological insight, to state the aims of education in a way that acknowledges the value system within which current changes are occurring, and at the same time does justice to the changes themselves. In the absence of this scholarly appraisal of cultural change and stability, there tend to occur extravagant statements about education which seem as much influenced by the spokesman's desire to outdo his rivals as to present a genuine explanation or prognosis.

Teaching educational philosophy to teachers and others who have a special responsibility for translating aims into practice has not been very successful in the past. One reason for this is that it has been presented simply as a history of ideas without interpretation in terms of modern social conditions. Another, and more telling, reason is that it has not been connected with objectives at the level of administration and practice. Because of this it has appeared to students to be a study with little relevance to practical realities. A renewed effort in the framing of courses in the history, sociology, and philosophy of education, and in comparative education, is one of the priorities of a period where the accent is on innovation. Out of this ought to come statements of societal aims which provide a more definite rationale for change.

There is also an obvious need to formulate objectives at the system or strategic level. These are the policy statements that guide the system. Typically they exist in incomplete or inconsistent form. Some are expressed, or implied, in educational legislation, others exist in statements of regulations and in official documents. Most perhaps have to be inferred from observation of the system itself. This method of inference from observation was employed by Professor R. Freeman Butts of the U.S.A. in his study of Australian education in 1956.[2] Having observed the system, he inferred the policies which sustained it. The method, as a way of getting at objectives, is open to question. It may seem reasonable at first sight to assume that a country's educational system is the product of deliberate policies. In fact, it is not quite reasonable. At least some of the things that are done are simply done because it is not possible to do otherwise. Butts' assumptions, however, because they are in sharp contrast to what many Australian politicians and educational administrators believe to be their policies, bring out clearly how vague these policies really are. Vagueness, and inconsistency between aims and practice, are more likely to be corrected if objectives are fully and clearly stated.

Explicit formulations of educational policy are more likely to be undertaken if adequate machinery for policy making exists, in the form of deliberative bodies representative of public and professional opinion. A common pattern for this in decentralized systems of education is a body at both central and local levels, in addition to parliament itself. Parliament is a deliberative body, of course, but its range of resonsibility is so wide that it is not a suitable body for formulating policy in detail, even though the major features of it may need to be embodied in legislation.

In centralized systems such as one finds in the six states of Australia, one is struck by the absence of such bodies. Policy making is a matter for the Minister of Education and parliament. The formal role of the administrators is to carry out this policy. This procedure is supplemented by the use of *ad hoc* committees set up to report on topics of special concern; but this is a fairly rare occurrence.

In fact, senior education officials influence policy considerably, by advice to the minister and parliament. They are then in the position of carrying out the policy officially which they helped to create unofficially — an unsatisfactory, ambiguous role to play. The voices that one would expect to be raised in formulating objectives at this high level, so close to the level of public policy — those of the public and the profession — are not heard except through the machinery of government, or through the mass media.

Cremin[3], in a critical comment on educational administrators in America, stresses their role in assisting in the process of defining educational objectives:

> 'They [the administrators] have been concerned with building buildings, balancing budgets, and pacifying parents, but they have not been prepared to spark a great public dialogue about the ends and means of education. And in the absence of such a dialogue, large segments of the public have had, at best, a limited understanding of the whys and wherefores of popular schooling. I think we need to train up a new kind of educational leader in this country if the great questions of educational purpose are to receive intelligent discussion by teachers and the lay public.'

We come now to objectives at the institutional level. No less at this level than at the policy level is it important to develop statements of objectives. Teaching procedures, like administrative ones, easily become traditional and resistant to change. Particularly for those who work in a system where prescribed syllabuses are used, or where teaching is evaluated by external examiners, there is little incentive to question objectives. For them, to teach something because it is 'in the syllabus', or because it may be 'in the examination', is sometimes justification enough.

The work by Bloom and his collaborators,[4] which has produced taxonomies covering both cognitive and affective educational objectives has had profound effects in guiding curriculum development, and in increasing precision of statement (and hence accuracy of communication) among examiners, teachers, research workers, and students.

In the taxonomies objectives are expressed in behavioural terms, such as analysing and valuing, and they are particularly appropriate for an interpretation of the educative process as the modification of the behaviour of the learner.

The influence of the taxonomies has been so great that it is necessary to make the cautionary comments that they do not concern themselves with the particular knowledge or values which might be included in a curriculum, nor do they make any pronouncement about what the objectives of instruction should be. Nor do they give a rationale for methodology. The statement of what is to be achieved is by no means the same as a statement of how the task is to be done, although it is an essential guide to it. To develop an appropriate method, the whole setting in which learning occurs must be taken into account.

Knowledge to be taught must be determined in accordance with societal goals, as must the desired modes of individual behaviour. When both of these are known, a taxonomy provides a valuable guide to the teacher who has to use suitable tasks to try to achieve them, and to the examiner who has to determine whether they have been achieved.

In the three-level model for objectives proposed, it will be seen that any statement of objectives must be *authentic* in that it is expressed in terms appropriate to its level, and *compatible* in that it accords with versions of the same objective at other levels. To formulate objectives in accordance with this double relationship is an exacting process. The task of 'translating' from one level to another is likely to be especially difficult, and up to now little attention has been given to it. It is certainly a much more complex task than identifying an educational aim in a taxonomy of such aims at a particular level.

If we can state objectives in harmony with the discipline in terms of which they are expressed practically, with the political, administrative, and legal policy statements in which thay are included, and with the more general aim from which their relevance is derived, we shall also be able to detect the incongruities that actually occur. A clear recognition of these incongruities would be very valuable at the present time when a solid basis for innovative action is so necessary.

REFERENCES

1. Henry M. Brickell, 'Two Change Strategies for Local School Systems', in *Rational Planning in Curriculum and Instruction*, National Education Association Center for the Study of Education, 1967.
2. R. Freeman Butts, *Assumptions underlying Australian Education, Austrailan Council for Educational Research*, Melbourne, 1956.
3. Lawrence A. Cremin, *The Genius of American Education* (Horace Mann Lecture), University of Pittsburgh Press, 1965, p. 117.
4. B. S. Bloom, *Taxonomy of Educational Objectives, Handbook 1: The Cognitive Domain*, Longmans, New York, 1956; D. R. Krathwohl, *Taxonomy of Educational Objectives, Handbook 2: The Affective Domain*, David McKay, New York, 1964.

Chapter 2

The Aims of Primary Education in England

The Plowden Report,[1] in its chapter on the aims of primary education, reported that many of the replies of expert witnesses regarding these aims seemed to have as much relevance to other phases of education as to primary. The point is not elaborated in the Report, but it does seem to be important, and may well serve as an introduction to a discussion of the wider social changes in England and their impact on primary education.

One of the striking changes that has taken place in England in recent decades is the greater opportunity that has arisen for less privileged sections of the population to participate fully and equitably in the various fields of social activity, such as employment, leisure, cultural pursuits, and government. The great demand for education is an expression of this trend towards social justice, and, in its turn, the increased provision of education has facilitated the social transformation. There is no need here to debate the question whether equality of opportunity has been achieved. It is likely anyway that notions of what constitutes equality will change with new knowledge about people's capacities and needs, and about the social environment and its influence on children.

The meaning of primary education today can be seen best against this background of social change. In a state of social inequality, when the levels of education are unequally available to different social groups and classes, education obviously serves different purposes at different levels. Until World War II primary education was a complete education for large numbers of the lower classes. It provided a training in literacy, and endeavoured to inculcate habits of industry and attitudes of obedience and loyalty that were deemed adequate for the lowly life and occupation in which the person was expected to serve. Increasingly opportunities for bright and ambitious children were created to enable them to receive a secondary-school education, and the expanding 'redbrick' university system opened up opportunities for professional training for increasing numbers. But for the ordinary boy and girl elementary education was an education complete in itself, with its objectives bounded by the very limited life for which it was a preparation.

With the passing of the 1944 Education Act this concept of elementary education* as a self-contained form of education was officially ended, and it became instead a first stage in education to be followed by a second stage for all. Since then the most pressing problem has been to devise a suitable system of secondary education for a whole age-group. The original conception was a tripartite scheme of schools, comprising the traditional academic grammar school, a new technical type of school, and a third, more unspecialized, kind with the emphasis mainly on general education. This last was called 'modern', an appropriate if somewhat unclear notion.

Sorting the children from the primary stage into the 'correct' stream proved to be a difficult and vexing problem. The 11+ examination by which it was done was administered with great care, and often with great ingenuity, but it was a dubious instrument because of the fact that the three types of school had little correspondence with any psychological or educational realities. The examination was, on the other hand, of great importance to teachers, pupils, and parents, because it guarded the entrance to courses which virtually determined the pupils' vocational prospects; and it is not surprising that it dominated the upper reaches of primary-school work, often with stifling results.

There were hidden factors which also affected selection. Many able children from poor homes did not make use of the new opportunities, sometimes for financial reasons, sometimes because of the more subtle influence of social class attitudes which kept aspiration at a level lower than was warranted by aptitude.

The secondary system has moved more and more towards a comprehensive one, alleviating, if not entirely removing, the problem of selection. Teaching in the primary school is now largely free from the influences of the process of selection for secondary school, and, although the problems of providing in the best way for a total secondary-school population are by no means solved, it could be said that the revolution in primary education is now achieved. It is no longer an education for the masses, complete in itself, but a first stage in education for all.

The witnesses to the Plowden Committee who stated aims of primary education that apply equally to other stages of education were implying a profound truth. In countries where education for the whole population through infancy, childhood, and adolescence is a reality, the major social aims of education at all these levels *are* the same. It is when objectives are stated in terms of administrative or teaching procedures that the special features deriving from the stage of development of the children and from the curriculum show up.

Seen in evolutionary perspective, the modern primary school is the first phase of a process of schooling aimed at (i) fitting children for work, according to their

---

* Following the passing of this Act the use of the term 'elementary' was discontinued.

aptitudes and interests, (ii) developing interests that may serve them in their leisure, and (iii) equipping them as citizens of a free democracy. To see it in this way is to see it most clearly, without any of the atmosphere of crisis that sometimes accompanies innovation.

The silent, social revolution[2] that has been described, and that has given a new meaning to primary education, has been accelerated and reinforced by the dramatic social changes since the war, particularly those arising from the great increase in scientific knowledge. This has had far-reaching effects in many aspects of life, but the effects have been most marked in industry, commerce, communication, entertainment, and military science. The pace of these changes has caught the educational system unprepared, and it is now engaged in a somewhat frantic attempt to catch up.

The most urgent objectives have been to revise curricula in the scientific subjects, and to retrain teachers to cope with the new knowledge. Less urgent, but of great importance, has been the setting up of machinery to ensure that curricula are kept under constant review, to revise the curriculum as a whole in conformity with the altered vocational pattern, and to revise the provision for citizenship education to match the increasing complexity of the civic role in a modern democracy, the special problems of race relations and international relations, and the modern need for literary and humanistic studies.

The immediate impact of these changes has been mainly at the secondary and tertiary levels, but the need to make consequent changes at the primary level has also been recognized.

The English have been rather reticent about stating educational aims, and the statements that have been made have been of a philosophical and historical kind.[3] Significant as these have been, they have not always acknowledged clearly the cultural presuppositions made, as Sir Fred Clarke[4] so eloquently pointed out, and they have not been very effective in providing specific objectives for teachers in the classroom. It is only recently that the attempt has been made to develop operational statements.

Nevertheless, English practice, in both administration and teaching, has tended to favour the cultivation of behavioural objectives — rather more effectively indeed than some countries which explicitly espouse them. The tradition in administration is elaborated in Part III in the discussion of the dynamics of innovation. The tradition in primary-school teaching, which has kept the emphasis on the nurture of the individual child, is expressed well in this statement in the Plowden Report.[5]

'A school is not merely a teaching shop, it must transmit values and attitudes. It is a community in which children learn to live first and foremost as children, and not as future adults . . . . The school sets out deliberately to devise the right environment for children, to allow them to be themselves and to develop in the way and at the pace appropriate to them .... It lays special stress on individual discovery, on first-hand experience and on opportunities for creative work. It insists that knowledge does not fall into neatly separate compartments, and that work and play are not opposite but complementary.'

Now there is a need to make explicit what is implicit, and to write these goals about the development of both teacher and children under conditions of freedom into statements about organization and teaching. This move is already evident in the case of priority subjects, mathematics and science, and will be so with other subjects being revised. In this task of spelling out objectives in the new curriculum development movement, England is benefiting greatly from the work done earlier in the U.S.A.

REFERENCES

1. Central Advisory Council for Education (England), *Children and their Primary Schools,* H.M.S.O., London, 1967, (Plowden Report).
2. The phrase is the name of a book dealing with educational changes in England: G. A. N. Lowndes, *The Silent Social Revolution,* Oxford University Press, London, 1955.
3. As examples, the following are given: Sir John Adams, *The Evolution of Educational Theory,* Macmillan, London, 1915; Sir Percy Nunn, *Education, its Data and First Principles,* 3rd ed., Arnold, London, 1945; M. V. C. Jeffreys, *Glaucon,* Pitman, London, 1950.
4. Sir Fred Clarke, *Education and Social Change,* Sheldon Press, London, 1940.
5. Central Advisory Council for Education (England), *Children and their Primary Schools,* H.M.S.O., London, 1967, (Plowden Report).

Chapter 3

The Aims of Elementary Education in the U.S.A.

In America the historic role of public education has been to promote social progress. Jefferson's oft-quoted statement linking education and social freedom has become a text for countless commentators, and the idea is deeply engrained in American thought and practice.

Popular education in Europe, as has been discussed in the case of England, had quite a different origin from higher education, and served different social purposes. But in the United States popular education was a democratic social movement virtually from the beginning, and, as the need for a longer period of schooling arose, it was extended to embrace secondary (and later even college) education with few of the complications involved in countries where elementary and secondary systems that had grown up separately have had to be united. The major traditions of elementary education in America may be regarded then as the traditions of public education itself.

Another distinctive feature of public education in the United States is the degree to which it is identified with the school, rather than with other agencies such as the church, adult education, or the mass media of communication. Probably no country has translated social questions into educational ones and educational questions into school ones as freely; probably no country has expressed such optimism about the power of the school to create or maintain a desired social order. It inverts the school—society relationship that Plato proposed in the *Republic*. Among tasks at one time or another set for the school are the following:

(i) combating illiteracy;
(ii) americanizing children of immigrant parents;
(iii) perpetuating and strengthening the social ethic;
(iv) preparing children for a free society;
(v) promoting social mobility;
(vi) improving the living standard of the community;
(vii) giving social and moral training done previously in the home;

19

(viii) strengthening racial tolerance.

D. W. Brogan[1] has called the public school 'America's formally unestablished church', and Max Lerner[2] describes it as 'a sub-culture, almost on a level with the family in importance'. He expresses this optimism in the power of the school very eloquently in the following quotation, and also something of the faith that sustains all dedicated teachers:

'. . . there are also teachers who are the only counterforce the growing child can evoke to oppose the crassness of the crowd culture. By instilling a love of books, a hunger for experience, a critical attitude towards the prevailing idols of the tribe, a generous one towards foreign peoples and alien cultures, such teachers have a disproportionate impact on each generation. They unlock for each the treasures of history and science, literature and the arts, and place in its hand that key to whatever has been felt and created which makes every educational system potentially revolutionary, and every good teacher by necessity an insurgent.'

In some utopian societies, and to a lesser degree in some actual ones, the various institutions which informally influence the course of individual development and the quality of social life are controlled in such a way that they support and enrich the formal educational institutions. Sir Fred Clarke[3] calls this an 'educative society'. He recognizes the problem of ensuring that freedom continues under such circumstances, and argues that, in a society which is planned, freedom also has to be planned. Plato's solution in the *Republic* for his educative society was to put the key institutions that might have an educational influence under the control of highly educated philosophers.

The balance of power of the school vis-a-vis other educative agencies has probably undergone a substantial shift since the advent of television, but the full significance of this is not yet understood. It is clear though that adult values are decisive in determining the ultimate effect of any education system, particularly where the control of education is in the hands of popularly elected citizens, and is exercised at the local level. How these values are vulgarized or elevated, reinforced or redirected by powerful media like television according to the hands into which they are allowed to fall, may well be an important key to the future of education in America.

An institution from which so much is expected is correspondingly vulnerable. There are so many things for which it may be blamed when they go wrong. In recent years the decline in morals and the increase in delinquency, the failure of the United States to be first into space, and racial intolerance are among the more serious matters for which it has taken more than its share of blame.

Social progress can be interpreted in different ways: its supporters seem to speak with two voices. In its idealistic interpretation it is the degree to which ordinary human experience is suffused with intellectual, moral, and aesthetic significance, enabling the common man to realize his destiny as a creative member of a free society. In its more practical and earthy interpretation it is measured by the material benefit that accrues to each person, and to society.

The first is the grand theme of American education. It assumes the importance of a free society, one that 'specifically delegates to its educational institutions the task of constant study and criticism of the free society itself'.[4] It teaches that all are capable of being so educated that they can live as free citizens, thus making power responsible, and ensuring the survival of free inquiry and the continuance of human values no matter how threateningly impersonal social organization becomes. To adapt a well-known statement by Bruner, quoted in full on p. 79, it assumes that democratic values and attitudes, and the knowledge that underlies them, can be taught effectively in some authentic form to all. How to do it is not fully known. Presumably it would require a balanced curriculum in the arts, sciences, humanities, and social sciences giving a continuous expansion of horizons. It would also require a successful cultivation of attitudes and values, an increasingly tolerant spirit, a distaste for discrimination and all forms of injustice, a love of inquiry, and a careful training in it in consideration of the many-sided problems — social, scientific, and individual — that are part of the world of the child growing up.

The great spokesmen for this tradition, like John Dewey, in part speak in an American idiom, but they also speak in more universal terms that are significant everywhere. Dewey's analysis of the relation between democracy and education has had great influence abroad.

The other interpretation of social progress stresses the cash value of education, or, to change the metaphor, its value as a ladder of opportunity for all who have the life goals of success or power. For the community it is a guarantee of collective prosperity and security. These practical and vocational objectives were fostered from the beginning by the system of control by small local groups which measured success in terms of practical competence and an effective initiation into local values and mores. Increasingly education has become aligned with wider-ranging interests and responsibility, and local authorities have themselves been brought more into the sphere of national influence; but localism is still present, and vocationalism is still strong.

Great stress has been placed on efficiency of instruction. More than any other nation, the United States has tried to build a science of instruction, following the lead given by Herbart in Germany. This approach has been characterized by a tough empiricism, with great attention to variables like amount learned and speed of learning, less to qualitative ones like personal style. Evaluation has flourished, and great effort and ingenuity have been devoted to devising scales to measure things that ordinarily are not quantified.

The movement has resulted in a great emphasis on the means to effective teaching, particularly the teaching of prescribed material. Devices of all kinds, using improved mechanical, optical, photographic, and electronic equipment, have been developed as aids to effective teaching. Programming of subject-matter has also gained ground, and is being further 'individualized' with the aid of computers. So efficient is some of this material becoming that it can be thought of as 'self-teaching', or 'teacher-proof' (a terrifying phrase).

The whole efficiency movement has been supported by a rapidly expanding body of psychological theory and research. To the educationist bent on human engineering, psychology is the queen of the sciences. Research and theory have ranged widely, making a major contribution to world knowledge in this field. The major emphasis in learning theory has been on one form or another of behaviourism, which is concerned with the modifications that can be made in human behaviour by manipulation of the environment. What might be called the psychology of habit formation has had major influence in the schools.

This dualism, between a society's view of education as meeting its need for cultural renewal and as economic investment, occurs of course in other countries, as does the individual's view of education in assisting him to learn the arts of a free man as well as to get on in the world. Perhaps it is because in America so much emphasis is placed on the school as the agency for achieving *both* that any incongruence that occurs between them is so marked. Perhaps it is that idealism has had to be set aside for a time.

One of the research studies before World War II that made a great impression on educationists outside America was the *Eight Year Study*. This was one of the most remarkable action research studies in the whole history of education, and some of the programmes developed by high schools, which were directed only by the injunction to give the children the best education possible, seemed from the reports of this research entirely in accord with the grand theme that has been referred to. The spirit of this period in education, so influenced by the traumatic experiences of the depression, the optimism of the New Deal, and the writings of Harold Rugg, was strongly supportive of a new social idealism in education.

It ended abruptly with the war (or so it seemed to a foreigner), and since then the United States has been involved in major national crises which might be expected to deflect attention to matters concerned rather more with survival than with spiritual and cultural growth. At home there have been the convulsions of the civil rights movement, and abroad, Korea, the cold war, and Vietnam. The key importance of economic, industrial, and military power in playing her international role has overshadowed other goals, and probably has intensified the utilitarian role of the education system.

In reviewing educational objectives in the United States in broad perspective, one is struck by the fact that they are expressed at the societal and institutional levels, rather than at the level of the system. The making of educational policy is in the hands of the state governments, and of state and local boards of education. The state is the legal authority, but may delegate responsibility to local school boards. The balance of responsibility between state and local authority varies from state to state, but in general there has been a strong tradition of local control; and a great deal of influence, if not legal power, rests with the local authorities. It is from these, then, in conjunction with the state, that the policy statements should come which express educational aims in terms of the system.

The fact that the study of educational administration has made such progress in the United States, and the fact that the senior officials employed by the authorities are likely to have had this training, would strengthen the expectation that such statements of policy would be made. One would expect these to show an appreciation of the societal aims in good perspective, and to express a strategy for how they would be realized, how the system would undertake innovative action, how decisions would be arrived at, what steps would be taken to canvass and also enlighten public opinion, and so on.

In fact this does not appear to be happening. The initiative in a number of vital matters, including research and development, appears to have come from the Federal government, some of it being expressed on a regional basis which corresponds to neither local nor state jurisdictions. There appears to be need for a redefinition of responsibility involving federal, state, and local authority in policy making. This matter is more relevant to a later chapter dealing with the innovative process, and will be taken up again there.

At the institutional level, it is to be expected from the striking development in education studies, and the opportunities provided in universities, colleges, and similar institutions to teach them and to undertake research, that there would be considerable attention given to the objectives of teaching; and this has occurred. Much of what has been written has been studied widely in other countries, and has affected research and practice there as well.

Elementary-school objectives have been stated in a variety of forms: in terms of subjects, of psychological processes involved in learning, of children's personal and social needs, of social demands, etc., stressing one or other of the major orientations of elementary education. Three of these are described briefly below. They have been chosen as being illustrative of such statements, and as being important in themselves.

One proposal that has been influential is that made by R. J. Havighurst,[5] in which the objectives of schooling (and development generally) are considered not in terms of subjects to be learnt but as tasks of development to be mastered. These tasks which the child encounters as he grows up are of major personal significance, and need to be accomplished successfully for effective further growth. The developmental task concept, of course, applies at levels other than that of the elementary school. They are listed below, but no further elaboration or evaluation of them is attempted.

(i) Learning physical skills necessary for ordinary games;
(ii) building wholesome attitudes towards themselves as growing organisms;
(iii) learning to get along with age mates;
(iv) learning an appropriate sex role;
(v) developing fundamental skills in reading, writing and calculating;
(vi) developing a conscience, morality, and a scale of values;
(vii) developing attitudes towards social groups and institutions.

Another, somewhat similar, approach is made by Stratemeyer[6] who proposes the following three 'persistent life situations' as a basis for curriculum development:

(i) growth in health, intellectual power, moral choice, aesthetic expression and appreciation;
(ii) growth in social participation, person-to-person relationships, group membership, inter-group membership;
(iii) growth in ability to deal with environmental factors and forces — natural phenomena, technological resources, economic, social, and political structures and forces.

One interesting curriculum statement involving behavioural objectives was proposed by the Virginia State Board of Education[7] as early as 1943. The overall function of the elementary school is stated in terms of the following eleven functions of social life:

(i) protection and conservation of life, property, and natural resources;
(ii) production of goods and services and distribution of the returns of production;
(iii) consumption of goods and services;
(iv) communication and transportation of goods and people;
(v) recreation;
(vi) expression of aesthetic impulses;
(vii) expression of religious impulses;
(viii) education;

(ix) extension of freedom;
(x) integration of the individual;
(xi) exploration.

The practice of stating objectives at length in order to give greater clarity and precision to objectives reached its most complete expression in the scheme of educational objectives proposed by Bloom and his associates, which has already been mentioned. Although it is likely that those who will frame statements of educational objectives in the future will want to use classifications different from those in these taxonomies, nevertheless all are likely to be profoundly influenced by them.

Concluding Comment

It is suggested that among the highest priorities in American education at the present time, when the tide of interest in innovation is running so strongly, should be a full restatement of educational aims. This should do justice to aims at the societal level and the administrative level, as well as at the level of organization and teaching; and should make very clear the interrelations of these three.

It is the first of these, the societal aims, that need restating most urgently, because in a time of national insecurity it is the idealistic goals that a society sets for itself that are most vulnerable. To live unquestioningly in the immediate present is to run the danger of being habituated to existing practice. Not that it is expected that they need revision in any fundamental sense; but they do need to be stated in the idiom of late 20th-century America, and in terms that touch the life of the young. To elaborate them in detail in the way that one does at the level of educational practice will require a courageous grappling with some controversial issues, and the destruction of some platitudes. The emerging society, although at present seen only through a glass darkly, is likely to require a major modification of vocationalism in the education system as this is at present practised, a renewed humanism, and a new kind of training for international relationships and responsibilities not yet faced by any nation.

The faithful translation of these statements of purpose into positive policy statements and effective procedural statements, with scrupulous regard for compatibility, will have a major effect on objectives at these levels.

The present lively study and research in the behavioural sciences give promise of allowing the task of teaching to reach levels of efficiency never approached before. But this will have value only if educational policy expresses clearly the social purposes that give point to efficiency, and if resolute administrative action is taken to create the conditions necessary to realize these social purposes. Among these conditions, of first priority is that there should exist a teaching force of high quality, and with high morale and a strong sense of purpose. 'In the end,' states Featherstone,[8] 'you always return to a teacher in a classroom full of children. That is the proper locus of a revolution in the primary schools.'

The great society will not be created by the school teachers of America. To act as though it will be is not only ineffective, but dangerous, in that it diverts attention from other necessary ameliorative social action. But it will certainly not be created without them.

The United States is hospitable to the idea of change in education. There is no great psychological battle to be won on that front. It has many of the techniques needed to deal with new forms of education, paper plans that have never really been brought to life in the schools.* What it needs most at present is a full-scale, ruthlessly honest review of what it is that needs to be changed, right from the level of social philosophy down to classroom practice.

---

* According to Featherstone New York City has tried out every good idea in educational history – once.

REFERENCES

1. D. W. Brogan, *The American Character,* Knopf, New York, 1944, p. 137.
2. Max Lerner, *America as a Civilization,* Simon & Schuster, New York, 1957, p. 738.
3. Sir Fred Clarke, *Freedom in the Educative Society,* University of London Press, London, 1948.
4. R. Freeman Butts, 'Public funds for parochial schools? No!' *Teachers' College Record,* 1960, p. 33.
5. R. J. Havighurst, *Developmental Tasks and Education,* Longmans, London, 1949.
6. Florence B. Stratemeyer and others, 'Developing a curriculum for modern living', *Rev. Ed. T. C.,* 1957.
7. Virginia State Board of Education, *Course of Study for Virginia Elementary Schools Grade 1–7,* 1943.
8. Joseph Featherstone, 'Teaching children to think', *The New Republic,* Sept. 9, 1967, p. 19. This is the third of three articles giving an American's impression of English primary education.

Part II

MODERN DEVELOPMENTS IN PRIMARY (ELEMENTARY) EDUCATION

Chapter 4

Modern Developments in Primary Education in England

There is considerable ferment in primary education* in England. The publication of the Plowden Report is both an expression of it and a further powerful stimulus to it. The most prominent activities are those that involve the curriculum, organization, and teaching methods in the primary school, and some of these are described and commented on in this chapter.

There are general features of these changes which may with advantage be stated at this point. They will help to bring out the significance of specific innovations.

First, there is evident a resolute attempt to interpret education in behavioural terms. This emphasis on nurturing the personal growth of individual children has shifted attention from formal lessons to the more frequent use of informal activities in which the children, individually or in groups, pursue their tasks. Teaching by guiding and stimulating the pupils has tended to supplement, and often replace, teaching as formal class instruction.

Second, there is a resolute attempt to relate the curriculum to the pupils' environment, to make clear the point that subjects are ways of ordering the environment, and of guiding new studies of it. By using subjects to explain, describe, and show appreciation of the environment, children learn to use mathematics, science, geography, art, English, etc., rather than just to learn about them. With this need in mind for children to use subjects, rather than to memorize factual content, there has been a searching reexamination of traditional curriculum statements. Most of these statements dealt with selected results, rather than with the basic concepts, structure, and methods of the subject. This reexamination has produced surprising revisions, particularly in science and mathematics.

Third, the interdependence of different innovations is being more thoroughly recognized. Changes in curriculum, in methods of teaching and examining, in school organization, and in school buildings, are all interrelated — and, by

---

* The term 'primary' refers to the age range 5–11 years. It is usually divided into two stages, 'infants' (5–7 years) and 'junior' (8–11 years).

reinforcing each other, they make a greater mobilization of resources possible.

With these guiding statements in mind we may pass to a description and appraisal of the new practices. These eleven practices are listed below under the headings of Curriculum, Method, and Organization. These are used for want of better categories: they certainly leave much to be desired, and make it difficult to avoid repetition. The terms express aspects of one functional whole, the setting in which the children learn. The pursuit of any particular objective usually involves all three, even though changes do not always occur together.

Curriculum	I.	The unified curriculum
	II.	The Initial Teaching Alphabet
	III.	The Nuffield Mathematics Project
	IV.	The Nuffield Science Project
	V.	The teaching of French
Method	VI.	Discovery learning
	VII.	Learning by expression
	VIII.	Learning by social interaction
Organization	IX.	Teaching individuals in unstreamed classes
	X.	Vertical or family grouping
	XI.	Cooperative teaching

Curriculum

There are no legal provisions governing the content of school curricula in England, except that the school day begin with an act of worship, and that religious education be given.* It is the responsibility of the individual school to provide a curriculum which is suitable for the age, ability, and aptitude of the children. What influences there are towards uniformity are the more informal pressures of professional opinion with which the school is in contact through publications of various kinds, in-service courses, and the visits to the school of advisers and inspectors. The examination which was taken at the end of the primary school (in the child's 12th year) and used as a basis for selection to different forms of secondary education did provide, in part, an unofficial curriculum for the upper classes of the primary school. But with the increasingly widespread introduction of a comprehensive system at secondary level, the need for the 11+ examination is less apparent, and many authorities have abandoned or substantially modified it. The head of a primary school in England, then, is unusually free from direction from outside his school, and is in a very privileged position in being able to determine what is taught in his school. Undoubtedly some heads do not use this freedom very adventurously, but on the whole it

---

* There are provisions which allow non-attendance at these according to freedom of conscience.

does result in a programme which varies from school to school. This fact should be borne in mind throughout this chapter: it will help to explain how some of the measures described here which involve choice based on children's interests or teachers' judgment can be achieved.

Prescribing a subject in a curriculum may mean a number of quite different things. The subject may be merely named and the details left to the professional judgment of the teacher, or the actual topics to be taught may be set out, and even the order in which they are to be done. The ultimate in course prescription yet devised is the Skinnerian programmed text. The question of the degree to which the structure of a subject is inherent, and is not open to children or teachers to vary, is an important one. It will be returned to later. Clearly the more prescribed a curriculum is, the less freedom of choice there is for children, and the more does the speed-of-learning dimension come to the fore. The less prescribed it is, the greater is the possibility that individual differences in other respects than in speed of learning will show up.

I. The Unified Curriculum

The unified curriculum is put first in this list because it is perhaps the most thoroughgoing departure from conventional school practice. It also illustrates well how difficult it is to separate the categories of curriculum, method, and organization in describing some school practices, and also how old a new idea can be.

A generation ago, the 1931 Hadow Report on the Primary School included this famous sentence, 'The curriculum is to be thought of in terms of activity and experience rather than of knowledge to be acquired and facts to be stored.' This concept has been both the hope and the despair of educationists who have struggled to make it a reality. Perhaps the posing of 'activity and experience' and 'knowledge to be acquired' as alternatives has led to misunderstanding. What really are being contrasted are 'active' and 'inert' forms of knowledge, a distinction that every teacher readily understands, but does not always adequately guard against. The unified curriculum is an attempt to express the curriculum in terms of activity and experience rather than in terms of subject matter to be learnt.

In trying to describe it one can only list a number of general features and make a number of explanatory comments; inevitably an idea like this takes on a different character according to the teacher using it.

(i) A substantial part of each day's work is devoted to projects, centres of interest, topics, units, studies, activities (however they may be named).

Examples of them are endless. One can start with a topic almost anywhere where interest and attention are captured, and follow it in all sorts of ways. Some of them will lead to complexities where children get out of their depth. But this is valuable. All too often with nicely ordered knowledge to be taught we give the impression that there is always an answer, which is in the book, or in the teacher's head. Three examples only are given (two of which were observed by the writer): the idea is a familiar one to most readers, and does not need labouring.

(a) *A study of time* (9–10-year-olds). This required a great deal of reading which has involved mathematical–astronomical–scientific–geographical ideas, a good deal of historical research (clocks through the ages), much writing (describing construction details, functions, origins, etc.), a great deal of calculating, experimenting, constructing, inventing, drawing.

(b) *A study of printing* (8–10-year-olds). This began with art and handwork, making designs, cutting them in various media (wood, linoleum, etc.), and printing them onto paper and materials, and led to a considerable amount of historical, geographical, and scientific study.

(c) A top junior class (11-year-olds) became interested in the problem of measuring the area of an awkwardly shaped field at the back of the school. The problem stimulated much learning about surveying and triangles. From surveying, interest passed to navigation. For one boy the work on navigation took the form of a story of encounters of pirate ships and men-of-war, and involved a great deal of calculation, history, geography, and English (example taken from Plowden Report, p. 199).

(ii) Projects may arise from something done or said by the teacher, or by a child; but in either case they are *accepted* by the children.

(iii) They may be pursued by a whole class, a group within the class, or an individual child. Commonly a group is involved, and individuals work on different aspects.

(iv) They may be pursued for varying parts of the school day, and for a varying number of days and weeks. Some pupils may use the greater part of the day, others a morning or an afternoon, depending on what other jobs have to be done. The teacher's 'control' of this kind of situation is very subtle and skilled indeed, and requires an intimate knowledge on his part of each pupil.

(v) While there is no timetable in the ordinary sense, there usually are some fixed commitments because of the use of common facilities such as the hall for dancing and movement, and, in some schools, the outside part-time specialist coming in to teach French. As will be pointed out later when the French course is being described, where class teachers are not qualified to teach French, use is made of part-time teachers. Criticism of this arrangement is often heard in those schools where a unified curriculum is used, because of the break in the unity. There are also commitments in the sense that the teacher has a general plan of what he wants to achieve, and commitments for individual children whom he knows need special work; but his route to these goals is not a fixed one.

(vi) Children improve in their effectiveness in working in this way by practice in it. Many of the 10- and 11-year-olds observed had never known any other way of working, and were quite skilled in using their time effectively. The presence of a visitor in the room, claiming the whole of the teacher's attention, made no observable difference to their absorption in their tasks.

(vii) As a concluding comment we may state the values which supporters of the unified curriculum claim for it. Most prominent among these are the educational experiences afforded the pupils: the pursuit of a significant task with interest and zest, the practice of a number of important intellectual skills (collecting evidence, analysing, reasoning, etc.), presenting results in writing and in mathematical form, increased self-reliance and responsibility, increased clarity of the meaning of subjects (mathematics, history, etc.) in the examination of the environment.

Less importance is attached to actual factual material learnt than to skills, insights, and attitudes. Because of this, the supporters of the method are not disturbed by the criticism that the knowledge gained by pupils may be somewhat unsystematic and fragmentary.

II. The Initial Teaching Alphabet (i.t.a.)

The Initial Teaching Alphabet is an alphabet devised by Sir James Pitman, consisting of 44 characters each with a constant sound. It is made up of 24 of the existing Roman letters (each being given a constant sound), and 20 new characters. The 44 characters cover all the sounds in the English language.

The 24 existing Roman letters are as follows: a (as in apple), b (as in bed), c (as in cat), d (as in doll), e (as in egg), f (as in finger), g (as in girl), h (as in hat), i (as in ink), j (as in jam), k (as in kitten), l (as in lion), m (as in man), n (as in nest), o (as in on), p (as in pig), r (as in red), s (as in soap), t (as in tree), u (as in up), v (as in van), w (as in window), y (as in yellow), z (as in zoo). (Note that q and x have been dropped.)

The 20 new characters are as follows:

ɑ (as in f<u>a</u>ther),	æ (as in <u>a</u>ngel),	aʋ (as in <u>au</u>thor),	ᴄh (as in <u>ch</u>air),
ee (as in <u>ee</u>l),	ie (as in t<u>ie</u>),	ŋ (as in ki<u>ng</u>),	œ (as in t<u>oe</u>),
ω (as in b<u>oo</u>k),	ꞷ (as in f<u>oo</u>d),	oʋ (as in <u>ou</u>t),	ᴏi (as in <u>oi</u>l),
ɾ (as in b<u>ir</u>d),	ʃh (as in <u>sh</u>ip),	ʒ (as in trea<u>s</u>ure),	ᴛh (as in <u>th</u>ree),
ʃh (as in mo<u>th</u>er),	ue (as in d<u>ue</u>),	wh (as in <u>wh</u>eel),	ꙅ (as in i<u>s</u>).

Note that many of the additional i.t.a. characters, for example:

ᴄh, ee, ʃh, ᴛh, oʋ, aʋ,

closely resemble the traditional digraphs. Lower-case and upper-case letters in alphabet have the same shape: they differ only in size.

The alphabet has been designed to assist children by eliminating the following inherent difficulties of traditional orthography:

(i) Some of the letters represent a variety of sounds. For example, a has a different sound in each of the following words: all, any, want, am, mate, rather. In each of the following words o has a different sound: do, one, gong, go, women.

(ii) The same sound is spelt in a variety of ways. For example, the sound i (as in bike) is spelt differently in each of these words: height, eye, buy, by, bye, guide, island, sign, lie.

(iii) There is great variety between the appearance of lower-case, capital, and script forms of the letters. Pitman has pointed out[1] that the traditional alphabet has not 26, but 66 characters: e.g., A, a, *a*, B, b, *b*, F, f, *f*, etc.

As will be clear from the description of i.t.a. given:

(i) Each letter has one sound only,

(ii) Most sounds are spelt the same way, and

(iii) each letter has only one shape, upper- and lower-case letters differing only in size.

As a medium for learning to read (assuming that the learning of the additional characters is not a great burden), there appears to be *a priori* evidence that the Initial Teaching Alphabet has a clear advantage over traditional orthography.

But a host of questions spring to mind.

(i) In fact, do children learn to read faster with i.t.a.?

(ii) How is comprehension affected?

(iii) How will spelling and writing be affected?

(iv) How do children transfer to traditional orthography (t.o.)?

(v) Is this a scheme mainly for backward readers?

(vi) Most children do learn to read using traditional orthography, so why bother?

(vii) Are there sufficient supplementary reading books in i.t.a.? And does one have to provide sets of reading books and library books in both t.o. and i.t.a.?

Undoubtedly there are more questions than completely satisfactory answers to cover the widely varying conditions, and the many countries, in which English is learnt as a native tongue, but there are preliminary answers to most of the obvious ones, and they do give some assurance to the half-hearted.

A major experiment with i.t.a. was undertaken by the University of London Reading Research Unit (in charge of Dr. J. Downing), in association with the National Foundation for Educational Research, with financial backing from several sources including the Ford Foundation. In its report[2] it made the rather unusual provision of critical evaluations of the results by twelve independent educationists from Britain, Australia, Canada, and the U.S.A. The results gave favourable support to the experimental group of children using i.t.a. as compared with the control group using t.o. The number of children used in the experiment is not large, but the results appear to be quite positive.

Three findings from this research do not need further elaboration and are reproduced below in graph form, A showing progress in reading the basic reader

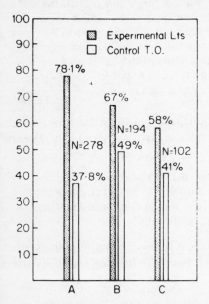

A. *Progress in reading Basic Reader Series.* Proportions completed the Series and advanced beyond. After 2 years at school.

B. *Comprehension in reading in t.o.* (Neale Analysis Test). Proportions having a comprehension-age equal to and higher than their chronological age. After 3 years at school.

C. *Spelling in t.o.* Proportions having a spelling-age equal to and higher than their chronological age. After 3 years at school.

series used in the experiment as the criterion of reading success, B showing a comparison, using comprehension as the criterion, and C showing a comparison of the experimental and control groups with regard to spelling.

This statistical statement may be supplemented by some comments of the Chief Education Officer for Southend, Donald Bartlett:[3]

'What results does Downing obtain? Are they borne out by the opinions of the practising teacher? Are they of value to the teacher not using i.t.a.? . . . The results . . . may be summarized briefly as follows. Can children learn to read more easily by i.t.a.? Results show that they can do so, whether judged on accuracy, speed, or comprehension. Can they transfer their training to reading in traditional orthography? Here there was shown to be a setback on transfer. After transfer are reading attainments in t.o. superior to what they would have been without the intervention of i.t.a.? The results show that the experimental group achieved scores in t.o. superior to those of the control group by the beginning of the third year. The fourth question is concerned with the fluency of written compositions with i.t.a., and the results show that the written compositions of i.t.a. pupils are longer and use a more extensive vocabulary than those of their counterparts using t.o. Spelling attainments are the subject of the last question, and here again those children who had started with i.t.a. proved better in t.o. than the control group of children . . . . These results are remarkable by any standards and show to the inquirer that i.t.a. is worth its place in the schools. The results which indicate regression at the transfer stage will cause comment particularly from teachers using i.t.a. Many have not found this at all to the degree indicated and notice little setback except for hesitancy on the part of the child for a few days.'

Dr. W. D. Wall, the Director of the National Foundation for Educational Research, surveying the evidence in the London study, was moved to comment as follows.[4]

'We are justified in concluding that the irregularity of English spelling is a cause of difficulty in learning to read for children between the ages of five and seven. It is, too, justifiable to add that i.t.a. itself simplified the learning task significantly.'

Other evidence is not so favourable to i.t.a. A three-year i.t.a.–t.o. study was recently completed in England by Terence Swales at Reading University. He concluded,[5]

'Children taught by i.t.a. for three years were neither superior nor inferior in reading achievements to those taught by t.o. from the outset . . . . i.t.a. produced neither more nor less backward readers than t.o.'

American research studies, supported by the United States Office of Education, have not established any superiority for i.t.a. Mazurkiewicz[6] reported in 1965 that at the end of the second year of his experiment, when most students would have transferred out of i.t.a., there was still very little difference in reading achievement between the i.t.a. group and the t.o. group in their scores on the California Reading Test.

The weight of recent evidence seems to be leaning towards the conclusion that there is very little difference in their reading abilities between children taught in traditional orthography and those who first learn the initial teaching alphabet.

Research results are of course subject to evaluation according to the methods used. Devotees of i.t.a. may take the view that research findings which do not establish the superiority of i.t.a. are a poor compliment to the quality of the research done.

Adopting a more objective view, it can be said that in experiments with large numbers i.t.a. is at least as good as t.o. as a medium for teaching reading. This in itself is a rather remarkable result. Perhaps in the hands of some teachers, and for some children, it may prove to be superior. Each year something of the order of six million children in the world begin to learn to read in English. Improvement in methods of teaching reading is obviously a field of immense importance.

Whatever its merits, a striking feature of i.t.a. is its rapid rate of adoption, considering the notoriously slow pace at which innovations in education usually occur. It was introduced to a handful of British schools on an experimental basis in late 1961. By mid 1966 it was being used in 1,765 schools all over Great Britain and in many more than this in the U.S.A., had spread in a limited way to many other countries, including New Zealand and Australia, and had been experimented with for the teaching of illiterate adults and of English as a second language. An i.t.a. foundation was set up in England by Sir James Pitman in 1962, and in 1965 an American foundation was established at Hofstra University, Hempstead, New York. Publication in i.t.a. has spread to thirty-five publishing houses, who have published among them seven beginners' reading schemes, three remedial reading schemes, and some three hundred supplementary reading books in the new medium.

III. The Nuffield Mathematics Project

The Nuffield Mathematics Project, sponsored by the Schools Council and financed by the Nuffield Foundation, was set up in 1964. Its establishment marked a ferment in the field of mathematics teaching which had been growing since the end of the war, and which was the subject of the first curriculum bulletin issued by the Schools Council.[7] The major pressure was obviously the nation's need for mathematicians, but the educational question was not just one of numbers of students. There was a growing realization that school mathematics courses were encumbered with a good deal of material that not only was of little value in itself, but also produced unsatisfactory attitudes among the children. There was also a clearer recognition that, although the problem was with secondary-school and university-level studies, the reform of the content and spirit of the subject in its introductory phase gave the best promise of improvement. The Mathematics project was aimed at this introductory work, but, in setting its age range at 5–13, and thus bridging primary and secondary education, it sought to ensure that a course was not abruptly altered at the point of transfer to secondary education after a promising beginning.

In the short time since it was set up the Mathematics Project has counted the following achievements to its credit.

(i) It has involved a great many schools, teachers, children, parents, administrators, and mathematicians in an approach to learning mathematics from the tender age of five through to thirteen which is so different from the arithmetic to which everyone had become accustomed as to be understandably called the 'new' mathematics.

(ii) It has stimulated a flurry of interest and concern that has sent teachers, inspectors, administrators (and, in many cases, parents) back to 'school' to ensure that they, as well as the five-year-olds, understand the new ideas.

(iii) It has produced ideas about concrete material for assisting the development of mathematical concepts that have produced such a volume and variety of improvised 'equipment' (pots and pans, sticks, marbles, scales, shells, etc.) as to change the appearance of the classroom.

(iv) It has produced a number of draft publications embodying the progress of its thought for comment and criticism, and, more recently, a number of 'permanent' publications which represent milestones in the development of the teaching of mathematics in Britain, and which undoubtedly will exercise an influence for some time to come.

The books are *I do and I understand,* an introductory book; *Teachers' Guides,* which cover three main topics – Computation and Structure, Shape and Size, and Graphs; *Weaving Guides,* which are single-concept books giving detailed instruction or information about a particular subject; and *Check-up Guides,* which will provide checks on the child's progress. The task of evaluating success and progress in a course such as this is an unusual one. We can gauge progress when the criteria are number of sums right, or speed of working on assigned tasks, but progress in such matters as interest, originality, and depth of insight is an unfamiliar object of measurement. The check-up guides are being prepared by a team from the Institut des Sciences de l'Education in Geneva under the general supervision of Jean Piaget.

(v) It has, while giving such an authoritative lead in a new venture, with great wisdom stressed the view that the books should not be looked on as guides to the only 'right' way to teach in mathematics, and that development from work in the guides is more important than the guides themselves.

It is difficult to decide whether to include a description of Nuffield Mathematics under the heading of curriculum innovation or methodology. The title of the key volume, *I do and I understand,* gives pride of place to the way in which the subject is learnt. It is dedicated to Jean Piaget, the Swiss psychologist, whose ideas of cognitive development have so strongly influenced it. Its chapter headings carry on the methodological orientation of the title, as can be seen from these examples:

Chapter 3   How children learn
Chapter 4   The significance of language

Its stated aim (in a general introduction) is 'to devise a contemporary approach for children from five to thirteen. The stress is on how to learn, not on what to teach. Running through all the work is the central notion that children must be set free to make their own discoveries and think for themselves, and so achieve understanding, instead of learning off mysterious drills.'

It should be stressed that the Nuffield material is not a syllabus for children to follow, nor is it a textbook. It is addressed to teachers, and aims to create a universe of discourse for them, richly illustrated with the kind of examples that teachers appreciate (namely, actual children's work) but not in the form of a set of models to follow. Mathematics is presented as an important way in which primary-school children may order their experience, and effectively communicate with one another and with their teacher, in a meaningful language involving words, symbols, pictures, or diagrams. Their growth in proficiency in using the medium is closely related to their experience, and to other school tasks, and to their wish to communicate. No ready-made problems are presented. Rather they are expected to arise out of the children's own interests, out of the tasks in other 'subjects' which are being pursued, and, of course, as developments of mathematical work going on. Many children become intrigued with mathematics as a 'pure' study, and spend a good deal of time working at such things as number series, sets, magic squares, and the geometry of unusual shapes, often with a sophistication that confounds our earlier notions of what children can understand.

The spirit of this approach is one that teachers of infant children find familiar. The change for them is mainly in the kind of material needed to enrich the classroom, and in the challenge to their own mathematical insight. For other teachers, habituated to the sterner realities of the mathematical world of 8–11-year-olds with its endless sums (whether in honest form or disguised as 'problems'), the difficulties of encounter and reconciliation are greater. There are promising signs that the number of teachers who see the point of the 'new' mathematics is increasing rapidly. Since it is in essence an approach, an understanding of the rationale which underlies mathematical operations, rather than a body of mathematical facts, it is bound to fail if the teachers do not appreciate this.

Characteristically, the Plowden Committee end their discussion of primary mathematics teaching with a reminder of the generative and regenerative power which must always come from the teachers, and this is a convenient note on which to end this section.

> 'It happens that our inquiry has coincided with a period of change in the teaching of mathematics, and we have been privileged spectators of it. While it must be evident from our remarks that we are full of enthusiasm for what we have seen, and of hope for the future, we must emphasize that the last thing we wish to see is a hardening of the new approach into an accepted syllabus supported by textbooks, workbooks, and commercially produced apparatus, and consecrated by familiarity. The rate of change must obviously slow down, but the initiative must remain firmly in the practising teachers' hands.[8]

IV. The Nuffield Science Project

The revision of the primary science course has many of the same general features which have been described in connexion with mathematics. These are summarized in the following six points.

(i) It was undertaken by a national committee sponsored by the Nuffield Foundation. There was close association with schools, and each step was taken only after satisfactory 'field' trials.

(ii) It takes the environment as its starting point and focus of attention. Previously in primary-school science attention was limited to biological phenomena. In this new approach, biological and physical phenomena are used, and the idea of the relatedness of science is brought out.

(iii) It advocates a discovery approach with great freedom in the type of topic selected, and in the depth and range of ideas invoked as the investigation proceeds.

(iv) Its deliberations cover children with an age range bridging primary and secondary years, from five to thirteen.

(v) There is stress on the link with other subjects, especially with mathematics and history, and on the skills of expression in written and diagrammatic form.

(vi) The materials produced are not intended to be followed by teachers as a syllabus, but rather to assist an understanding of the new approach, and to help by suggesting the type of investigation likely to be successful with children and the type of equipment that might (at least to start with) be acquired.

The keeping of animals, fish, birds, and other pets in school, and the study of the botanical environment (often with the aid of horticultural or agricultural plots), the keeping of weather records, and similar projects, have been an accepted part of primary-school science for many years. These activities are now extended to include phenomena that might be classified as falling within the scope of physics, chemistry, geology or astronomy; and simple apparatus such as magnets, cells, basic chemicals, are provided. Observations, measurements, experiments are supplemented by science from history, or contemporary description. History is full of exciting science stories, many of which cannot be, or should not be, repeated. They may be too expensive (the conquest of space for example) or too dangerous (the conquest of dread diseases for example).

Interesting as the facts of science may be to primary-school children, the importance of the study lies in the influence it can have on their maturing mentality. The scientific knowledge gained by the age of 12 amounts to little in comparison with what has to be learnt; and it is likely that much of it will be modified later. But the attitudes engendered, and the intellectual skills associated with the methods which science uses, can have an enduring value, carrying the student on to more mature studies in the subject, and transferring more generally to other studies.

Pervading all the observing, experimenting, constructing, speculating, testing, and recording that go on in the pursuit of primary-school science is the practice of the important intellectual skills that underlie scientific thinking: accuracy in observation, precision in the handling of evidence, hypothesizing, and generalizing.

For those who are going to use science professionally this introduction in the primary school may well be crucial. But the scientific method, being applicable to many kinds of problems, is relevant to everyone. All need to be able to distinguish fact from opinion, to know what evidence is and what the weight of evidence is in a particular situation, and to know when doubt is called for, even if it cannot always be resolved. All need to catch some of the scientist's passion for seeking truth, and, because they have done so, to be impatient of careless or imprecise observations or inferences that lead to error or half-truth, and to abhor procedures which lead deliberately to error.

The chief concern of education is with the establishing and disseminating of truth. In this it finds itself in collision with anti-educational exploitive influences, concerned with securing some personal or group advantage. If, in our schools, our children can be taught more effectively to think like scientists, to be touched with their scrupulous regard for truth, and to be made more sensitive to humane values through humanistic studies, they will be less tolerant of exploitation than many of their elders at present seem to be. A course in science which has behavioural objectives of this kind, and is not content merely with presenting scientific facts, may not be so new; but it is a novelty if taught well enough to succeed. It is too early yet to say whether this kind of success is being achieved in English primary schools. After all – the idea that *everyone* should be able to think for himself, and to apply rigorous tests to distinguish fact from opinion, is new in any society.

V. The Teaching of French

Most commonly in England the learning of a foreign language used to be regarded as a task for the secondary school, although some private preparatory schools did begin it earlier. Now there is a widespread acceptance of the idea that it is better to begin it in the primary school, and use the language as a means of dealing with ordinary situations, as one uses the mother tongue.

The commonest language taught is French, partly because France is England's nearest neighbour (although one suspects that this reason is something of a rationalization), and partly because there is a tradition of French teaching in England, and more teachers of French are available.

Not that teachers are available in adequate numbers. On the contrary, the average primary-school teacher does not have the competence needed, and a great deal of the effort involved in introducing the subject has gone into providing emergency courses for teachers. The result is that part-time teachers, often with a background of secondary-school teaching, have been employed.

There are a number of courses in vogue — *Bonjour Line*, a course on film strip made for the Ministry of Education in France, *Parlons Français*, a course on moving film made in the U.S.A., and *En Avant*, the Nuffield course. The French and American courses have the advantage of being first in the field, but it is expected that the Nuffield course will gain in popularity, and to a degree displace the others.

En Avant is a five-year introductory course, bridging the primary and secondary years. It is designed for pupils in the last three years of the primary school (9+, 10+, 11+) and the first years of the secondary school (12+, 13+). Its objectives are to teach pupils to speak, read, and write French, to introduce them to French customs and institutions, and to widen the general educational experience of the children. It is arranged in four stages, stage 1 being completely oral, stage 2 introducing some reading and writing, and stages 3 and 4 developing reading and writing and leading to composition. For each stage an appropriate teacher's guide and supporting materials are published (or are to be published). For stage 1, for example, the material is as follows:

(i) Teacher's book. This contains the text and the teacher's notes for twenty lesson units with suggestions for exploitation of the material presented.The full text of all the recorded material is included. The book also contains an introductory unit, a list of French names and of classroom phrases, and an index of the vocabulary and sentence patterns which occur in these units.

(ii) Flannelgraph figurines in colour. These sheets of figurines which are to be cut out depict the objects and people which occur in the stage 1 lessons.

(iii) Flashcards, printed in two colours — two sets numbering twelve and ten cards respectively. The first set depicts animals and the numbers 1 to 12, and the second illustrates the verbs of action included in the first 20 lessons.

(iv) Tape recordings. Twelve tapes (at 3¾ i.p.s. half track). These are made by native speakers, male and female, adults and children. They include the presentation of sentence patterns and vocabulary, songs and exercises, etc.

(v) Three films (sound, colour, running time 7½ minutes). These are regarded as ancillary, but are closely linked to the course, and use the structures and vocabulary which it introduces. They depict the adventures of three puppet characters, Boupah, Nigot and Fléon. The text and tape recording of the sound track of the films can be purchased separately. Instructions are also provided for making the puppets and a puppet theatre.

The Nuffield course is a notable contribution to the teaching of modern languages in England, expressing in a practical way ideas about introductory teaching which have been gaining currency there and elsewhere for some years. It is hoped by many, however, that it will come to assume a more background role than at present, and that as teachers become better qualified in foreign languages (including ones other than French) they will follow a particular course less and less, and take advantage of ideas in the existing courses to develop their own. The 'step by step' presentation of these courses, with controlled vocabulary and sentence structure, represents a formalism from which the primary school in other aspects of the curriculum has been freeing itself. The recent change in mathematics teaching was a major step in this direction in a subject which has been noted for its fixed sequential treatment. It would be something of a regression if foreign-language teaching, transferred from the secondary school, brought back with it a formal approach to its teaching.

Concluding note on developments in the curriculum

It is perhaps not surprising that, when so much attention has been given in the last decade to mathematics and science, it is these subjects that are so prominent in the reform of the primary-school curriculum.

But there is a great deal to admire in other aspects of the curriculum. One may mention especially the greatly increased output of children's writing obtained by associating it with many activities in the curriculum, and the environment studies in social studies. The work in English is likely to be further stimulated as the Nuffield programme in linguistics and English teaching comes to completion and begins to exert its influence. This project was set up in September 1964, and based on the Communication Research Centre, Department of General Linguistics, at University College London; it is due to complete its work in 1970.

In the development of physical and art education since the war many of the modern concepts of primary education have been successfully incorporated. The individual creative expression of children in pictorial art, in crafts, and in movement and dance, and the linking of this with speech and drama, literature and music are particularly admirable. The work is impressive, however, rather than new, and is not listed among recent innovations.

Methods of Teaching

In this section three elements of the teachers' observed manner of working are distinguished, and commented on: namely, *their reliance on discovery by the children, their emphasis on encouraging the children's expressive activities, and their use of supportive social relationships among the children.* None of these methods is new in the literature of educational psychology. What may be considered to be new is the more effective alignment of them with curriculum provisions, and with school organization.

VI. Discovery Learning

In spite of the fact that learning by discovery is referred to very frequently in modern English educational writing* and by teachers, the idea is by no means a clearly defined one. We contrast it with an idea like 'imparting knowledge directly', but the distinction at a conceptual level is not as clear as it may look at first sight. One way to make the distinction clearer, at least in practical terms, is to describe the kind of teacher behaviour occurring in each case. This is done on facing page, where two teaching styles are distinguished, and commonly associated behaviour is listed in parallel columns. Each is named by reference to the *learning* of the children, but each involves planning and goal-oriented activity on the part of the teacher, and may properly be considered to be *teaching*.

Teacher-directed learning is consistent with, if not explicitly based on, psychological theory, which has as its central concept the modifiability of human behaviour through appropriate control of the environment. Behaviouristic theory, with its emphasis on habit formation, and its concepts of simple and operant conditioning and of reinforcement, has obvious relevance to this style of teaching.

Teacher-facilitated learning is more consistent with genetic theories involving hormic or purposivistic concepts and with psycho-analytic theories dealing with the springs of human action. On the intellectual side, it is consistent with the developmental theories of such psychologists as Baldwin, Luria, Bruner, and Piaget, which deal with the growth of cognitive structures.

English education on the whole has been pragmatic, and not explicitly based on theorizing of any sort. The main role that theory appears to have played is to support procedures sanctioned by usage and 'common sense'! In the first third of this century Froebelian influence was perhaps the strongest, and was exploited effectively by those concerned with the education of young children.

* A discussion of the same idea within the American context is given in Chapter 5.

Teacher-directed learning

(i) The lesson content to be covered is planned by the teacher (with or without the use of a syllabus).

(ii) The order of presentation is planned, and adhered to, except in unforeseen circumstances.

(iii) The presentation is assisted by such devices as these:
(a) using some form of motivation;
(b) using the blackboard, or other audio-visual aids;
(c) questioning;
(d) recapitulating and reinforcing.

(iv) The class organization is planned. This may mean that the class is organized as a whole, into groups, for individual work, or in some combination of these.

(v) Some evaluation of this 'reception' learning is planned.

Teacher-facilitated learning

(i) The teacher relies on the child's interest in making an inquiry or engaging in an activity.

(ii) This interest is 'assisted' by the creation of a stimulating environment for the child to work in. This may be done by providing books, telling stories, encouraging children to express their interests and bring materials to school, keeping animals and birds in school, providing equipment of various kinds, posing problems, asking critical questions that redirect a child's endeavour, etc.

(iii) Investigations are allowed to take their course, but are supervised, assisted and checked by the teacher.

(iv) Records and reports are made. These may take a variety of forms, and may involve the use of reference works, e.g. encyclopaedias. The sophistication of these records and reports depends of course on the stage of development of the children.

(v) A high degree of variety in content is accepted by the teacher.

(vi) A flexible use of time is accepted. Clearly, children working in this way will vary greatly in the amount of time they devote to a particular task.

(vii) A flexible class organization is accepted; informal social interaction is permitted.

(viii) Appraisal by the teacher is continuous, and on an individual basis.

The education of infants through free discipline and play has been a feature of English education for the past thirty years. Those concerned with older children, on the other hand, for whom it was believed more didactic teaching was necessary, have not had the same kind of support. More recently, however, the writings of Piaget have been influencing English education strongly. The theory of a progression in cognitive development through levels with qualitative differences accords well with the 'common-sense' notions that teachers have about children's mental development from concrete to abstract forms. It is in harmony, too, with the main features of infant education, and so helps to bridge infant and junior work. And it stresses the importance of the interaction of the learner with his environment, and of self-generated interests − restoring the confidence that many previously had in projects by which they had later been disillusioned.

R. F. Dearden,[9] in a careful examination of discovery learning, distinguishes three versions of it, which he calls pre-school learning, abstractionism, and problem solving. *The pre-school model* is described as 'the learning of the pre-school child as he trots around the garden, plays with his friends, or explores the neighbourhood'. *Abstractionism* is the (supposed) learning of concepts from merely handling structured materials such as Dienes' blocks or Cuisenaire rods, in which the concepts are 'embedded'. *Problem solving* leaves the result of the learner's activity open in some important respect, so that what is to be learned has indeed to be found out and not imparted; but it does draw in the active, verbal participation of the teacher in framing problems, suggesting, discussing, or instructing. Dearden is critical of the first two, and dubious about the third.

His third version of discovery learning is rather more directive than some teachers would practise, at least in some kinds of school work. His examples of learning tasks are drawn mainly from mathematics, and to a lesser extent from science, subjects which may specially require the active guidance of the teacher. Possibly his three categories are needlessly sharply drawn; and perhaps there is an excessive 'hardening of the categories' as his description proceeds.

The line between 'imparting knowledge' and 'discovery' may be quite fine. Active participation by the teacher may block the child's route to discovery; non-intervention may leave the child confused and aimless. Socrates, whom Dearden quotes approvingly, may be able to say* honestly, 'Be ready to catch me if I give him any instruction or explanation instead of simply interrogating him on his own opinions,' but teachers have in the past been very prone to do this without being caught. Undoubtedly the teacher has to judge how this

---

* To Meno in Plato's dialogue. Socrates is teaching a slave that a square double the area of a given square is to be constructed on the diagonal of the given square, and not by doubling the length of its sides.

intervention best serves the child's progress towards understanding. Many teachers in England, with the recent history of formal education in mind, are now more inclined to err, when in doubt, on the side of non-intervention.

VII. Learning by Expression

We may learn through listening, reading, speaking, writing, constructing, calculating. All are important, but it is a truism that active learning is most likely to be effective. Passive, or servile, learning, leads easily to lowered concentration. Expressive activities make what is attempted explicit, and heighten concentration.

Moreover, expression provides an immediate *test* of learning. Children who express ideas in speech or writing are using them publicly; they are exposing them to evaluation by others. Children who paint or model or construct do the same, although the nature of the evaluation may be different. Whatever thought or creativeness the expression achieves is thus made known. There is much less likelihood of failing to realize that one does not understand. It is by no means uncommon for a child who has learned something from a book or teacher to believe that he understands it until he has to express it. Teachers are frequently surprised by the inability of children to express to them things which they appear to have learnt.

The 'output' of a modern primary class can be astonishing. They fill the room with their stories, paintings, graphs, models, costumes. In an earlier day they used to work in books, each neatly labelled for its purpose, and the books were inspected by the teacher. Now they publish in a form that all can see. These are not formal answers to set tasks, but various modes of experimenting with thought and feeling. They employ words, sentences, colour, expressions of quantity, shape and form; they aim to achieve statements of relationship, factual communication, dramatic effect, humour, imagination. In making these statements the children are identifying themselves by the things they can do. Whatever they can do will of course be greatly influenced by the impressions made on them by the thought of others, as it should, but in expressing it they have a chance at least of becoming something more than a spurious replica of someone else. They have a chance of developing some authentic awareness of identity, and a genuine sense of personal style in expressing it.

VIII. Learning by Social Interaction

One of the great benefits that flows from an informal method of working is that it generates a high level of interest and involvement in school tasks through social interaction among the children. Children like to learn together. To be allowed to do so increases their zest for learning. The old-fashioned classrooms gained orderliness at the expense of interest and verve; it was too high a price to pay.

In English classrooms conducted on informal lines, the children talk to each other quite freely, discussing what they are doing, what has been achieved, what must be done next, and so on. They work in school in much the same way as they play with their friends outside. Some of the exchanges made between children no doubt are irrelevant or redundant, considered strictly in relation to achieving the task in hand, but these are a natural accompaniment of informal groupings of this kind, and have value in assisting to maintain morale.

The social group increases greatly the opportunity for effective expression. As such it may be considered to be a natural ally of the teacher who wishes to use discovery as a method, and to secure as much 'output' from each child as possible.

There is no virtue in noise as such. If classes working in this way are noisier than traditional classes, they are gaining by the educational process involved, not by the noise. Modern English classrooms are becoming better planned to combat noise. With the setting up of areas for special activities, and the use of simple sound-absorbing materials in the construction and carpet on the floor (except in those areas where water, clay, paint, etc., are used), this problem is lessened. Perhaps it is because the writer is excessively noise-sensitive that the provision of carpets on schoolroom floors appears to him as one of the really significant innovations of modern times. It is pleasant, and surprising, to learn that it appears to be economically feasible to use them.

Class and School Organization

The features of organization brought to notice in this section are alternatives to the 'streaming' which has dominated English education for the past thirty years. It is not easy to give them a title, as they have not assumed any definite or permanent pattern. The keynote of present experiments in organization is flexibility, to accord better with the spirit of the changes in curriculum and method. There is a very adventurous spirit abroad in these experiments. We shall use the titles 'Teaching individuals in unstreamed classes' and 'Vertical grouping' in describing these changes. Associated with them are novel ways of using staff, and this will be dealt with under the heading 'Cooperative teaching'.

In its history the idea of streaming in primary education has had social class overtones, and these have been strengthened by its association with a selective secondary system of education. In recent years this has changed. It would be fairer now to judge streaming on educational grounds, and ask whether it increases equality of opportunity or limits it, whether it increases efficiency in learning or decreases it. The present reaction against it, which is mounting rapidly, is partly a criticism of its efficiency, and partly a criticism of measures that have become associated with it.

Streaming is a somewhat vague general term for the classification of children (either into classes, or into groups within classes) by attainment or ability. Its purpose is to create more effectively teachable groups by making them more homogeneous. The groups obtained obviously depend on the criteria used to determine attainment and ability. Obviously too, the homogeneity attained can only be approximate, as identity of performance over a whole group is unlikely to occur. In fact what is achieved is a narrowed range of performance on the criterion measures. The usual criteria used are the child's performance in a variety of forms of command of English, his performance in arithmetic, and his achievement in some test of general mental ability: these commonly are combined. At best, it will be seen that the grading achieved is a rough and ready index of homogeneity. The selective secondary system, with its limit on grammar-school places and the 11+ examination used to allot these places, bolstered up the streaming arrangement.

Any form of organization tends to create its own climate, and to become associated with particular practices. An interesting description of streaming from this point of view is given in a comprehensive research study undertaken by the National Foundation for Educational Research.[10] It reported that in streamed schools, as contrasted with unstreamed schools, the teachers were older; they used formal sums and problems in arithmetic more frequently and practical arithmetic less frequently; they used tests more frequently; they had a less permissive attitude to children's behaviour; more were in favour of physical punishment; more had a lower tolerance to noise; more favoured the bright (A-stream) children, were in favour of the 11+ examination, and believed in streaming. Obviously the supporters of streaming are expressing a whole cluster of attitudes about education concerning the curriculum, discipline, academic achievement, and so on; and, just as obviously, the opponents of streaming oppose the things that go with it.

Because streamed and unstreamed schools embody different philosophies, it is difficult to evaluate the practice of streaming in isolation. What research there has been has not helped greatly to settle arguments or dispel doubts.

Yates and Pidgeon[11] concluded in 1959 from their summary of the research on streaming that it was not possible, on the evidence available, to establish a case for or against it. More recent research by Daniels[12] and by Jackson[13] did not significantly alter this conclusion. Wiseman's study in Manchester[14] showed that streamed schools have better records of attainment (attainment being measured by objective tests of English and arithmetic), and the study by the N.F.E.R. already referred to showed that, on a straight comparison between streamed and non-streamed schools, pupils in the streamed schools had slightly higher mean scores on the attainment tests (attainment being measured by tests of reading, English, mechanical arithmetic, and problem arithmetic of the kind usually demanded of juniors by teachers and education authorities). The differences were greater the more the test reflected 'traditional' educational practices; they were largest for mechanical arithmetic and smallest for reading.

The mounting concern about streaming has been based on more general grounds than its effectiveness in preparing pupils for tests of the 11+ examination type. Indeed the opponents of it appear to regard its success in doing this as evidence of its restricted approach to primary schooling. The following summary expresses the doubts and antipathies that have become increasingly articulate in recent decades. Those who are experimenting with the newer forms of organization see the need for new alternatives in terms of some or all of these.

The relation of streaming to curriculum objectives

As already mentioned, the usual basis for streaming is the pupil's achievement (or promise) in English and arithmetic. These are used because of their intrinsic importance, because of their relevance to success in other subjects, and because of their relationships with intelligent behaviour, particularly when expressed in the usual academic forms. They are supplemented by a test of general intelligence, but this usually relies for its content on similar linguistic–numerical concepts to those used in the study of English and arithmetic.

It would be foolish to criticize streaming by trying to minimize the educational importance of language and number. Whatever form the organization of classes may take, the importance of these ought to be recognized, though they may be interpreted more richly than as the stereotyped forms which they have taken in at least some schools. But undoubtedly, if pupils are classified for teaching, the criteria used for classifying them inevitably do indicate the main objectives of the teaching, and they tend to intensify interest in these objectives. If other objectives were prominent in primary education (for example, physical skills or music), presumably these would be considered an appropriate basis for streaming.

Historically the system of streaming is associated with a restricted view of the function of the primary school — as a preparation for secondary education, and as a test of fitness for it. The modern concept of primary education is radically different from this. It is now seen as a rich and stimulating experience in which children may indeed take the basic preparatory steps in gaining academic skills and insight and become aware both of the richness and variety of the social and physical environment and of the creative impulses of the human spirit — but where they may also explore their own interests and talents.

In the face of such a broadened range of objectives streaming appears to lose much of its point.

The validity and reliability of the streaming procedure

There are some practical questions here involving argument of a technical kind which we shall avoid, but they require definite, non-technical answers.

The N.F.E.R. study found that after the initial assignment of children to a class in the first year of the junior school (aged eight), the chances of a pupil's being transferred are very slight. One may well ask then whether the validity and reliability of the measures used to grade the children are such that accurate selection can be made at the end of the infant school, and whether it can be assumed that this selection will hold good for four years.

The effects of teaching in altering the streaming. and the related question of the influence of the stream itself on the aspiration and achievement patterns of the child, also require illumination, whatever the answers to the first questions may be.

Looking at these issues from the standpoint of someone trained in educational measurement, one would be tempted to think that in fact streaming was an *ad hoc* form of grouping (varying from school to school) whose validity was taken for granted, but whose reliability was obscured, both by the later use of similar types of measures with the children concerned, and by the tendency of the children, chameleon-like, to assume the characteristics of the group they were put with. To put it in this way is no doubt unkind to the conscientious headmaster, and probably inaccurate for the insightful one, but, viewing the matter generally, it may not be very far from the truth.

The possible tendency of streaming to encourage class teaching methods. Since it is designed to secure 'homogeneous' groups, it may be assumed that advantage will be taken of this to use teaching methods directed uniformly at the class as a whole, rather than ones which deliberately involve individuals separately. To elaborate further the picture the writer has of class teaching, a description from an earlier publication[15] is repeated:

> 'He [the good class teacher] is one who can hold his class of 30 or more children together during a "lesson" in smoothly functioning unison. The questions he asks are accepted by each child as directed at him. The responsibility for framing an answer (even if someone else is asked to give it) is accepted by each. The teacher is sensitive to the reactions of each child. A significant glance corrects momentary inattention here, a few words clear up a lack of understanding there. The progressive clarification of the lesson topic occurs through the contribution of everyone, teacher and children alike. The teacher is like the leader of an orchestra. It is his initiative that sets the process in motion; it is his drive that sustains the process at a high pitch of intensity.'

In fact the N.F.E.R. research[16] supports this assumption. In this study two types of measures were developed: a *traditional lesson scale* which showed whether the teacher used class-prepared compositions, spelling lists, formal grammar, and rote-learning of tables, and a *progressive lesson scale* which indicated whether the teacher used projects in which the child did his own 'research', whether he allowed pupils to work together or help each other, whether he allowed them to do practical arithmetic, e.g. measuring or apparatus work, and to engage in free activities. Teachers in streamed schools proved to be 'traditional' and 'non-progressive', those in unstreamed schools were 'non-traditional' and 'progressive'. This difference may of course be due to the teacher's conception of teaching rather than to the organization in which he finds himself. Undoubtedly some teachers, if given a streamed class, will endeavour to teach it without any special regard for the fact that it is streamed. But, as will be pointed out later when discussing the alternative schemes, the fact that it is streamed is likely to result in the children making similar intellectual demands on the teacher simultaneously, and to create the typically 'impossible' situation where one teacher has to try to deal with thirty or more pupils individually.

As noted earlier, ideas of curriculum, method, and organization go together. Streaming seems to accord best with a prescribed curriculum, and with class teaching aimed at uniformity in standards.

Possible adverse side effects of streaming on teachers' and pupils' attitudes. It has been argued that, even if it were effective on other counts, streaming can affect teachers' and pupils' attitudes to an extent which calls it seriously into question.

There is a good deal of informal evidence on this matter which suggests that divisions created by streaming often create feelings of unworthiness in 'lower' groups. More definite is the fact that in streamed schools the older and more experienced teachers are generally assigned to the brighter classes. Definite also are the findings of the N.F.E.R.[17]:

> (i) that girls in classes under a pro-streaming teacher displayed more anxiety about being tested than similar girls under an anti-streaming teacher;
> (ii) that teachers who were in favour of streaming had more isolates in their classes;
> (iii) That teachers who were opposed to streaming rated more pupils as being 'a pleasure to have in the class'.

This aspect of the Foundation's research is being continued. It is an area where it is easy to get impressionistic data, difficult to get measured data. The Plowden Committee, having surveyed the evidence open to it, concludes as follows:[18]

> 'Schools which treat children individually will accept unstreaming

throughout the whole school. When such an organization is established with conviction, and put into effect with skill, it produces a happy school and an atmosphere conducive to learning . . . . We welcome unstreaming in the infant or first school, and hope that it will continue to spread through the age groups of the junior and middle schools'.

The critical point in this conclusion of the Plowden Committee is the attitude which teachers have to children. It cannot be overemphasized as the key to making teaching more individual, and hence more effective. This point is stressed in the N.F.E.R. Study.[19] 'A mere change in organization — the abandonment of streaming, for example — unaccompanied by a serious attempt to change teachers' attitudes, beliefs, and methods of teaching, is unlikely to make much difference either to attainments or — though this is less certainly based on the present evidence — to the quality of teacher—pupil relationships.'

It is heartening to report the reply made to the writer by a distinguished Chief Education Officer in England when asked what he thought was the major change in English primary education in recent years. His reply was: the changed attitude of English teachers to teaching; there is a growing acceptance of the need to teach individual children, not classes.

IX. Teaching Individual Pupils in Unstreamed Classes

The description given below is a composite one, built up from observations of many classrooms. What the children were doing, and how they were going about it, differed refreshingly from class to class, but there were underlying similarities which may be used as the basis for this description.

(i) The rhythm of the day's work is varied between group and individual activity. No mention of groups is made in the title of this section. This does not mean that groups, including the class as a group, are not used. On the contrary, they are used extensively. But the purpose always is that the individual should learn, whether he works at a task with the class, or in a group, or alone. The major emphasis is on the small group, and on individual work. In the observations made, it was an uncommon event to see a class taken as a whole, except for physical education and French.

(ii) Different groups and individuals pursue different activities at the same time. This arrangement seems to achieve three important objectives: (a) it takes care of the factor of variation in speed of working by different children at the same tasks, because there is no set time for starting or finishing tasks; (b) it takes care of the factor of variation in special interests by allowing different children to work at different tasks; (c) it produces a pattern of working which allows the teacher to divide his time among the children in the most effective manner, as not all the tasks need his attention equally.

The apparent 'chaos' of the scene that a class working in this way presents, particularly to a visitor used to sterner things, gives way to understanding when the hidden art of the teacher is revealed, as he explains what each is doing, what attention each needs, what special gifts or weaknesses each has, and what each ought to be doing tomorrow. Some teachers keep written records which show what each child has accomplished, others seem to find the evidence of the child's work sufficient. (One of the unofficial advantages of this manner of working is that a visitor can talk to the teacher. In other circumstances to do so is to cause an interruption that is near-fatal.)

Undoubtedly this method works only by taking a very flexible view of what should be learnt. It is definitely inconsistent with a closely prescribed curriculum.

(iii) The children, once launched, are to a degree, and for a time, 'self-operating': they are carried along with the task. To achieve this a teacher needs a lot of assistance with materials, books, and other equipment. The classrooms that form the background to this description are like workshops in an advanced state of disarray. But it is the disarray of a busy group, and is soon rectified.

The revolution that has occurred in the production of books and other educational material for schools is an important factor in the teacher's success in teaching in this more informal way. It may well be a decisive factor. Much of the material now is 'structured', so that with suitable assistance from the teacher it guides the child's discovery. Little use is made of programmed learning at this stage, and there appears to be no great interest in it at primary level. Perhaps some new techniques in presentation will alter this.

One reason perhaps for this lack of interest is the distrust generally felt for a textbook approach with heavy reliance on verbal learning and on 'predigestion' of the material by the writer. Short programmed presentations on a very wide variety of topics which can be used by pupils as reference material may have more success.

(iv) There appear to be few disciplinary problems in classrooms where children work in this way. The tensions often created when the class is taught together seem to be absent. No doubt such common irritating features as inattention and reproof by the teacher for failure to understand are more likely to occur when a teacher is trying to keep the work of a class together. Teachers, when questioned on this point, confirmed that the children were more relaxed. The teachers also were more relaxed, but certainly no less busy.

X. Vertical or Family Grouping

The unstreamed class discussed in the previous section most commonly is uniform with respect to age. A variation of this which is becoming increasingly popular in the infant schools is the formation of classes from two or three different age levels.

Entry to infant school is permitted at the age of five years, and there are in most cases three times in the year for entry — in January, April and September. Those entering in January spend two years and two terms in school; those in April, two years and one term; and those in September, two years only. There are thus three age groups concerned — five, six and seven.

Three patterns of organization are found. We may refer to them as (i) traditional grouping by age and/or ability, in which each age level is kept separate, and parallel classes within the age group are based on age or ability; (ii) transitional mixed grouping in which one 'exit' level of children aged six to seven years is separated from the lower level which is mixed (in this arrangement there are no separate reception classes for new pupils); (iii) vertical age grouping in which there are no levels, but each class is composed of some children from each age group. Under this arrangement the class is just an administration unit that periodically loses some older children, and gains some younger ones. The diagrams on the next page illustrate these three types of organization for a school with eight classes of about forty children, which is a common size in English Schools.

Some of the advantages claimed for vertical grouping are as follows:

(i) The children are more secure with fewer changes of class.

(ii) The new ones come into a stable, on-going group, and are quickly initiated. It is easier to make very flexible arrangements for initiation. For example, timid beginners might come only for an hour, or for half a day.

(iii) Competitiveness between the children (perhaps for the attention of the teacher) is reduced to a minimum; cooperation between children of different ages is enhanced.

(iv) The children can be better known to the teacher, as they are with him over a much longer period.

(v) The children's progress is not geared to the work of a year, but can be managed appropriately within the whole infant period.

(vi) Learning situations are more natural. Children with ability work at their own pace, and indirectly influence other children.

(vii) The teacher's problem in trying to meet the needs of forty children at about the same stage, and needing the same kind of attention, is lessened.

It might be asked why one needs classes at all under this arrangement, since all the usual criteria on which classes are formed are disregarded, and the actual teaching depends very little on the class as a group. In fact, this question has been answered by the actual establishment of a number of schools that have no classes and no classrooms. One of these new buildings observed by the writer embodied the concept (advocated by the Plowden Report) of a 'first' school, an extended infant school covering the age range of five to eight years. The

Traditional grouping by age and/or ability

	R 40	A 40	A 40

January Entry

R = reception class for entering pupils.

	R 40	B 40	B 40

April   Entry

Sequences RAA, RBB, RC indicate that
children are promoted by age.
Alternatively they could be graded by
ability at 2nd and 3rd levels.

	R 40	C 40

September   Entry

Transitional mixed grouping

No separate
reception
classes

5 mixed classes
for 5- and 6-
year-olds, each
with 24 entered
in September,
8 in January,
and 8 in April

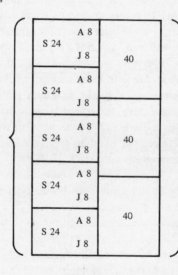

3 graded classes (mainly by
age) to prepare children for
promotion to junior school.

Vertical grouping

8 classes all parallel,
all mixed, each consist-
ing of 30 children who
entered in September,
5 in January, and 5 in
April.

S 30	S 30	S 30	S 30	S 30	S 30	S 30	S 30
A 5	A 5	A 5	A 5	A 5	A 5	A 5	A 5
J 5	J 5	J 5	J 5	J 5	J 5	J 5	J 5

architectural idea was 'open-plan', with all facilities communal, and including an assembly hall, a dining area, work-spaces for such activities as reading, mathematics, science, art, crafts, and construction, and a home area for each 'class', but no classrooms in the ordinary sense of that word. To see such a school in action, with its sense of family and community, was a delightful experience – but it left one very thoughtful about one's ability to define a school, at least by using the classical form for definition, *per genus et differentiam.*

The experiment with mixed age grouping for older children is also occurring. The spread is usually restricted to two age groups, but middle schools on the open plan may well come into existence. Once the need for homogeneity is relinquished, and heterogeneity is not only accepted but seen as an advantage, there is no knowing where it may end.

XI. Cooperative Teaching

Traditionally the primary-school class has been taught by one teacher. This practice arose at a time when the work of primary-school teaching was at such a simple level that specialized teaching was not considered necessary. A number of positive arguments have been used to support it – the need that younger children have for the interest and support of one person, and the advantage that the teacher has in coordinating the curriculum to give children a unified view of knowledge. Whether these arguments have arisen to make a virtue out of necessities or not, they have not been seriously questioned. However, there has arisen the need to reconsider the role of the primary-school teacher because of the increasing level of scholarship required as primary-school curricula are revised, and to recognize the individual differences of the staff no less than those of the children. There has also been an increasing disposition to accept the view that even young children profit from contact with a wider range of adults, so long as a stable environment for them is established. To these educational considerations can be added the practical problem that is brought about by the greater use of part-time teaching staff. These teachers, inevitably, will not be able to take full responsibility for a class.

The most familiar model for cooperation among staff is that of specialization by subject, as practised in the secondary school. This has had only limited appeal at primary-school level in England, and indeed the need for modifying it at the secondary-school level has been seriously considered, particularly for the lower forms.

The other model is the American one of team teaching; and although there is no enthusiasm for the idea of massing young pupils* for teaching, other features

---

* Senior pupils in American elementary schools are often older than senior pupils in English primary schools. This may be relevant.

of this model are favoured, notably the association of teachers with one expert and experienced person, the use of para-professionals, and the general idea of sharing of work.

Cooperative teaching, as it is usually called in England, is developing on a number of fronts.

(i) The most significant is the most informal: the increasing number of ways in which members of a staff find they can cooperate with each other, once the idea of being self-sufficient in one's own classroom breaks down. Cooperation has gone furthest in those schools where it is facilitated by the architectural features of the building, but it can occur in the conventional building as well. The cooperation that occurs supplements and reinforces rather than replaces. Children may go to another teacher to hear more about a certain topic, because that teacher is an expert on it, to get a demonstration from another because he has special skill, to see some work done in another class, or to use equipment housed in another room, and so on. Increasingly it is the school as a whole, not the classroom, which is the functional unit.

(ii) There is acceptance of limited specialization with interchange of staff, so long as it does not disrupt the unity of a class's work.

(iii) A form of cooperation of considerable importance is the use of a staff member as consultant to the staff in a particular subject. This has been occurring unofficially since the recent curriculum changes have increased demands on teachers, and the Plowden Committee supports it. A teacher may have a special interest in a subject and special qualifications, and be able to give leadership in it in the school. Previously the headmaster carried out this function for the whole curriculum, but this is now less likely, although of course the headmaster may wish to be considered as the consultant for one of the subjects! It is important that the teacher remain in this consultant role, and does not become directive. There is no wish to see the primary schools becoming departmentalized by subjects.

(iv) It is appropriate under the general heading of cooperation to comment on the provision of auxiliary staff — part-time teachers and para-professional staff. Both are at present used in a limited way, and their use is likely to be extended. Practices vary a good deal in different parts of England. It is common to find teaching staff employed on a part-time basis, in excess of basic establishment. These teachers assist in various ways: spending part of the day with particular teachers (e.g. new young teachers), taking individual pupils for additional assistance in some subject, relieving the deputy or headmaster, taking a special subject (e.g. French), and so on. Non-teaching staff are also used: secretaries, meals assistants, and welfare assistants. The last-named work with the kindergarten children, assisting with non-teaching tasks. Most of the work of this auxiliary staff is done outside the classrooms, though, particularly in the case of the welfare assistant, by no means all of it. The cooperation of these auxiliary staff in carrying out non-professional and marginally professional tasks is extremely valuable, and frees the teacher to play his proper professional role. It has long been a complaint of teachers that a lot of their time is wasted on non-professional tasks.

To extend this kind of assistance the Plowden Committee recommends that a new type of auxiliary staff be appointed to be called a 'teacher's aide'. The kinds of assistance it is envisaged that they should be able to give[20] are these:

(i) to assist with the children's play and their reading, to supervise their use of individual equipment, to accompany them on out-of-school excursions, and help in and out of the classroom with the preparation of materials;

(ii) To supervise children after school while they are waiting for their parents.

The Report recommends that aides be appointed at the rate of one full-time aide for two infant classes, and one for four junior classes.

Critics of the proposal express the fear that the aides may become second-class teachers, and that authorities will be tempted to solve problems of teacher shortages by increasing the appointment of teacher's aides. Certainly, should these things happen, it would be a serious matter. It will be a pity, however, if such a fruitful proposal fails through fear of its being abused.

Concluding Comment

These then are the innovations in English primary schools. Recollected in tranquillity, and written down, they seem to appear more ordinary than they are.

They are some of the ways being taken to make the curriculum more relevant, and the methods and organization more in harmony. They are likely to ensure a supportive and stimulating environment in which little children growing up may develop their powers, enlarge their vision of the world, and begin that important initiation into the intellectual and moral tradition which underlies all civilized life; and, without too great a fear of failure, explore and test their own view of themselves. They will increase the chances that schools can become educative communities in which pupils can discover and strengthen a sense of identity, and learn to respect the need and right of others to do so too.

REFERENCES

1. Sir James Pitman, *As difficult as ABC: the case against the traditional orthography as a learning medium,* Pitman, London, 1966.
2. J. A. Downing, *The i.t.a. Symposium,* National Foundation for Educational Research in England and Wales, Slough, 1967.
3. Comments on the i.t.a. Symposium (mimeographed).
4. *ibid.,* p. 164.

5.   Quoted in 'Initial Teaching Alphabet : a look at the research data', *The Educational Magazine*, Melbourne, Feb. 1968, p. 43.

6.   *ibid.*, p. 43.

7.   *Mathematics in Primary Schools* (Schools Council Curriculum Bulletin No. 1), H.M.S.O., London, 1965, Revised 1967. The approach in this bulletin emphasizes exploratory methods rather more than the Nuffield scheme does.

8.   Central Advisory Council for Education (England), *Children and their Primary Schools*, H.M.S.O., London, 1967 ('Plowden Report'), p. 239.

9.   R. F. Dearden, 'Instruction and learning by discovery', in *The Concept of Education (Ed. R. S. Peters)*, Routledge & Kegan Paul, London, 1967.

10. National Foundation for Educational Research, 'The organization of junior schools and the effects of streaming': Preliminary Report, 1966, in *Children and their Primary Schools*, Vol. 2 pp. 545–594.

11. A Yates and D. Pidgeon, 'The effects of streaming', *Educ. Res.*, Nov. 1959.

12. J. C. Daniels, 'The effect of streaming in the primary school', *Br. J. Educ. Psychol.*, Feb. 1961.

13. B. Jackson, *Streaming: an education system in minature*, Routledge & Kegan Paul, London, 1964.

14. Manchester Survey, reported as Appendix 9, *Children and their Primary Schools*, Vol. 2.

15. G. W. Bassett, *Each One is Different : teaching for individual differences in the primary school*, Australian Council for Educational Research, Melbourne, 1963, p.22

16. *Children and their Primary Schools*, Vol. 2, p. 559

17. *ibid.*, Vol. 2, p. 579

18. *ibid.*, Vol. 1, p. 291.

19. *ibid.*, Vol. 2, p. 576.

20. *ibid.*, Vol. 1, p. 330.

Chapter 5

Modern Developments in Elementary Education in the U.S.A.

The innovations discussed in this chapter are not necessarily well established in the schools. America is so vast and varied that quantitative assessments of this kind about its education system are difficult to make without a major survey. Undoubtedly all of them are practised to some extent, and some of them (particularly some of the new curricula) are reasonably well established.

It is less likely that any comprehensive observation of American teachers would reveal a widespread use of teaching methods and class organization that emphasize individual learning, discovery and inventiveness by children, and self-discipline, although there are brilliant examples of all of these. The present temper of American education in its striving after quality education appears to favour a higher degree of formality in the teaching of elementary-school children than was practised a decade or so ago, when there seemed to be the same trend towards greater freedom of expression as is at present evident in England.

Perhaps, as teachers gain more confidence in meeting the academic demands that the new curriculum schemes have introduced into the various subjects, they will become disposed to teach again in ways that emphasize the spontaneity of the student rather than the constraints of the curriculum.

The main basis of this statement on modern developments is to be found in the work of curriculum committees, in the research publications of theorists, and in the deliberations by educationists in conferences and publications, rather than in classroom practice. It is the new ideas that are stated, and the question whether they have been accepted in practice is not pursued too closely. Most of the ideas are about practice, that is about what teachers should do and what they should teach, and undoubtedly they will affect practice increasingly. It is likely too that the increasing evidence built up from practice will give greater clarity to the ideas themselves. An idea like team teaching, for example, means many things at the level of practice, and will not be really clear until this elaboration in terms of operational examples has taken place.

The same threefold division (curriculum, teaching method, and school organization) is used in this chapter as was used in the preceding one. The

59

innovations in the three categories selected for discussion are as follows:

Curriculum	I.	Mathematics projects
	II.	Science projects
	III.	Modern foreign language projects
	IV.	Social studies projects
	V.	English, the arts, health & physical education projects
Method	VI.	New theoretical aspects of instruction for productive thinking
	VII.	Educational technology
Organization	VIII.	Non-grading
	IX.	Team teaching

New ideas in school architecture are not described. This is not because they are unimportant, but because they require a discussion of technical matters and the presentation of plans and drawings that are outside the scope of this book. Suffice it to say that new ideas in educational practice tend to find expression in school architecture no less than in the behaviour of teachers, children, and administrators, and outdated school buildings hamper innovation no less than outdated ideas held by teachers and administrators. The concern with using the new technology effectively, with team teaching, and with the movement and grouping of children within and between classrooms, is affecting school design most. A group of classrooms with common access to an instructional resources centre (books, equipment, materials) is a common new feature; adjoining classrooms with movable screens instead of separating walls, and acoustic treatment of interiors with carpets and with wall and ceiling tiles, are others. The architects of the new schools have an assured place on the roll of innovators.

Nor is included a number of new developments such as the Headstart Program for pre-school children (particularly in culturally disadvantaged areas), Educational Parks designed to secure a greater integration of races and social groups at school, and a host of novel practices of varying (and to an extent unknown) degrees of educational significance proposed and being practised under Title III of the Elementary and Secondary Schools Education Act of 1965,* (which is called PACE – Projects to Advance Creativity in Education). Many of these novel programmes are particular expressions of more general principles raised under the headings of curriculum, method, and organization, or they are rather too limited in significance to be described in a general statement such as this.

* This Act is dealt with more fully in Chapter 8.

This threefold division, into curriculum, teaching method, and school organization, has the merit of being significant in its scope, and in line with the way in which innovations in England were discussed in the previous chapter.

Curriculum

Development in curricula has produced the most striking recent change in elementary education. A brief survey of some of the major projects is given in the following pages. There are a number of general features of this movement which may with advantage be reviewed before the survey is introduced.

(i) The first is the prominence given to the subjects which were identified in early federal legislation as priority subjects, namely mathematics, science, and modern foreign languages. These were the subjects for which federal funds were made available after World War II. These have dominated the field of curriculum development, with concentration on them first at the secondary level, and then spreading downwards into the elementary school. As the reform movement continues, other subjects are being brought under review, but the sense of urgency appears to be less.

(ii) One is struck by the subject-by-subject approach to curriculum reform, with little attempt to produce an overall plan. No doubt this has occurred because of the lead taken by outstanding mathematicians, physicists, and other scholars, whose concern has been with their own subjects.

Educationists have long been concerned with the fragmentation of knowledge that occurs in schools, and the inert learning that takes place when children are unaware of the connexion of what they are studying with other objects, events, and relations. The degree to which specialized subjects may be correlated has been a matter for inquiry and debate, as has been the stage at which different subjects are best introduced, the range of subjects to be taken by all, the optimum extent of an optional system, and so on. These important questions, concerned with the structure of the curriculum as a whole and with the progression of studies, have not been prominent in the recent ferment about curriculum. Perhaps they will become so again when the revisions within subjects are better established.

One way in which an undue emphasis on separate subjects may be avoided is by the method of teaching used, and by the type of class organization. As was pointed out in discussing the changes in English elementary education, an effective education programme requires the harmonious union of all three: curriculum, teaching method and organization.

While it is essential that the logical nature of the individual subjects be understood by teachers, it is not necessary that they should be presented to young children in the same form. The child's curriculum is likely to consist of the observations of phenomena, social events, objects, ideas in books, etc., and these may be interpreted for him *through* subjects. Dealt with in this way the pupil's 'curriculum' consists of selected aspects of the environment, and his intellectual development is a progression towards the conceptual schemes that subjects represent. Teaching the child to see what is in the environment is by no means the same as teaching him the environment in the form of a number of subjects.

An approach which uses scientific, mathematical, historical, aesthetic, and other appropriate modes of thought in helping the child to understand and appreciate experience implies that curriculum statements are made for the benefit of the teachers, not the children. In fact, however, most curriculum projects prepare parallel material for the children in the form of workbooks or textbooks, and these (particularly the textbooks) keep their attention restricted to the separate subjects. The textbook approach seems deeply ingrained in American school practice, even at elementary-school level. More than any other feature it casts a shadow on the school which goes a long way towards eclipsing the spontaneity of the work.

(iii) The interest taken in the curriculum of the elementary school by university scholars has already been mentioned. In some cases this interest has derived from a previous encounter with a secondary-school project, and in others the necessity to plan a continuous curriculum through both elementary and secondary school has been accepted at the outset. An examination of the curriculum projects described later in this section reveals the frequency with which they are located in universities, and how commonly the leader of the project is a distinguished scholar in the subject concerned. Typically, teams for the development of curricula have consisted of a director who is the subject specialist, psychologists who assist with learning theory, people with special skills in design, layout, construction, illustration, etc. who prepare materials, and cooperating teachers who carry out trials in schools. The curriculum specialists, in most cases, appear to have been bypassed.

The control of these projects by subject-matter specialists has had a number of important effects. One is that the content of the courses of study has been brought into line with the most recent developments in the subject, and that out-of-date material has been discarded. Attention has been concentrated on the logical structure of subjects which gives them their distinctive character.

According to Paul Hirst,[1] forms of knowledge fall into one or another of a number of domains. These domains can be distinguished by the concepts that characterize the different bodies of knowledge, by their occurrence within different networks whose relationships determine what meaningful propositions can be made, and by the different type of test they require for the validation of propositions. He distinguishes science, mathematics, history, morals, aesthetics, philosophy, and religion, but admits that the logical autonomy of some of these domains might be disputed. Beyond dispute however, he claims, is that 'the history of the development of knowledge is the story of its progressive differentiation into a number of logically distinct forms, each providing unique understanding because of the uniqueness of its concepts, its conceptual structure, and its criteria for validity.'[2]

In America, Bruner has been very influential in stating the importance of structure in the learning of subjects. He writes[3] ' . . . the curriculum of a subject should be determined by the most fundamental understanding that can be achieved of the underlying principles that give structure to that subject.' Being so determined, he claims, makes the subject more usable in later applications, more intellectually satisfying in the process of learning, and more likely to be remembered.

Bruner's way of stating the importance of structure gives it double support. Scholars are quick to say that a subject must be studied in a way that makes the structure clear because in fact there is no other way in which it may be studied with understanding. But to this Bruner adds the values to the student of greater utility by 'non-specific' transfer to other matters, and of more lasting retention.

The case for a process of education that leads, among other things, to an understanding of the structure of knowledge is unanswerable, and scholars who have associated themselves with the schooling of little children have done a valuable service in insisting on the treatment of subjects at this level with intellectual integrity. But the methodological questions as to how this may best be achieved are still open ones. They are also crucial questions so far as the success of these new curricula is concerned. There could be a danger, if the wisdom of the teachers and the appropriateness of their methods do not match the sophistication of the curriculum content, that the new mathematics and the new science could become simply a series of formal exercises distinguished from earlier ones mainly by the fact that they are more difficult.

Surprise and pleasure have been expressed by teachers at the unexpectedly inventive approach made by some children who have been stimulated by the new courses. The high achievement reached by these children in the elementary school when released from pedestrian constraints has been noted in both England and America. If this occurs under an effective form of individual teaching which encourages the more gifted children without requiring the others to take such speculative leaps, no harm can result. Indeed there is great merit in the fact that pupils capable of creative thought in a subject can be encouraged to test the limits of their imaginative power. On the other hand, if teachers are unwilling or unable to introduce forms of teaching which permit genuine individual progress, it could easily happen that undesirable pressure on less able children will result. The prospect of gifted five- or six-year-olds experimenting with abstruse mathematical ideas is one thing; that of ordinary youngsters being forced to think conceptually when they are quite unready for it is another.

Some critics of the new programmes are claiming that they are being introduced competitively, and with an accompanying anxiety that is having bad effects. Some parents, who misunderstand the new courses, think of them as avenues to greater and quicker success for their children. Even the Federal Government's Headstart Program (the name is unfortunate, giving as it does the impression of competition in a race) for children under the age of five has been interpreted by many as an opportunity for earlier introduction of formal academic work.

Donald McNasser[4] believes 'that it is incredible that in less than a decade we should have lost prescriptions so painstakingly learned in half a century about mental health in the growing years.' 'The reactions of younger children and their parents,' he writes,[5] 'are well known to school counselors, administrators and physicians. The child's every move at school is under constant scrutiny by parents; the grades he receives, the teachers he gets or doesn't get; the special class opportunities he receives or misses; his comprehension of the new math; the incessant questions by parents who are on the lookout night and day for any slippages, any discrimination. These children must sometimes feel they are standing trial. Criticalness and doubt become the main substance of the parent-child relationship. Listen to parents as they talk and think about their children. Do they sound like people who enjoy their children?'

A different emphasis to curriculum objectives is proposed by James McDonald,[6] who claims that a great many more activities should be undertaken in a spirit of play, not in a frivolous sense, but as a spontaneous expression of human vitality and imagination. Schools should not be used as 'training grounds for the production of role players who will become doctors, lawyers, teachers, engineers, scientists, etc.' McDonald's ideas are very much in accord with those of Peters of the University of London, whom he quotes approvingly:[7]

'Education can have no ends beyond itself. Its value derives from principles and standards implicit in it. To be educated is not to have arrived at a destination; it is to travel with a different view. What is required is not feverish preparation for something that lies ahead, but to work with a precision, passion, and taste at worthwhile things that lie to hand.'

Many of the new curricula do in fact express this creative spirit that McDonald identifies with play. To be fair to those who framed them, it should be reiterated that in the hands of teachers who understand them fully, and with parents who do not abuse them as devices for trying to get their children ahead, reflecting their own anxiety, they are likely to be beneficial rather than harmful.

(iv) An important feature of modern curriculum projects is the production of materials that assist the teacher to bridge the gap between the generalizations of a course statement and the actual tasks for the pupils. These materials take a variety of forms; for many projects it is likely that all or most of the following are prepared.

(a) Teachers' manuals which make clear the objectives of the course, its scope, and appropriate methods. They are designed to increase the teacher's understanding of the subject.

(b) Workbooks for the children with appropriate tasks. These may be prepared for use instead of textbooks, or in addition to them.

(c) Textbooks for the pupils in which the course is set out in sequential form.

(d) Teaching materials such as apparatus, charts, pictures, films, slides, tapes, records, complete with instructions for their use. Programmed material is sometimes included.

(e) Tests, or suggestions for evaluation.

(f) Films for use in in-service training of teachers which explain the new course and demonstrate it.

Those who prepare these materials take different views about their purpose. For some they are means by which the curriculum is made 'teacher-proof', increasing the prospect that poorly qualified teachers may use it successfully. For them the material is so structured that it scarcely requires the intervention of the teacher. For others they are additional tools for the teacher to use to realize the objectives of the course.

Another feature of modern curriculum development is the attention given to learning theory in deciding the form in which the curriculum is presented, and the type of material prepared for the students. It will be convenient to defer the discussion of this to a later section where methods of teaching are discussed.

Some summaries of curriculum projects in the various subjects are now given.

I. Mathematics Projects

Mathematics was one of the first subjects to be caught up in the new curriculum reform movement, and it has undergone major changes at both elementary and secondary level. As has happened in England, the changes in courses made by mathematicians have thrown a very great strain on the teachers at all levels, and particularly in the elementary school. The success of these courses will depend greatly on a transformation of pre-service training for elementary teachers, and a massive re-training of present teachers. It is relatively easy to take the formal step of adopting the new mathematics; but it is much more difficult to build up an authentic programme using the new ideas and new materials. If children are to 'get the feel' of mathematics, the teachers must learn to do so too. 'The true flavour of mathematics,' comments R. B. Davis[8] is subtle and elusive.' 'It is not derived from memorized facts. Rather it is like Mark Twain's remark about his wife's swearing, "she knows all the words, but somehow she can't get the right tune." '

A few of the new courses are described in brief below, and others are listed at the end of this section.* They have some things in common. First, there is the way in which the statement is made so that major concepts like set, number, function, field measurement, and proof are made focal, and the logical structure of the subject is stressed. Second, some topics have been introduced to children much earlier than in previous curricula, and some material has been omitted. Third, there is agreement that the student's method of study should enable him to use inductive methods as well as formal deductive inference. Finally, there is a large measure of agreement that the language of the subject should be precise, and free of ambiguity.

The variety of courses that have been developed brings home the point that the 'new' mathematics is not a single thing. It is clear, too, that there will be more versions of curricula, and that the problem of choosing the 'right' one will increase. A related problem is the articulation of work in the elementary school with that of the junior high. With the diversity of courses the problem of articulation could be acute. Some of the schemes anticipate this problem by preparing a course which spans the elementary and secondary grades.

The School Mathematics Study Group (SMSG) This group was sponsored by the American Mathematical Society in 1958, and financed by the National Science Foundation. The total cost of the project for the first five years was six million dollars.

The SMSG course is widely known and widely used. It is planned as a comprehensive course from kindergarten to grade 12, with textbooks at each level. The planning is from top to bottom, the opposite procedure from that adopted by the Nuffield group in England. Preliminary editions of the texts are produced first, and progressively replaced by revisions as evidence accumulates from classroom testing.

The approach emphasizes that mathematical concepts apply to the subject as a whole, and not only to sections such as algebra and geometry. The course is organized into units, each unit dealing with a topic that involves some weeks' work. The topics recur at different levels, and are treated with increased sophistication. Teachers' manuals, programmed books, and films have been developed to assist the teachers with the course, although it is not by any means revolutionary in its content. The familiarity of teachers with many of the topics may be one of the reasons for its popularity.

---

* Readers especially interested in mathematics and science curricula are referred to the following publication, *Information Clearinghouse on New Science and Mathematics Curricula*, J. David Lockard, Director. This is produced jointly by the American Association for the Advancement of Science, and the Science Teaching Center, Universtity of Maryland, College Park, Maryland. The third report was published in 1965.

The University of Illinois Arithmetic Project Based at the University of Illinois under the directorship of David Page, this project has received support from the National Science Foundation and the Carnegie Corporation as well as the University of Illinois.

The emphasis of this project is on mathematical invention, and on capturing the interest of students and teachers who see the subject as a stimulating field for intellectual curiosity and creativeness rather than as a body of facts and skills. The approach is similar to that of the English Nuffield course, and is well expressed in the words of Franz Hohn:[9]

> 'The true mathematician, as contrasted with the expert in computation, is uninspired by the prospect of performing routine, repetitive tasks, just as the true artist would not wish to paint many copies of the same picture—the mathematician's primary creative activity is the study of patterns, relationships, forms and structures in systems of numbers, geometrical figures, functions, and other objects of interest.'

Page uses what he calls 'intermediate inventions' to provide a focal point for a teacher and a group of children to explore mathematics. For example, a table of numbers may be used in this way. The children invent principles and hypotheses without being directed towards a specific problem with a specific solution. In this way they feel at home with the subject, much as children may feel at home with poetry by free composition of it. No fixed sequence is determined for the topics. As is stated in the official information sheet[10]:

> 'The University of Illinois Arithmetic Project is not looking for an ideal curricular sequence for elementary-school mathematics. The main obstacle facing schools today in determining a better curriculum is that there are not enough well-developed and classroom-proved alternatives to choose among. Day-to-day here-is-something-to-try suggestions are needed which combine to form a body of teachable alternatives reflecting important ideas of mathematics. Only when there are more than enough significant alternatives to choose from can the search for the best possible curriculum— if such a thing exists—be usefully begun.'

The project can be regarded not as a complete course of study, but as an experiment with appropriate materials for the teaching of elementary school mathematics in a way that encourages interest and inventiveness.

The Madison Project This project is sponsored by the National Science

Foundation and the U.S. Office of Education. The director is Robert B. Davis, at the Department of Mathematics, Syracuse University, New York. The name is taken from the Madison school in Syracuse where the project's earliest experiments were made.

The course is designed for both elementary and secondary grades, and is recorded in teachers' manuals, individual workbooks, films, and audio tapes for teachers. It is a supplementary course, an hour a week being suggested as the time allocation. According to Professor Davis,[11] the materials are founded on the belief that 'good mathematics is somewhat akin to good jazz,—it must be experienced, and the spirit is more important than the outward form.'

The approach is one in which the child is assisted in his discovery of the intrinsic structure of the subject through undertaking instructional tasks for which no method is prescribed and by the teachers' use of questions which lead the child to solutions dictated by the subject. The objectives of the course are to capture the interest of the children, while at the same time presenting a version of mathematics that is honest, modern, and intellectually exciting. How these objectives are attempted can be seen from the following practical guidelines which are suggested for teachers.

(i) Ask questions — the student learns by thinking the question through himself, not by being told.

(ii) Concentrate on concepts — try to get the student to think about the basic concepts as early as possible.

(iii) Conduct conversations, not lectures — every effort should be made to get the students thinking and talking, not listening and accepting.

(iv) Provide success experiences — attempt to respond to every student answer as a scientist might; it is an answer and deserves respect.

(v) Practise the light touch — you and the children may explore the fascinating concepts of mathematics as long as they continue to fascinate. When they threaten to become routine, turn to a new topic. They can be returned to later.

The Madison Project is somewhat similar in spirit to the Illinois Arithmetic Project.

The Suppes Experimental Project in the Teaching of Elementary-School Mathematics Patrick Suppes' work at Stanford University's Institute for Mathematical Studies in the Social Sciences has been sponsored in its different phases by the National Science Foundation, the Carnegie Corporation, and the U.S. Office of Education. He has undertaken a number of studies, some of which have concentrated on computer-assisted teaching. The one referred to here has involved the earliest elementary-school grades first, but is planned as a complete course to grade 6.

The key concept used by Suppes in developing materials for the earliest grades is that of set. He considers that sets, and operations on them, are more appropriate for young children than numbers in that they are more within the child's experience, as well as being more mathematically fruitful. As he puts it,[1][2] 'a set is simply any collection or family of objects . . . . sets are more concrete objects than numbers. At the same time operations upon sets are more meaningful to the student than manipulation of numbers . . . . the prior introduction of sets permits a clear, simple and precise characterization of numbers as properties of sets.'

The work is experimental in design. Material is made, taught and tested under controlled conditions. There is considerable stress laid on precision in the use of technical language.

Pupils' tests and teachers' guides in the *Sets and Numbers* series from kindergarten to grade 2 have been developed.

Other Mathematics Projects

(i) *Geometry Project of the Department of Mathematics at Stanford University* (Stanford University, California; National Science Foundation support).

(ii) *Foundations of Mathematics for Elementary School Teachers* (Department of Mathematics, State College of Iowa, Cedar Falls, Iowa; National Science Foundation support).

(iii) *Introducing Mathematics, I: Vision in Elementary Mathematics,* by W. Warwick Sawyer (Penguin Books, Baltimore, Maryland).

(iv) *Mathematics for the Elementary School* (Colorado Department of Education).

(v) *Minnesota Mathematics and Science Teaching Project* – MINNEMAST (University of Minnesota, Minneapolis).

(vi) *Number Work for Nursery School* by Joy C. Levy, 102 Russell Road, Princeton, New Jersey).

(vii) *The Greater Cleveland Mathematics Program* – GCMP (Educational Research Council of Greater Cleveland, Cleveland, Ohio).

II. Science Projects

The great upsurge of concern about teaching of science since World War II has had its impact on the elementary school no less than at higher levels. Five-year-olds are now expected to include science in their curriculum as naturally as they do the singing of songs or listening to stories.

A great deal of thought has been given in America to the construction of suitable courses for young children. There has been a variety of approaches, but with some common ground. The following objectives, with varying degrees of emphasis, might be considered to apply in all the courses:

(i) to introduce science to young children in a way that brings out the main concepts of the sciences;

(ii) to give an appreciation, through the methods of teaching and learning, of the methods and skills used by scientists;

(iii) to prepare appropriate materials (manuals, workbooks, films, equipment, etc.) to assist the teacher and the children;

(iv) to try to solve the problem posed by the fact that there are a number of special sciences, not just one; and the related problem that some sciences, such as geology, astronomy and meteorology, have usually been neglected.

Four of the well-known projects are briefly summarized below, and others are listed.

The Elementary Science Study (ESS) This course of study is being prepared by Educational Services Incorporated (ESI), or, as it is now called following its recent merger with the Institute for Educational Innovation (IEI), the Education Development Center Inc. (EDC). EDC is now one of the regional laboratories authorized in the 1965 Elementary and Secondary Education Act. ESI is well known for its early work in curriculum development, particularly in connexion with the secondary course Physical Sciences Study Committee (PSSC). Its steering committee includes well-known university people such as Bruner of Harvard and Zacharias of the Massachusetts Institute of Technology.

The project to develop materials for teaching science from kindergarten to 9th grade was begun in 1960.

The spirit of the course is to appeal to each child's understanding in science as a significant component of modern life; it is not intended to appeal merely to students with special interest in science and aptitude for it.

It encourages active participation by the child, open enquiry combined with experimentation. 'We want students not only to recognize scientific authority, but also to develop both the confidence and the skills needed to question it intelligently. For this reason we feel it is necessary for the student to confront the real world and its physical materials directly, rather than through intermediaries such as textbooks.'[13]

The work is arranged in units dealing with a particular topic or activity. The units differ a great deal in scope and approach, drawing their material from a number of sciences, and are suitable for a range of ages and abilities. Some require special equipment which is supplied, or ordinary materials that can be acquired easily or made. They may be planned to be done in the classroom, in the playground, or away from school. They involve children in collecting, observing, constructing, testing, problem solving, as well as in reading, writing, and calculating. They are supplemented with teachers' guides, classroom kits, films, and other material.

The units are not rigidly prescribed. It is considered that the teacher has an important role to play in assisting students to observe accurately and interpret what they see, in stimulating their interest, and in sustaining the children's discovery approach.

ESS is a good example of a course which is based on activity, experience, and discovery by children, rather than on textbooks; one which is not rigid in its sequences, and which relies on good teaching.

The University of Illinois Elementary School Science Project This project was inaugurated in 1960 by a grant from the National Science Foundation. It has been directed by J. Myron Atkin of the College of Education, University of Illinois, and S. P. Wyatt of the Department of Astronomy.

This curriculum is of special interest in that it is based on astronomy. According to its directors a curriculum of this kind provides the opportunity to deal with fundamental principles of science and to make connexions with other sciences and with mathematics.

The main criterion used in selecting topics is the scientific one – their significance as seen by an astronomer. Thus there are in the course such topics as: the measurement of distances in space; the construction of models of the movements of objects in the solar system; gravitation; theories of origin of the universe, our galaxy, and the solar system; and stellar evolution.

Project books for the pupils and teachers' guides are supplied but the method of teaching is left to the teacher.

The Elementary School Science Project The Elementary School Science Project was launched in 1959. It is supported by the National Science Foundation and is centred at the Botany Department of the University of California, Berkeley.

In this course units are selected from mathematics and science, and coordinated loosely. The sciences concerned are chemistry, botany, physics, physiology, palaeontology and zoology. The units are distinctive in being substantial topics or strands that run through the course. For example, the unit *What am I?* (a study in human physiology) is divided into four parts as follows:

'How I Began' (embryology) for grades 1–3;
'How I Move' (skeletomuscular system) also for grades 1–3;
'How I Know' (nervous system) for grades 3 and 4;
'How I Keep Alive' (metabolism) for grades 5 and 6.

Examples of other units are Animal Coloration, Coordinates, Structure and Properties of Matter, Wave Motion, Population Dynamics, Plant Morphology.

The units are given grade allocations, but it is suggested that the teacher should vary these to suit the situations, and also select from the various strands of the course to give a balanced curriculum. No substantial contribution is made in this course to the vexed question of integrating knowledge from a number of different sciences.

Teachers' manuals are provided.

The Science Curriculum Improvement Study (SCIS) Another group, which began working at Berkeley in 1966 on a science course for the elementary school, is directed by Robert Karplus, an eminent physicist. The project is supported by the National Science Foundation.

The SCIS, in the words of its director, is 'an attempt to develop a teaching program whose objective is the increase of scientific literacy in the school and adult populations.'[14] It is the hope of the author that the course constructed will provide a pattern that can be understood by teachers rather than one which will be blindly followed by them, a hope that every educationist with the well-being of the schools at heart will applaud.

Its approach is to confront the very youngest children with intellectual challenges in connexion with natural phenomena, and continue this as the child moves through the school, evaluating the programme continuously. The key constructs that are needed for the development of the study of science, and that are considered to be within the grasp of young children, are the following: matter, living organism, variation within a population of similar individuals, physical system, and interaction. Trial units using these constructs have been produced and tested in the schools.

The general goals of scientific literacy and intellectual development are pursued by extensive direct contact with natural phenomena from both physical and biological science, an encouragement of observation and discovery by the children leading (with the assistance of the teacher) to abstract relationships at the various levels. First-level abstractions are the concepts of matter, living matter, and conservation of matter. Second-level abstractions are the concepts of interaction and relativity. Third-level abstractions are the concepts of energy, equilibrium, steady state, behaviour, reproduction, and evaluation of living organisms. The curriculum structure is designed to follow this hierarchical relationship of concepts.

The development of the project illustrates well a general problem faced by those who try to produce the 'ideal' curriculum: how to steer between the spontaneity of response and of initiation of ideas by children that is so natural an accompaniment of curiosity and discovery, the logical growth of science according to its perceived structure, and the nature of cognitive development according to some preferred theory (for example that of Piaget, Bruner, or Hunt, all of whom Karplus quotes with approval). The CSIS is an interesting attempt to do this.

Other Science Projects

(i) *Elementary School Science Improvement Project* (grades 1 and 2) (Utah State University, Logan Utah; National Science Foundation support).

(ii) *Minnesota School Mathematics and Science Teaching Project* – MINNEMAST (grades k–6) (University of Minnesota, Minneapolis, Minnesota; National Science Foundation support).

(iii) *Physical Science and Mathematics Project* (grades 2–9) (Washington University, St. Louis, Missouri).

(iv) *Quantitative Approach in Elementary School Science* (grades 1–6) (State University of New York, Stony Brook, New York; National Science Foundation support).

(v) *Science – A Process Approach* (grades k–9). (Commission on Science Education, American Association for the Advancement of Science, 1515 Massachusetts Ave., N.W., Washington, D.C.; National Science Foundation support).

(vi) *The Science Curriculum k–12 Approach* (National Science Teachers Association, 1201 16th St., N.W., Washington, D.C.).

(vii) *Science Manpower Project* (grades k–12) (Teachers' College, Columbia University, New York; supported by 34 American industries).

III. Modern Foreign Language Projects

The revitalized interest in the learning of foreign languages in America since World War II has already been noted. This was sharpened by a rigorous examination of language instruction undertaken by the Modern Languages Association with support from the U.S. Office of Education and a Carnegie Foundation grant. It led to legislation supporting a new emphasis on foreign language study (the National Defense Education Act of 1958). The learning of modern foreign languages by children had come to be recognized as a significant element in the defence of America!

The new movement has brought many significant changes.

(i) An extension of the range of languages studied from the traditional French, German and Spanish to include Russian, Asiatic languages and Arabic.

(ii) A lengthening of the typical two-year sequences in high schools to cover more of the high-school grades, and to begin in the elementary school. Projects covering as long a period as nine and ten years of study have been initiated.

(iii) An intensification of interest in methods of teaching languages, stimulated by the experience of direct teaching methods in the war. While there is by no means a consensus of opinion on methodology among the experts, there is a measure of common ground. The methods most commonly used are these:

(a) An audio-lingual method stressing listening and speaking. The first few hundred hours of foreign-language learning are devoted primarily to oral communication, with the teacher stressing oral accuracy within a limited range of structure and vocabulary. Reading and writing are given only as reinforcement of the oral work, and play a very minor role at the elementary school level.

(b) Systematic and regular practice to build the skills involved.

(c) The use of equipment which permits the child to practise privately as much as he wishes, and which increases the range of speakers and models — particularly native speakers, records, tapes, language laboratories, films.

(d) Emphasis on the pupils' understanding in all oral practices. Rote learning is believed to hinder the free and spontaneous use of foreign languages.

As is the case in England, the inadequate number of qualified teachers is a major problem in implementing the new ideas. According to Birkmaier,[15] a teacher using the audio-lingual approach should have:

'a near-native competency in the four language skills, listening, speaking, reading, and writing. He should also be well versed in the cultural ways of the foreign country. He must have an understanding of how a particular language works, and where the crucial points of interference lie between his native language and the foreign language. He must also have an understanding of the ways and means he can use to facilitate acquiring the language by the student.'

Teachers like this, in anything like the numbers needed, are going to be hard to come by!

Curriculum development in foreign languages is being undertaken on an interdisciplinary basis, involving the linguistic scientist, the cultural anthropologist, the educated native speaker, the language specialist, the technologist, and the teacher; and the typical course is produced in the form of teachers' guides, tapes, visual aids, textbooks, workbooks, tests, and supplementary reading materials. Not all of these would be needed at the elementary-school level.

An example of a project in teaching French is given below. The course *Bonjour Line,* prepared by the research centre at the Ecole Normale Superieure de Saint-Cloud, is also used in America. This has already been referred to in the description of modern developments in England.

The Modern Language Project 'Parlons Français' This was initially sponsored by the Ford Foundation, N.D.E.A., the Massachusetts Council for the Public

Schools, and 21-inch Classroom; and later by the Health de Rochemont Corporation. It is located at 9 Newbury Street, Boston, Massachusetts.

This is a three-year course for grades 4, 5, and 6, and is prepared for television. It includes two 15-minute programmes each week, with provision for 15 minutes of practice on each of the non-TV days. The teacher is expected to give 45 minutes per week of additional follow-up. Recordings are used as a review and reinforcement. Native speakers, both adult and children, are used.

Other Foreign–Language Materials
Below are listed additional materials prepared mainly as a guide to teachers. The leadership exercised by the Modern Languages Association in this work is clearly evident.

Modern Languages Association Elementary School Modern Language Guides (Darien, Connecticut: Educational Publishing Corporation). Listed below are a series of teachers' guides and materials in French, German, and Spanish for the elementary grades developed by the Modern Language Association Foreign Language Program.

Beginning French in Grade 3, Teachers' Guide, revised 1959: Disc recording.
Continuing French in Grade 4, Teachers' Guide, revised 1960: Disc recording.
Beginning German in Grade 3, Teachers' Guide, 1956.
Continuing German in Grade 4, Teachers' Guide, 1959.
Beginning Spanish in Grade 3, Teachers' Guide, 1958: Disc recording.
Continuing Spanish in Grade 4, Teacher's Guide, 1958: Disc recording.
Continuing Spanish in Grade 5, Teacher's Guide, 1958: Disc recording.
Continuing Spanish in Grade 6, Teachers' Guide, 1960.
Students' Book for *Spanish in Grade 6:* Reading units 1–7.

Films Dealing with the Methods of Teaching Languages
(i) *Audio-Lingual Techniques for Teaching Modern Foreign Languages* – 60 minutes, 16mm., sound, b & w (Modern Language Association Program Research Center, 70 Fifth Avenue, New York 11, N.Y., 1962). A series of four films, each based on an individual language – French, German, Russian and Spanish.

(ii) *The Minnesota Second Language Teaching Films* – 30 minutes, 16mm., sound, b & w (University of Minnesota, Minneapolis, Minnesota). A series of 25 films in French, German, Spanish, and Russian.

(iii) *Principles and Methods of Teaching a Second Language* – 32 minutes, sound, b & w (Teaching Film Custodians, 25 W. 43rd St., New York 36, N.Y.,1961-1962). A series of five films: 'The Nature of Language and how it is Learned', 'The Sound of Languages'; 'The Organization of Language'; 'Words and their Meanings', 'Modern Techniques in Language Teaching'.

This series is sponsored and produced by the Modern Languages Association of America and the Center for Applied Linguistics.

IV. Social Studies Projects

The academic trend so noticeable in the new science and mathematics courses is also very apparent in the revisions being made in social studies. Today it would be much more appropriate to refer to this subject as social science.

The approach to teaching is scholarly, logical, conceptual, and analytical. There is an emphasis on primary source materials, research, evaluation, and comparison. The explanatory concepts of the behavioural sciences have replaced descriptive information, and fundamental concepts have taken priority over current problems as a focus of study. In keeping with this trend, social sciences not ordinarily taught at school have been proposed for study – for example anthropology and sociology.

Few of the curriculum projects devoted to work in the elementary school have been developed sufficiently to enable a detailed appraisal of them to be made. Some of the most interesting projects designed for the elementary grades (or including them) are briefly summarized below:

Greater Cleveland Social Science Program This course is designed as a continuous one from kindergarten to grade 12, and is sponsored by the Educational Research Council of Greater Cleveland.

Content is selected from history, geography, sociology, philosophy, economics, and government to give a course that conveys the central values of American culture, and encourages attitudes of respect for free society and social responsibility.

Elkhart Indiana Experiment in Ecomomic Education This project is sponsored by the Department of Economics of the School of Industrial Development of Purdue University and by the School City of Elkhart, Indiana. The director of the project is Laurence Senesh of the Department of Economics, Purdue University, West Lafayette, Indiana.

The central idea in the approach is to test whether fundamental concepts in economics can be related to the child's experience on all grade levels, and be treated developmentally through the grades.

Committee on Curriculum Guide (kindergarten – Grade 12) Geographic Education This is a project on the National Council for Geographic Education, U.S. Office of Education, Department of Health, Education and Welfare, Washington, D.C.

A curriculum guide for planning courses in geography for kindergarten to grade 12 has been prepared, led by a committee of geographers. New ideas on materials, evaluation, and geographic skills are included.

Elementary Sequence in Behavioural Sciences This project is sponsored by the American Council of Learned Societies and Educational Services Inc., and directed by Douglas Oliver, Massachusetts.

It is designed for the elementary school and is planned to give the students accurate, objective materials from the behavioural sciences, and an understanding of their methods.

Improving the Teaching of World Affairs This project is sponsored by the Glen Falls Public School, New York, and the National Council for the Social Sciences; and directed by H. M. Long, Glen Falls Public School, Glen Falls, New York.

As its title suggests, the focus of the project is on increasing the pupils' understanding of other peoples. The course expresses a concern for an international outlook which is strangely lacking in other projects.

Other Social Studies Projects

(i) *Development of a Model for the St. Louis Metropolitan Social Studies Center* (grades k–12) (Graduate School of Education, Washington University, St. Louis, Missouri, U.S. Office of Education support).

(ii) *Preparation and Evaluation of Social Studies Curriculum Guides and Materials for Grades k–14* (College of Education, University of Minnesota, Minneapolis, Minnesota; U.S. Office of Education support).

(iii) *Preparation of Teaching Guides and Materials on Asian Countries for Grades 1–12* (Department of Education, University of California, Berkeley; U.S. Office of Education support).

(iv) *Development of Economic Education Programs* (grades k–12) (Joint Council on Economic Education, New York).

(v) *Economic Education Activities* (grades 1–12) Joint Council on Economic Education, New York).

(vi) *Elementary School Economics Program* (Industrial Relations Center, University of Chicago, Chicago, Illinois).

(vii) *Development of Sequential Curriculum in Anthropology for Grades 1–7* (Department of Sociology and Anthropology, University of Georgia; U.S. Office of Education support).

V. English, the Arts, and Health and Physical Education Projects

Developments in the remaining subjects have not been comparable with those in the subjects already mentioned. Although it has been recognized that 'in the eyes of posterity, the success of the United States as a civilized society will be largely judged by the creative activities of its citizens in art, architecture, literature, music and the sciences',[16] there has not been the sense of urgency in stimulating creative activities in schools, except in mathematics and science.

There have been promising moves outside the schools to raise the cultural level. The action of the Federal Government has been of great significance. It has created a National Foundation for the Arts and the Humanities, amended the National Defense Education Act to allow Federal support to subjects other than science, mathematics, and foreign languages, and it has increased its support to libraries. The Ford Foundation has decided to expand its programme of support to the arts. Research into creativity has intensified. Examples of studies being done are the Aptitude Project at the University of Southern California directed by J. P. Guilford, the work of the Institute for Personality Assessment and Research at the University of California at Berkeley directed by Donald McKinnon, studies of creativity in elementary-school children, by Paul Torrance at the University of Minnesota, J. W. Getzels and P. W. Jackson at the University of Chicago, and Kenneth Beittel at Pennsylvania State University.

Robert F. Hogan [17] makes a nice distinction between curriculum changes in English on the one hand and those in mathematics, science, and modern languages on the other hand. 'English', he says, 'is in a state of "fermentation",' whereas the other subjects are undergoing 'revolution'. This fermentation has directed attention to such questions as the use of mass media in the classroom — including paperback books — a freer approach to controversial books, and the use of structured linguistics in place of traditional grammar. The emphasis has been on secondary courses, but interest in the elementary school is growing. A major project, *Project English,* has been sponsored by the U.S. Office of Education under the Cooperative Research Program to promote research and experimentation in English teaching. This project covers the whole range of teaching from kindergarten to the graduate school.

Programmes in health and physical education have not changed greatly. Concern with health education is a continuing one, and takes new turns in changing circumstances. Teaching about smoking, narcotics, and other dramatic ways of endangering health is a feature of the present scene. Health education seems to be aligning itself with the sciences, perhaps as part of the movement towards higher academic standards.

Physical education seems to vacillate between objectives of physical fitness, aesthetic expression, recreation, and a holistic view of personal development. The main emphasis at present seems to be on physical fitness, and the subject moves uneasily in the new academic climate.

Three curriculum studies in health and physical education of national significance merit special mention.

(i) *The School Health Education Study,* sponsored by the Samuel Bronfman Foundation, which is studying curriculum materials for health education.

(ii) *The California Study,* sponsored by the Dairy Council of California and directed by Otis J. Cobb at Stanford Universtiy, which is studying the relation between student problems and school performance.

(iii) *The AAHPER Curriculum Commission Study,* being undertaken by the American Association for Health, Physical Education and Recreation, which is concerned with identifying and formulating concepts from problem areas in the curriculum. Some of the problems of the '60s and '70s identified by the Commission include accidents, venereal diseases, smoking, alcohol, teenage diets, obesity, poor mental health, lack of fluoridation, medical economics, and the lack of evaluation of health information, diseases, and disorders.

Concluding Comment

The thought given to the improvement of school curricula is most impressive, and the interest taken in the task by top-ranking university professors of mathematics, physics, and the rest equally so. It is a pleasing recognition of the importance of the foundations of learning by scholars who usually come into direct contact with it only at its advanced levels. The phenomenon of the 'Professor of Education without portfolio', as these scholars have been called is a fascinating one.

What is needed to derive full benefit from their contribution, and to raise the quality of American schooling to present aspirations, is an equally bold approach to teaching method and school organization.

Effective teaching can occur only in a 'behaviour setting', to quote an expression used by Barker and Wright,[18] in which curriculum, teaching method, teaching style, children, and organization are in functional harmony. We shall now turn to the new ideas about teaching methods and organization.

Teaching Method

VI. New theoretical aspects of instruction for productive thinking The strong emphasis on the structure of subjects which has been so evident in recent curriculum revisions has aroused a correlative interest in the search for suitable teaching methods, and in relating learning theory more specifically to teaching. As Bruner points out:[19]

'The psychology of learning has only been tangentially concerned, until very recently, with the optimal means of *causing learning to occur.* Very little of learning theory is given over to the designing of optimum orders of encounter for the learning of materials . . . . How can material of a certain kind be so presented and so sequenced that it will be readily and most transferably learned? The results of such theory would provide a basis for a *theory of instruction* that is complementary to a *theory of learning*.'

This problem of creating a theory of teaching which makes the most effective relationship between learners and learning tasks has been a persistent one in educational theory. It seems obvious that a subject has characteristics which exist apart from any mental processes involved, either in those who produce the subject or in those who try to understand it. The structure of the discipline is one thing, and the individual learner, with his particular aptitude, maturity, and motivation, is another.

As has been stated, a subject is most clearly described in a way that brings out its structure, showing the relationships between basic terms and propositions and those derived from them. This may not, however, be the best way to arrange it for teaching. A proposition that is logically simple may be harder for a child to understand than one which is logically secondary, because it is more unfamiliar to him. The development of knowledge is usually away from primary experience to abstractions, away from particular objects or events to general propositions. Accordingly it is to be expected that the order in which knowledge is taught, particularly in the elementary school, will differ from the order in which it is most systematically expressed.

Dewey makes this distinction the basis for two different kinds of teaching, which he calls the logical and the psychological methods. The former is described by him as follows:[20]

> 'Pupils began their study of science with texts in which the subject is organized into topics according to the order of the specialist . . . . Laws are introduced at a very early stage . . . . The pupils learn a science instead of learning the scientific way of treating the familiar material of ordinary experience.'

The psychological method he describes in these words:[21]

> ' . . . by following, in connection with problems selected from the material of ordinary acquaintance, the methods by which scientific men have reached their perfected knowledge, [the student] gains independent power to deal with material within his range, and avoids the mental confusion and intellectual dictates attendant upon studying matter whose meaning is only symbolic.'

Countless commentators, adherents and opponents of Dewey, have taken up the same theme and dealt with it in their own way. In the hands of some the psychological method, with its emphasis on the children (and with a rather sentimental psychology to match), has resulted in needlessly undisciplined learning and low levels of scholarship. In the hands of others the logical method, with its emphasis on the subjects to be learned (and with a rather ruthless or uninformed view of children to match), has resulted in undue pressure on children, and the setting up of undesirable attitudes to learning.

In the present period there are a number of new approaches to teaching (or new versions of old approaches), which could bring about changes in the actual behaviour of teachers which will do better justice to the current emphasis on student insight and higher productive academic achievement. Four will be pointed out, and examined briefly, namely (i) the stress on studying the structure of subjects, rather than on learning their results; (ii) the stress on appealing to higher mental processes in teaching; (iii) the relevance of intrinsic motivation to higher cognitive activity; and (iv) the stress on exploratory or discovery methods by the student. Although enlightened practitioners have always paid due attention to these aspects of teaching, the present concern is more among the theoreticians than the practitioners.

(i) *The stress on the structure of subjects* The distinction between the structure of a subject and the statement of the subject as a body of results may be expressed as a contrast between a body of knowledge seen as dealing with certain concepts and sequences, and as validating ideas in certain ways, and one seen as a formal statement of axioms, propositions, and proofs. Learning the first may be likened to learning to play a game, learning the second to learning the rules of the game; or, to bring this distinction more fully into context, the first is like learning to think and act like a mathematician, the second is like learning about mathematics. Thinking mathematically, if pushed far enough, will of course lead to a grasp of the subject seen as a comprehensive statement of results. But it is not necessary to assume this comprehensive statement, or the order in which it is expressed, in order to practise thinking like a mathematician. This point is effectively brought out by Hirst in the following quotation.[22]

'To grasp a valid proof or explanation is to recognize, in the end, an overall pattern of logical relations between propositions that satisfy certain criteria. To insist that this sequence of truths can only be grasped as truths by temporally building on previously adequately established truths, is to take the characteristics of what is to be achieved as an end for the characteristics of the process by which the end is achieved. Maybe the analogy with a jigsaw puzzle is valuable here. In a valid explanation the elements must fit together as if to establish the pattern of the puzzle; but there is no one temporal order in which the pieces must be fitted together to produce the pattern.'

Teaching a subject as a body of results, and teaching it to bring out its structure and methods of inquiry and proof, are likely to be very different. The first lends itself to expository methods, the study of textbooks, programmed texts, and similar materials in which the subject is arranged in logical sequence, the prescribing of set tasks to be covered, and the testing of the students' grasp of detail. The second rather suggests confronting the student with problems through which he explores what the subject is about, encouraging inventiveness instead of directing him to a conclusion, and evaluating his attitudes and methods as well as the results he achieves.

(ii) *The appeal to higher mental processes* The appeal to higher mental processes is closely related to the concern with understanding the structure of knowledge. Since Bloom[23] set out so explicitly the cognitive objectives that may guide the teacher, the methods used by teachers have been more frequently scrutinized with these objectives in mind. The verdict has been quite definite. Existing emphasis is mainly on the reproductive processes involved in information learning, rather than on the higher cognitive processes of analysis, synthesis, etc., on which problem solving and inventiveness depend. Moreover, the existing emphasis is buttressed by conventional learning theory with its stress on drill and reinforcement. As Snygg points out,[24] this learning theory has almost nothing to offer a teacher who wants to do more than teach the facts we already know:

> 'In its most widely accepted form, reinforcement theory simply attempts to explain why an act is repeated. This question, which was crucial when we were trying to teach children the answers to problems someone has already solved, or to keep on doing something they did not want to do the first time, has no relevance to a teacher or curriculum planner who is trying to develop creativity, initiative, and the ability to deal with new problems. It is impossible, by definition, to reinforce an act which has not yet been committed.'

The preoccupation with increasing the student's understanding of the nature of knowledge, and with the higher cognitive processes involved in productive thought, is leading to a new wide-ranging exploration of the various facets of teaching-learning situations,* particularly from the standpoint of the teacher's role. It should lead to a clarification of the nature of effective teaching, and dispel much of the confusion that has grown up in the last few decades about this.

(iii) *Intrinsic motivation* One aspect of students' learning to think like

---

* As an important example of this concentration of effort may be cited the conference on the nature of learning sponsored by the U.S. Office of Education in 1963 which was attended by some of America's most distingushed specialists in learning and child development. This conference was recorded in J.S. Bruner (Ed.), *Learning about Learning*, U.S. Government Printing Office, 1966.

historians, scientists, etc., rather than simply learning history, science, etc., is that their interest in the subject is self-sustaining, and derives directly from the experience of working in the subject.

How completely intrinsic motivation can be effectively used with different students is problematical. Bruner takes the view that 'totally dispassionate problem solving is probably limited to a few saints',[25] and talks rather of an 'optimum' balance between intrinsic and extrinsic rewards. Many teachers would agree with this view.

On the other hand the child's capacity for spontaneous, playful behaviour is obvious even though it has not always fitted neatly into motivational theory. Caron[26] has drawn attention to the discrepancy between behaviourist motivational theory and the fact of children's spontaneous activity. He writes as follows:

> 'The notion implicit in S—R drive theory — that the aim of all behaviour is quiescence and relief from stimulation — could scarcely be reconciled with the child's inordinate appetite for play and tomfoolery, his inexhaustible motility, his persistent questioning about matters that bear no possible relevance to his biological well-being, indeed, a vast range of investigatory and intellectual activities that seem to have no other purpose than their own occurrence.'

It is this readiness to engage in 'investigatory and intellectual activities with no other purpose than their own occurence' that is being seized on, and studied, in that it fits the present concern with achieving productive rather than reproductive thinking so much better than the appeal to extraneous goals such as social approbation, gold stars, high grades, or threat of failure. It is of course recognized that extrinsic motivation can be very effective in influencing children to learn, but the cost, in terms of permanence of learning, the transferability of what is learnt to other tasks, and, above all, the attitudes engendered, is being counted more realistically. The price in terms of inert knowledge and inert students may well be too high.

Neo-behaviourist approaches to the motivation of thinking such as those of Berlyne[27] and McClelland,[28] depict the organism as seeking not a quiescent state but an *optimum* level of activation above and below which the drive to restore equilibrium occurs. A concept such as this makes better sense of the state of boredom, and how activity may be initiated from it, than does the model of motivation based on viscerogenic needs.

Disturbance of this level of activation happens when unexpected occurrences take place in the environment. Glaser[29] reports that research, much of it with infra-human organisms, has indicated that the strength of exploratory behaviour is positively related to the degree of change in the stimulus situation provided by novel, unfamiliar, complex, surprising, or incongruous situations introduced into the environment.

The common element underlying these situations, according to Berlyne,[30] is that of conflict. In the case of knowledge-seeking behaviour ('epistemic' behaviour, he calls it) the conflict is conceptual, i.e. it occurs among beliefs, thoughts, attitudes, etc. He writes as follows:

'Various considerations suggest strongly that intrinsic motivational states and rewards can, if skillfully utilized, enormously increase (1) retention of new material, (2) understanding of new material . . . , (3) active search for information, (4) ability to solve problems by directed thinking, (5) recognition of a solution to a problem once attained.'

The teacher may use surprise, doubt, difficulty, and contradiction to stimulate conceptual conflict. Not that these tactics will automatically be successful. Children have to accept the conflict by seeing the point of it. The congruence between logical conflict and the perception of this conflict by the student is perhaps a little too facile for many teachers faced with pupils obstinately impervious to 'conceptual conflict'.

The use of intrinsic motivation, to be effective, at least with some children, is likely to require a flexible approach to curriculum content, accepting the child's interests rather than prescribing too closely what 'should' interest him. For other children habituated to act in terms of 'ego-motives' such as need-achievement, specific training in responding to motives other than achievement may be necessary. Alpert[31] points out that curiosity is at present lower in the motivational hierarchy than need-achievement, and suggests developing a sequential programme through the 12 years of school in order to develop and strengthen self-propelling intellectual motivation at the outset, rather than trying to dislodge motives based on social tension after they become well entrenched.

The relevance of early childhood experiences to the success of such a programme is obvious. Children who have learnt to think and act mainly to please their parents, or for some other instrumental purpose, will find the school's message of intrinsic satisfaction in school work rather strange. They are more likely to look to their teachers, and to their peers, for approval.

(iv) *Discovery learning* This topic was discussed at some length in the English context in the preceding chapter. It is an equally central topic in American thinking about teaching strategies. Some of the American viewpoints about it are in this section.

Bruner, who is regarded as one of the leading proponents of learning by discovery, writes as follows:[32]

'It is, if you will, a necessary condition for learning the variety of techniques of problem solving, of transforming information for better use, indeed for learning how to go about the very task of learning. Practice in discovering for oneself teaches one to acquire information in a way that makes that information more readily viable in problem solving. So goes the hypothesis. It is still in need of testing. But it is an hypothesis of such important human implications that we cannot afford not to test it — and testing will have to be in the schools.'

Later, he writes,[33]

'I am not quite sure I understand any more what discovery is, and I don't think it matters very much,' and he adds, 'but a few things can be said about how people can be helped to discover things for themselves.'

Cronbach[34] also expresses uncertainty:

'In spite of the confident endorsements of teaching through discovery that we read in semi-popular discourses on improving education, there is precious little substantial knowledge about what advantages it offers, and under what conditions these advantages accrue. We badly need research in which the right questions are asked and trustworthy answers obtained.'

He thinks it is time we put aside the polemic question 'Is teaching through discovery better than didactic teaching?' and asked more subtle and more limited ones.

A rather more extreme view (that of Kendler[35]) is that 'discovery' has become a nine-letter dirty word, and should be eliminated.

Wittrock[36] has made a useful analysis of the various confusions and ambiguities bound up in the expression 'discovery learning'. The statement below is based on this analysis.

(i) Discovery as a way of learning the structure of subjects is different from discovery as a way to teach problem solving. Putting this another way, we may distinguish *learning by discovery* from *learning to discover*. Discovery is both a means and an end, and the two should be distinguished. Otherwise, in asserting or testing the value of discovery learning, it is easy to fall into error. 'When learning and discovery are measured by one event, discovery cannot be given as a cause for learning. It does no good to say tautologically that those who discover learn.'[37]

(ii) What is to be discovered? Is it rule, generalization, or a more specific bit of information? Discovery may differ in its usefulness as a way to learn these different things.

(iii) Discovery learning is commonly equated with inductive learning, where the subject proceeds from the specific to the general. It is just as plausible to assume that the learner by discovery begins with a higher-order generalization from which he derives specific conclusions. Induction has no exclusive identity with discovery learning.

(iv) The benefits claimed for discovery learning are multiple — transferability, economy, retention, problem-solving ability, and various attitudes. In research studies the particular dependent variable concerned needs to be specified.

(v) There is a lack of operational definitions and objective indices for the term 'discovery'. Is it a discovery method because the teacher poses specific problems, but avoids rules or generalizations? Is it a discovery method when he uses vague or very general cues and avoids specific ones?

We may add some queries not raised by Wittrock. Do discovery methods have equal value for different children? Cronbach[38] is 'tempted' by the notion that pupils who are negativistic may blossom under discovery learning, whereas pupils who are anxiously dependent may be paralysed by demands of self-reliance. To what degree can children learn to use discovery methods? Is discovery learning (appropriately defined) equally useful in learning subjects other than mathematics and science? — a great deal of the current discussion of educational method seems to assume that the whole curriculum consists of these two subjects.

It may be concluded from this examination of the term that, although there is a strong feeling in the U.S.A. that learning by discovery is a hypothesis of great significance, there is a great deal of confusion in its meaning and use, and that considerable redefinition and reformulation are needed to increase its usefulness as an educational concept.

More positively, Gagné's definition[39] may be quoted:

> 'Within an act of learning, discovery may be said to occur when the performance change that is observed requires the inference of an internal process of search and selection. What is sought for and selected varies with the kind of learning that is taking place.'

His idea of the implications that discovery learning has for educational practice is well worth reporting:[40]

> 'First is the idea that discovery is an integral process for varieties of learning. It is not a panacea for learning effectiveness, nor is it an essential condition for all kinds of learning situations. Second, when discovery does occur, it is obviously dependent upon internal events

generated within the learner. This means that if one is interested in promoting the occurrence of discovery to achieve some educational objective, he must somehow see to it that prerequisite capabilities have been established. In other words, there must certainly be a lot of attention to the preparatory plan of instruction, if discovery is going to take place.'

In a review of the conference recorded in the publication *Learning by Discovery* from which quotations by Wittrock and Cronbach have already been taken, Keisler and Shulman[41] state what seems to be warrantable about the concept 'learning by discovery' and what needs to be done to make it more useful. The following statement is adapted from their review.

Four categories are proposed within which to evaluate the concept, namely classroom practice, curriculum development, the psychological study of learning, and research strategy. Each is a distinct universe of discourse within which discovery learning needs to be examined.

First, then, how is the behaviour of teachers affected? How much and what kind of guidance should teachers give to children? The answer is clear, but unhelpful: the degree of guidance varies from time to time along a continuum, with almost complete direction at one extreme to practically no direction at the other. Great significance however is attached to *preparing* students to profit from a learning experience.

Bruner[42] suggests six ways in which the teacher may prepare pupils for discovery.

(i) He can encourage them to believe that they *can* solve problems, that they *can* go beyond the evidence. 'You must wait until *they* are willing reflectively to turn around before you begin operating with the abstractions. Otherwise they will become obedient and non-comprehending.'[43]

(ii) He should expect them to be intrinsically interested. 'You can corrupt them too easily into seeking *your* favour, *your* grades'.[44]

(iii) He can help the children to find the connexion of what is being studied with what they know.

(iv) He can give the pupils practice in the skills related to the use of information and problem solving. One of these skills is pushing an idea to its limit; another is that of hypothesis making; another is training in being concise (Bruner talks of the overwhelming prolixity that hinders children's thinking, a problem that can be echoed by most thoughtful teachers).

(v) He can help children to turn round their own behaviour, to see it reflectively, to make explicit what is implicit — Bruner calls this the 'self-loop' problem.

(vi) He can help the children to explore contrasts, and by so doing help them to organize knowledge in a fashion that helps discovery.

The question whether the right amount of guidance is given is a critical one; it can best be answered by individual teachers who are able to gauge whether pupils are able to deal effectively with a broader class of problems as a result of the teaching.

We turn now to the theme of discovery learning in relation to curriculum development. It is not easy to reconcile a concept of curriculum development embodying objectives, an ordered sequence of topics, and materials, with that of discovery learning. The first suggests a well-planned and signposted route, the second an unknown place with few direction signs. Achieving this reconciliation is probably the most serious challenge faced by the curriculum planners. It requires a clear recognition of whether the course is aiming at knowledge which may be taught either didactically or by discovery; or whether it is aiming at behavioural objectives which can be acquired in no other way than through the experience of exploration. If the latter, then curriculum planning must give genuine scope for novelty and unpredictability, restricting itself mainly to what Bruner has described as preparatory exercises, i.e. ones that facilitate the productive flow of the students' ideas.

One qualifying statement that should be made is that no method of learning used exclusively is likely to be successful, nor indeed is it appropriate. The scholar, whose activity is often taken as a model in recent writings on the curriculum, does not engage continuously in discovering new knowledge. He engages in a broad range of behaviour, some of it involving invention, some reception. What underlies them both is his characteristic knowledge-seeking attitude. Curriculum planners could well take cognizance of the purposes which different topics may serve, and accept the fact that the teacher's judgment must be trusted.

One of the major questions posed in the conference referred to was the direct one: what conclusions can be drawn from the research evidence to date as to the effectiveness of the method of learning by discovery? The answer is clear, but disappointing: the question as stated is not amenable to research solutions because the discovery method is far too ambiguous and imprecise a concept to be used meaningfully in an experimental investigation.

The position will not be improved until research does justice to the magnitude and complexity of the problem, and clearer descriptions are given of events that comprise the treatment, or lesson. Cronbach's proposal[45] to focus on a narrow problem under limited circumstances with a well-defined population, rather than attempting definitive tests of the overall hypothesis represents one interpretation of how the position could be improved.

Those who favour a form of teaching that 'opens up' the child tend to take a similar view of appropriate research strategy for studying this problem. The traditional hypothesis-testing model is for them too limiting. Fruitful research in dealing with forms of human behaviour that are difficult to identify reliably, and to measure accurately, come from a more general exploratory approach.

The controversy over discovery learning has many aspects of partisanship about it. The phrase has become something of a slogan. Without doubt, however, there is some substance in it which has attracted gifted teachers over the centuries. Without doubt, too, this substance is peculiarly relevant today, when educators are searching for means to improve the quality of learning, and particularly to increase the pupil's creativeness and to strengthen his zest for learning. It would be a great pity if the difficulties (semantic and otherwise) over discovery learning were to be interpreted by teachers as indicating that the idea is discredited, even in part. Many significant ideas in education are hard to define, and difficult to experiment with.

Bruner's theorems for a theory of instruction Having commented on the salient ideas of current writing about teaching method, we may conclude this section with a summary of Bruner's recent statement[46] of the scope of a theory of instruction. It sets out in a comprehensive way the elements of teaching method suitable for the new objectives of schooling.

There are according to Bruner, four aspects to a theory of instruction:

(1) The optimal experiences or encounters that predispose a learner to learn;
(2) the structuring of knowledge that is optimal for comprehension;
(3) the optimal sequences of presentation of materials to be learned;
(4) the nature and pacing of rewards and punishments.

Each of these is amplified in the sections below but in much shorter form than in the original.

1. *Predispositions to learning*

(i) Teaching should have as one of its objects the opportunity for the pupil to explore alternatives, subject to the conditions

(a) that the risks involved in exploration should be minimized,
(b) that errors should be made as informative as possible, and
(c) that previously established constraints on exploration (e.g., from the effect of family or culture) should be vitiated.

(ii) The relation between the one who teaches and the one who is taught affects the nature of the learning that occurs.

(iii) The child must have minimal mastery of the social skills necessary for engaging in the instructional process.

(iv) Early training in elementary intellectual skills, such as language and simple manipulative skills, is critical for later development.

(v) Instruction always involves a decision about the best use of a given culture pattern in achieving educational objectives. Culturally deprived children would at least not be taught from the same point of origin as middle class children.

(vi) Optimization of learning results from a matching of learning materials to the style of the learner.

2. *Structure of knowledge*

(i) A set of statements about a subject can be reduced to a simpler set that is more economical to learn, and more generative of new knowledge. This reduction is most apparent in mathematics and science, less in history and literature.

(ii) The economy and generative power of a set of statements about a subject are dependent, however, on the mastery already attained by the user.

(iii) Any structure of propositions that effects a productive simplification of a body of knowledge can, similarly, be restated in a simpler form that is both powerful and effective in the sense of being within reach of a learner. In short, any subject can be taught effectively in some intellectually honest form to any child at any stage of development.

(iv) What one knows about something cannot be separated from the order and manner in which the knowledge was acquired.

(v) At a very minimum, any body of knowledge can be presented in three ways:

(a) in terms of a set of actions to be performed to achieve certain results;

(b) in terms of certain summary images that 'stand for' the subject in the sense that a diagrammatic triangle 'stands for' the concept of triangularity;

(c) in terms of a set of symbolic or logical propositions strictly governed by well-defined laws of formation, transformation, induction, implication.

(vi) The three general systems of representing or structuring knowledge can be described as parallel in the sense that doing, picturing, and symbolizing can be pursued without interference by one in the others.

(vii) But it is possible to translate each system of representation into any other; the burden of evidence points to the fact the the translation of a body of knowledge into the three systems of representation has the effect of altering and enriching each of the systems.

(viii) Where an individual is starting to learn a body of knowledge completely from the beginning, the task of instruction involves some optimal orchestration of the three systems of representing that knowledge.

(ix) Subjects vary in the degree to which they have been subjected to effective and economical representation. Some are tightly summarized by general propositions (e.g. physics), others loosely summarized (e.g. social studies). It does not follow that because a subject is highly developed it should be introduced to a learner in this way. It is often the case that a manipulative and picturable knowledge of phenomena is necessary before a learner can grasp the referents of a symbolized representation. The curriculum can be in spiral form.

3. *The nature of optimal sequence*

(i) Sequences of learning can be devised to optimize the achievement of different objectives. One cannot, therefore, speak of *the* optimal sequence for presenting a body of knowledge. Different objectives may be:
(a) a particular form of presentation (as in 2 (v));
(b) a type of learning (for example one that is as quick as possible, or as proof as possible against disruption by stress); or,
(c) the conversion of knowledge into economical conceptual structures, or the recognition by the learner of the transferability of what has been learned to new situations.

(ii) For the kind of learning referred to in 3 (i) the following hypotheses are proposed:
(a) it is better to learn the basic conceptualization of a set of facts by induction from particular instances.
(b) The learning of a conceptual structure seems to require that there be contrast between a positive and negative instance.
(c) Premature symbolization of a conceptual relationship may have the effect of leading a learner away from the relationship between symbols and things symbolized.
(d) The size of step that one should employ in presenting a sequence of material to be learned varies with the present ability of the learner, and depends too on the kind of eventual ability that one wishes to produce.

(iii) It is rare for everything to be learned about anything on one encounter. Because of this too the curriculum should be a spiralling one.

4. *Reinforcement and information*

(i) Two terminal states that may follow upon an attempt to master some task may be distinguished. They are success or failure, and reward or punishment.
(a) Success followed by strong external reward will have the effect of increasing the likelihood of the same kind of performance another time. (This result may or may not be desirable.)
(b) Error with consequences of punishment from outside is more likely to disrupt behaviour than to provide a basis for correction.
(c) There is a dual function provided by success and failure on the one hand (a function of informativeness) and by reward and punishment on the other (a function of need reduction).

(ii) The balance between the intrinsic reward of problem solving and the external rewards that come as a sequel poses a threefold problem: a problem of the nature of the balance, a problem of phasing the balance over time, and a problem of segmentation. Each involves a compromise between intrinsic and extrinsic rewards. Each is dealt with below.
(a) In most cases learners require some reward for intellectual work other

than the joy of using the mind to tackle and master problems. What is needed is an optimum balance between intrinsic and extrinsic rewards.

(b) Studies of latent learning, where external motives are minimal, indicate that information achieved in such a state can later be organized for instrumental activity leading to specific rewards. But studies of learning under excessive drive for external reward suggest that what is lost in learning cannot be easily recovered. The asymmetry is not trivial.

(c) It is often necessary in initiating learning to resort to an initial regimen of praise and reward for each successful act. The danger lies in letting the learner become dependent upon the reward and the rewarder to keep the behaviour going. Optimum phasing requires a gradual process of giving the rewarding function back to the task and the learner.

(d) Segmentation refers to the nature and size of an act, and raises the question of where opportunities for success and for reward should be provided. Determining optimum units of this kind is almost as obscure as it is important.

Conduct and affect

Bruner distinguishes between a theory of instruction, which is concerned with the mastery of a body of knowledge, and a theory of belief and its inculcation. He claims that there is often a conflict when the same institution is charged with the forming of convictions and with the imparting of knowledge, and the latter suffers. His views regarding the relation between learning and conduct and affect are given below.

(i) One objective of learning, over and beyond the mastery of a body of knowledge, is to create a better or happier or more courageous or more sensitive or more honest man. The conduct of life is not independent of what it is that one knows nor is it independent of how it is that one has learned what one knows.

(ii) Knowledge is instrumental to values; it does not of itself predispose one to either decency or its opposite. Curricula should be constructed in terms of the instrumental assistance that knowledge imparts to the exercise of values, rather than in terms of the values the curricula impart.

(iii) The effectiveness of values depends not only upon knowledge of the instruments of their expression, but also upon a sense of the alternative ways in which one can succeed or fail in their expression.

(iv) Instruction in the values of society or in the values of a profession or group or family is based upon the acceptance or rejection of axiomatic or unprovable propositions about preference.

Concluding comment on Bruner's theory of instruction

Bruner's theorems for a theory of instruction have been summarized at some length, both because of their intrinsic importance and also because they exemplify the new concern in America with efficient teaching by scholars outside the 'establishment' of professional educationists.

Bruner modestly claims that there is bound to be some foolishness in such a preliminary exercise. Certainly there are things that are not new (and his comment 'yet it does provide something of a beginning'[47] is scarcely necessary); there are things that are inconclusive (for example, the 'optimal' conditions need to be actually determined not merely stated to be necessary); and there are things that are controversial (particularly the suggestion that a theory of instruction can be separated from a theory of belief, even when the latter is concerned with the rules or morals of thinking).

The new emphases of educational theory are likely to displace the influence of earlier learning theories, which (at least as interpreted by teachers) have made imitation, repetition, reinforcement, and extrinsic motivation the main guides to method. In a country where teaching is approached more as a science than an art, it is important that the theoretical basis for change be laid. It is always difficult to change the thinking and practice of a vast body of practitioners, even if the rationale for change is clearly understood and convincing. Without such a rationale it would be virtually impossible to do so.

VII. Educational Technology

Perhaps the most arresting evidence of modernity in American education is the invention or adaptation of machines for use in teaching. Few aspects of education have caught public interest as much as this.

To the ordinary person teaching holds few secrets; it has none of the mystique that surrounds medicine, aeronautics, and the rest, with their unfamiliar techniques and their complex equipment. Now that the technologist has moved into the educational field, new ways of doing old and routine things are possible, as well as new and exciting things. It may help to give teaching a little of that glamour that comes from being in tune with the spirit of the age.

A discussion of educational technology has relevance to all three divisions of this chapter — curriculum, teaching method and organization. The major emphasis will be given to its role in assisting the teacher, and for this reason it is included in the section on teaching method.

The scope of educational technology is obviously wider than its use in elementary education. Indeed many of its major uses are mainly, if not exclusively, found in secondary and higher education, in research, in library organization, and in administration.

Its scope, even within elementary education, is very wide, and a section such as this can be begun humbly with the words of Ely[48] in mind:

'No one can speak authoritatively about all the new developments in educational technology. The new frontiers are too vast, too complicated, and changing too rapidly.'

We have become used to the idea of audio-visual aids in education, the use of projectors, tape recorders, records and the like which enrich the teacher's presentation.* These are of continuing importance, if not now considered as innovations.

The new trends with this older equipment are such as to increase its effectiveness or convenience in use. With the increasing use of transistors, equipment is being made lighter and more compact. It is also becoming easier to use, with fewer controls, and tasks such as the threading of tape simplified by the use of cartridges. Combinations of equipment are also a modern development, for example the combined slide projector and tape recorder.

In America educational technology is thought of as being much more than an aid to teaching. It is regarded as a complex integrated organization of machines, procedures, and management. The technological aspects that are being experimented with are not optional extras which may be employed at the discretion of the teacher, but are integral to the process of teaching. Indeed a great deal of theorizing about the processes of instruction is being prompted by the requirements imposed by television lessons or teaching machines.

Most attention in this treatment of educational technology will be given to the use of the computer in teaching, because this is the major innovatory trend. Some other types of equipment will also be briefly described, either because of their special interest or because of their novel character.

'Button pressing' instead of 'hands up' A time-honoured method by which students have responded to the teacher's instructions or questions has been for them to put their hands up. From this simple act, teachers learn a great deal: who knows the answers, whether the same people are consistently answering or not, which questions are hard and which easy, and so on. This gesturing is a primitive kind of external signalling of a hidden, cerebral process.

There are the following machine versions of this 'hands-up' prototype of pupil response, as reported.

(i) A device on each student's desk allows him to press buttons which switch on lights of different colours visible to the teacher. 'All hands up' using this device would become 'all lights green!' A sophisticated version of this is reported as being installed in 500 auditorium chairs at Chicago Teachers' College North. As the students react to various questions from the lecturer, the distribution of responses is shown at his podium on meters calibrated in percentiles. A

* The Educational Media Index (published by the McGraw-Hill Book Company) lists over 60,000 items – charts, maps, films, kinescopes, filmstrips, flat pictures, models, mock-ups, records, audio-tapes, programmed materials, slides, overhead transparencies, and video-tapes. There are also microfiche film cards (and readers) for the convenient storage of filmed references, articles, etc.

computer enables the responses to be recorded, evaluated and printed, giving a picture of the performance of the group as a whole, as well as an individual record of each student's responses.

(ii) Another version is called a 'teletest system', and may be thought of as the up-to-date equivalent of an examination book. Each student has a responder unit, and these are wired into a system which includes the teacher's unit and an electric typewriter. The question is asked, an agreed period of time elapses (during which a light is visible to the student), the response is made, and recorded by the typewriter.

(iii) An even more complex system allows for the connexion of remote-controlled projectors. By means of a series of buttons, it is possible for the teacher to prearrange the use of the projectors or tape-recorded material. Digital counters, one for each student, are provided, and also a device that allows weighting to be given to particular questions. Once the system is programmed, the teacher's presence is not needed.

These responding units are an interesting example of the imitation of ordinary patterns of student-teacher behaviour. They attempt to cater for what is ordinarily done in teacher-student interactions in formal lessons, and improve on it by making the student responses more immediately apparent, and by recording and analysing them more effectively.

The language laboratory In 1955 there were no language laboratories in America. In 1962 there were 10,000, and at present there are many more than this. Many of these are in the elementary schools.

It was the new interest in foreign-language learning after World War II that brought the language laboratory so quickly into prominence, and it was the Federal Government's funds, provided in the National Defense Education Act that brought them into the schools.

Basically the language laboratory is an intercommunication and recording system which allows a number of students to listen simultaneously to the one person (teacher or someone else, live or recorded), to respond individually, and to record their own responses. Different versions of it encompass a variety of physical arrangements of the equipment (fixed booths within a room, around the perimeter of a room, in a mobile unit, etc.) and a variety of additional facilities coordinated with it, making it more appropriately named a communications centre (reproduction of tapes and records, motion picture films, television, video-tape recorders, etc.).

While the concept of a language laboratory arose in connexion with foreign-language teaching, it has spread beyond this. The facility is equally suitable for work in music appreciation and in the native tongue, and various other aspects of English.

Programmed instruction Programmed instruction, as is well known, dates back to the early work of Pressey in 1926, but its popularity today results from the work of Skinner in 1958, who envisaged the teaching machine as an autonomous device not requiring the assistance of a teacher.

It is unique among the major technological devices in that it was developed specifically for educational use. It is closely linked with the psychological theory of learning and teaching. 'Since programmed instruction is an active approach to teaching, it forces the development of theoretical notions about instruction, because instructional decisions must be built into every program.'[49] Without doubt the programmed instruction movement has done a great deal to make explicit the various steps and processes involved in the effective presentation of materials, and to clarify the processes of instruction, whether performed by teachers or by mechanical means.

A review of the steps involved in the formulation of a programme as seen by Lewis[50] will help to clarify this point.

(i) Specific and clear objectives for the programme must be established at the outset.

(ii) The body of content involved in reaching the goals must be identified.

(iii) Content must be broken down into small bits of learning that are easily understood and mastered by the learner.

(iv) Increments must be arranged in learning sequence, together with the insertion of 'cues' and 'prompts' and review increments to assist in the assimilation process.

(v) Each increment is arranged to be followed by a challenge in the form of a question to be answered, a problem to be solved, or a function to be performed.

(vi) Provision is made to inform the learner of his success, or to provide reinforcement after each challenge has been met.

There are differences of opinion as to how steps (iii), (iv), and (v) in this sequence are best done. The 'linear' programmes of Skinner are one version, the 'intrinsic' or 'branching' programmes of Crowder are another. Some students find the small steps of the Skinner-type programme boring, others find the larger steps in the branching programme too difficult. Catering for individual differences with prearranged programmes is not without its problems.

Yet its use in individualized instruction is one of the major claims made for it. Ely sets out this claim in these terms:[51]

(i) Every student is continuously involved with the task, a condition seldom obtained in the classroom.

(ii) Learning is completely self-based; the learner can proceed as slowly or as rapidly as his ability requires.

(iii) Motivation to learn becomes very great as the result of continuous success built into the programme.

(iv) The teacher is relieved of his responsibility for ensuring routine learning, thus leaving time for the development of creative and critical thinking skills. Stolurow[52] stresses the same advantage:

> 'Programmed instruction has many different, but specific, implica-
> tions for educational practice; one of the most important is
> individualized education . . . . It is probably most adequately de-
> scribed as a philosophy for the education of the individual student
> which is based upon a psychological analysis of the teaching–
> learning process as it takes place through the use of an educational
> dialogue between teacher and student. Programmed instruction is an
> innovation in the individualized or tutorial instruction.'

One of the major issues in connexion with programmed instruction concerns the role of the teacher. Where large segments of work, or whole courses, are programmed, the teacher either becomes redundant or serves merely as a supplement to the machine. A practice that is gaining ground is the use of short units that deal with particular themes or topics, and which can be used flexibly by the teacher to supplement work being carried on by other methods. Programmes of this kind seem to be particularly appropriate in the elementary school. It is hard to envisage young pupils following through a lengthy programme with any degree of verve; but short programmes, used as information sources in connexion with a topic being studied, are obviously useful.

The most striking use of programming is in computer-assisted teaching, and this is taken up in a later section.

Educational television Educational television is by no means a recent innovation in America, and there are some well-established systems in operation, both broadcast and closed-circuit. It is, however, a developing field, and may be regarded as a new medium, particularly for the elementary school.

Probably the best-known and most unusual of the broadcast systems is the Midwest Program on Airborne Television Instruction, known as MPATI. This is a project of the Ford Foundation, costing in excess of $7 million to put into operation. Television programmes are sent to 17,000 classrooms in a large area of the Middle-West from two transmitters installed in an aircraft. Programmes extending from the lower elementary grades to college level have been provided. Other large networks based on states or regions have been established, with a number of production centres feeding programmes into the system.

Smaller, more local systems have been made possible by the Federal Communications Commission's authorization in 1963 of channels for education purposes in the 2,500-megacycle band. These systems operate with low-powered transmitters with a coverage of 10 to 15 miles. This 'decentralized' approach to the provision of educational television is more attractive to some than the large network.

Closed-circuit television for instructional use is common in institutions of higher learning, but is also used by some school systems. Coaxial cable is used to link schools together so that they can take a programme from a central source.

A major development in educational television has been the production of relatively low-cost video-tape recorders. The video-tape recorder adds greatly to television as an educational medium. It enables programmes to be stored for use when needed, and to be repeated. It makes it possible for the student's actions to be recorded and played back to him, a technique of obvious value in many aspects of school work, and one with a great variety of uses in the hands of imaginative teachers.

There is a sharp contrast between the 'amateur' use of television by teachers using TV equipment in their own classrooms with students or having their own lessons recorded, and the professional approach to television based on commercial standards of production. In most countries in which ETV has been used there is some difference of opinion between the teachers or audio-visual specialists on the one hand and the professional broadcasters on the other, and this controversy exists in America. The broadcasters use methods that have been successful in television as a mass medium, and insist on a well-rehearsed presentation. The audio-visual specialists approach the television lesson as a televised classroom lesson, making only those concessions to the medium that are necessary to ensure that the viewing audience see and hear all that is necessary. Less rehearsal time is needed with this method, and of course the costs are less. Mistakes, or unrehearsed variations, are accepted in the same way as they would be accepted in 'live' lessons. Indeed this kind of spontaneity is regarded as an advantage. The major responsibility for the presentation, except for the technical aspects involved in lighting, camera technique, etc., is assumed by the teacher.

The distinction is analogous to that between the making of films using specific techniques appropriate to cinematography and the making of films by photographing live theatrical performances that would be ordinarily played on a stage. Just as the film technique permits features which are not possible on a stage, so the television technique permits things that are not possible in a classroom.

The Department of Audio-Visual Instruction of the National Association (DAVI), which has been very influential in promoting the use of audio-visual aids in American schools, represents this view of television as a classroom device. Both approaches are being used in America, and both seem to be successful.

The use of television as a teaching medium should no doubt vary according to the level at which the instruction is attempted, the subject being taught, and the purpose of the teaching. Care needs to be taken that it does not become an inflexible medium of instruction, reintroducing to teaching much of the formality and disregard for individual differences that better teachers have been able to overcome.

So far as the use of television in the elementary school is concerned, it could be said that there is some limited room for didactic teaching, especially if it is on tape and can be taken full advantage of by the teacher, and that there is room for more general programmes that enrich the child's understanding and experience. The most exciting prospect, however, is its use for the recording and playing back of children's activities. In this way it could create great interest in the children, and be a powerful analytic tool.

For it to be possible to put the producing of television programmes into the hands of teachers and children, there needs to be a reduction in the cost of equipment, in its size, and in the complexity of its operation. Fortunately there are trends in all three of these directions.

The use of the computer in education Foremost among the machines in the van of educational change is the computer. It may also prove to be the most significant. Its most obvious use is in the administrative tasks of education – in the processing, storage, and retrieval of data, be they salaries, library materials, students' marks or research measurements. Less obvious, but potentially of great significance, is its use in instruction. It is in this connextion that it is discussed here.

Computer-assisted instruction is more a research theme than accepted practice, although in a limited way it is already a reality. The idea is familiar enough, however, to be known around America by its initials CAI, and it is thus that it will be referred to here.

The world of CAI has its own devotees, and its own language which contains a strong injection of engineering–psychological jargon. The educationist who prefers ordinary English (or his own kind of jargon) may be repelled by this, but he has to come to terms with it if he is to understand CAI properly and judge it fairly. A sample (only moderately obscure) of this language is given below. It is a description of the sequence of events in a CAI programme in initial reading.[53]

'The computer pulls in from a disc unit the necessary commands for a given instructional sequence or program. These commands involve directions to the terminal devices to display a sequence of alphanumeric symbols and specified pictorial symbols on the CRT, to present a given image on the projector, and to play a particular audio message. After the appropriate visual and auditory material has been presented, a ready light comes on to tell the student to respond. Once a response has been entered it is evaluated by the computer and (on the basis of this evaluation and the student's past history) makes a decision as to what material is to be presented next. The time-sharing nature of the system allows for a cycle through these evaluation steps in less than one or two seconds.

As each response is input to the system, it is recorded in a canonical form that identifies the student, the particular problem he is working on, the response made, and the response latency. Thus a complete history is available on each student which can be used on-line to make decisions regarding the instructional sequence, and off-line for research purposes.'

Adams,[54] writing of the capability of CAI, states that it can do the following:

(i) Engage in two-way communication with a student by means of natural-language messages;

(ii) Guide the student through a programme of tasks, helping him where he has difficulty, and accelerating his progress where he finds little challenge;

(iii) Observe and record significant details of the student's behaviour, including steps undertaken in performing tasks, time taken for particular steps, and values of varying physiological and environmental quantities;

(iv) Simulate the operation of a physical, mathematical, or social process responding to variations in parameters;

(v) Analyse and summarize performance records and other behavioural records of individual students, and also of groups of students.

Although it has a fixed repertoire of responses (and cannot devise impromptu solutions to problems), this repertoire may span a great range of difficulty in the exercises programmed. Pupils can thus work on materials appropriate to their ability over a wide range of individual differences. The 'logical' power of the computer permits complex processing of student responses, and can indicate the order in which assignments in the program should be given.

Thus, in a significant way, the computer may be regarded as creating the opportunity for individualized teaching, *so long as this is interpreted as the treatment of a prescribed learning task at alternative levels of difficulty, at alternative speeds, and with alternative diagnoses of pupil deficiencies in performance*. It cannot provide for individualized teaching when this is interpreted as the opportunity for children to be exploratory and inventive in proposing unprogrammed responses, or in ranging outside the universe of discourse set up in the program.

A great deal of thought has been given to the requirements of programs for computerized instructional sequences. They require an analysis of the objectives in teaching a subject and of the appropriate cognitive process involved in a learning sequence, and an integration of these with sufficient elaboration of specific tasks for the student to provide the number and range of steps and illustrative examples needed. Such a planned pattern of display (as it is called) by the computer and response by the student is called an *interface*. For those experimenting with CAI, it is the creation of the interface that is the critical task.

The Research and Development Center at the University of Pittsburgh, which specializes in the study of learning, has given considerable attention to CAI, and has set out[55] an analysis of the design of an instructional interface for mathematics, reading, and science in the elementary school. This stage of schooling is chosen deliberately, as it is considered that the concern of the elementary school with general habits of thinking makes it very suitable for a computer approach. As an illustration of the type of analysis employed in the construction of an interface, the properties of elementary mathematics and the requirements for learning it are given below.

Demands made on children learning mathematics

According to the authors of the report, mathematics imposes the following cognitive demands on children learning the subject in the elementary school: (i) making the correspondence between sets of objects and a numerical presentation; (ii) discriminating numeral shapes; (iii) performing arithmetic operations as defined by the number system; (iv) recognizing patterns in the operations which can be performed with numbers and objects; (v) discriminating spatial properties and relating numbers to the properties of space; together with the computational skills relevant to these concepts.

Interface requirements for stimulus presentation and student response

Each of these conceptual demands of the subject has to be worked out in terms of the display provided and the varieties of possible student response. A brief statement of this follows.

(i) *Making the correspondence between sets of objects and numerical representation*: presentation of arrays of objects such as discs, sticks, toys, and matching the numerals with the proper set of objects by various response modes, e.g., by writing numerals, by selecting from alternatives, or by oral statement.

(ii) *Discriminating numeral shapes:* in order to teach the numerals which correspond to the number property of sets of objects, the interface must have a visual display mode. When the student has mastered the ability to relate arrays of three-dimensional objects to a number, two-dimensional presentations of arrays of dots, squares, pictures of animals, etc., may be used.

(iii) *Performing arithmetic operations:* similar visual display and type of response may be used for these as for teaching the correspondence between numbers and numerals.

(iv) *Recognizing patterns in the operations that can be performed with numbers and objects:* an important area of learning in mathematics is the search for pattern in numerical and spatial relationships. Through the search for pattern, students can be led to consideration of the operations involved in addition, subtraction, multiplication, division, and various combinations of these. He can also be led to generate his own sophisticated relationships. Exercises such as investigating series of numbers are used, e.g.:

If you say	3	7	1	4	9	2	17	8	5	10
I answer	8	20	2	11	26	5	50	?	?	?

(v) *Discriminating spatial properties and relating properties of numbers to properties of space:* in order to deal with the properties of space the interface suggested is as follows:

(a) to develop the ability of the student to respond to three-dimensional figures, e.g., sphere, cylinder, etc.,

(b) to abstract the properties of three-dimensional figures when presented with a two-dimensional stimulus,

(c) to use two-dimensional representations to visualize the properties of a three-dimensional object,

(d) to use the two-dimensional representation to develop the point-by-point properties of space – this involves the problems involved in the calculation of surface areas.

Instructional procedures

In the preceding section the requirements of an interface suggested by the demands of the subject have been enumerated and briefly elaborated; in this the additional requirements suggested by learning procedures are discussed. There are seven procedures that are considered necessary in the report under discussion, namely (i) determination of entering behaviour, (ii) participation in terminal behaviour, (iii) generalization display, (iv) gradual progression, (v) reinforcement, (vi) guiding of learning and (vii) withdrawal of guidance. A brief commentary on each of these is given in the following paragraphs.

(i) *Determination of entering behaviour*: by this is meant assessment of what the student already knows about the material which will be taught in the programme. Account can be taken of this assessment in prescribing a course which is designed for the pupil's individual interests and abilities.

(ii) *Participation in terminal behaviour*: this refers to the early introduction to the student of the end product of the instructional sequence to assist learning and to enhance interest. A simulation (for example of flying an aircraft, performing a diagnosis, singing a song, reading a sentence), in which the student has the feeling of participation in the terminal behaviour, gives the student a familiarity with the terminal behaviour without having to accept any consequences of error. A similar result can be achieved through the use of stories, films, and dramatizing devices.

(iii) *Generalization display*: this has to do with the process by which concepts are formed. The pupil learns to respond to similar elements in different learning situations, and to make appropriately different responses to different stimulus situations.

(iv) *Gradual progression*: the planned progression through the material must be gradual enough to minimize wrong responses, and at the same time allow for errors to be used as effective learning experiences.

(v) *Reinforcement*: reinforcers may be extrinsic (gold stars, praise), or intrinsic (knowledge of success). Intrinsic reinforcers are preferred when they are effective.

(vi) *Prompting and guidance of learning*: in many states of instruction efficient learning requires a hint or guide to the appropriate response to be learnt. A prompt which can be used as mediator in future learning is to be preferred to prompts which are unrelated to future tasks.

(vii) *Withdrawal of guidance*: the prompting referred to in (vi) may be withdrawn as the need for it diminishes. The need for guidance may be inferred from the time it takes the student to respond after the presentation of a stimulus.

University of Stanford's Projects in CAI Stanford University is another important centre for the study of computer-assisted instruction. At the Institute for Mathematical Studies in the Social Sciences there, a number of studies are in progress. Reference has already been made in the section dealing with mathematics-curriculum projects to the work of Suppes, who is the Director of the Institute.

Another study is reported by Atkinson and Hansen.[56] This one is concerned with instruction in initial reading and was quoted from at the beginning of this section. The importance of setting up a computer-based system of instruction in initial reading is seen in the testing of its feasibility, and in providing a school-based laboratory in which research and evaluation on the curriculum may be carried out. Such a laboratory would be free of many of the limitations which at present detract from curriculum experiments, such as imprecise specifications of instructional materials, and insufficiently detailed records of each student's performance.

The reading curriculum was developed by a team consisting of two psychologists, a linguist, two specialists in reading, and several teachers and advanced graduate students. The materials produced were developed within the framework of a set of theoretical propositions based on recent developments in psycho-linguistics and learning theory. These propositions provide a fairly detailed descriptive explanation of the acquisition of coding schemes that permit the initial reader to pronounce correctly any permissible string of English orthography.

It is reported that more than 200 lessons have been written. They are organized into six basic levels, each level containing about 35 lessons. The time taken over a lesson by a student would of course vary. The typical lesson contains the following types of instructional materials:

(i) Letter discrimination and identification, achieved mainly by matching single- and multiple-letter strings to models, and making same–different judgments about paired strings of English orthography.

(ii) Initial vocabulary acquisitions, introduced with an appropriate visual display.

(iii) Word decoding tasks, stressing common elements of alliteration and rhyming in simple monosyllabic words – bag, bat, ban, rag, rat, ran, etc.

(iv) Syntactic and intonation practice with phrases and sentences, providing the pupil with systematic presentations of eight basic types of English sentences and their associated intonation patterns. Initially the material is presented with such introductory words as 'I'll', 'It's a', 'That's a', 'They can', etc.

(v) Syntactic and semantic practice with phrase and sentence material, providing practice in vocabulary and its meaning, and recognizing word function (noun, verb, etc.) and the relation of subject and predicate in sentences.

(vi) Information processing tasks, requiring the retrieval of certain information from simple stories involving simple recall, or inference.

It is the hope of the authors that the procedures adopted in their research, and those suggested by future research, will help to lay the groundwork for a theory of instruction that will span the diversity of concepts and skills found in an elementary-school subject such as reading. They comment as follows:[57]

> 'Such a theory will have to be based on a rich and highly structural theory of learning, plus an optimization strategy that follows logically from the theory, and is compatible with current educational goals.'

Description of CLASS (Computer-based Laboratory for Automated School Systems) As another example of the interest in CAI, the 'automated classroom' of the Systems Development Corporation at Santa Monica, California, is worthy of mention. This is described by Bushnell[58] who is closely associated with the Corporation. CLASS is described as 'a new facility for the research and development of a complete educational system that would provide optimal learning conditions.[59]

It accommodates 20 students, each of whom receives an individualized sequence of instructional materials adapted to his particular needs, or learns in a group mode of instruction mediated by the teacher or computer. Each student has a manually operated film viewer containing 2,000 frames of instructional material. In addition, he has a response device which indicates the sequences of slides to be seen by the student: this enables the student to respond to questions, and presents knowledge of results to the student in the form of coded lights. CLASS is more than a multi-channel teaching machine. It will permit instruction through different media, including television, films, and slides, as well as by conventional lecture and textbook methods.

One of the most important aspects of automated teaching is the record which the student leaves of his learning experience. As students are required to respond actively at frequent intervals by filling in a missing word or selecting a multiple-choice answer, they leave accurate and detailed records which provide a basis for revising the education programme so that it may be improved. Provision is made in CLASS for two teachers. Each teacher is able to determine at any time the present progress of an individual student or a group, and is alerted by the computer to students who are performing unsuccessfully in their lessons.

Bushnell sees in the capability of the computer to perform the more routine and straightforward tasks of teaching a major contribution to efficient teaching. He states:[60]

> 'Liberated from most record-keeping, paper-grading tasks, and the basic necessity of packing students with factual material, the teacher can concentrate on the extension of student understanding, on stimulating student imagination, and on providing individual help and counsel.'

Concluding comment It is natural to wonder about the future of CAI. Is it a major new factor in education, or an interesting fad that will pass?

Dr. Senshu[61] suggests the possibility of feeding the output of the teaching machine directly into the brain, without first having the information processed by the senses. All that is necessary is to find the input terminals in the human brain, and the necessary code!

But without such a development, bordering on science fiction, it seems reasonable to predict that CAI will become a major research interest and will have significant repercussions on educational practice. A prediction such as this can be made, quite irrespective of any intrinsic merit that CAI may have in improving the efficiency of instruction or in providing a substitute for teachers. It obviously has great research potential because of the effectiveness of the experimental controls it can exercise, and because of the scope of its recording power and the range and subtlety of its analytic power.

Moreover, it is in line with the major tradition of instruction in America, which expresses such faith in a structured presentation of subject matter and in a wedding of logical and cognitive structure. It is in line with the American faith in educational technology, and – perhaps not least of all – it has had the support in the form of major investments, of a number of the giants of the educational business houses. It is likely to continue and expand as one of America's most interesting innovations in education.

School Organization

The main innovations in school organization are directed towards catering better for individual children, and are adequately summarized in two movements, namely non-grading and team teaching.

The first is proposed as a way of permitting children to work better at their educational level, whether it is below or above the normal standard for their age; the second as a way of bringing the resources of a staff to bear for the greatest benefit of each child.

Neither of these measures will of itself ensure that children are well taught. Good teaching needs a good curriculum and good methods. But these organizational measures make it possible for the curriculum and the methods to be more effective.

Elementary education traditionally has been organized on a grade basis, and the idea of standards of achievement in each subject for each of the grades is firmly embedded in American thinking, both lay and professional. The idea of having one teacher responsible for the work of a class is also traditional. Thus both non-grading and team teaching are major departures from established practice. It is not surprising that they are being approached cautiously.

VIII. Non-grading

The modern concept of non-grading may be said to have been put forward first in 1959, when Goodlad and Anderson published *The Nongraded Elementary School*.[62] Since then the idea has been discussed at great length; and in a limited way, and with varying interpretations of its meaning, put into practice. Some definitions and descriptive statements of it are given below:

> Anderson:[63] 'Nongradedness refers to two dimensions of the school and its atmosphere: the philosophy (or the value system) that guides the behaviour of the school staff towards the pupils, and procedures by means of which the life of the pupils and teachers is regulated.'
>
> Brown:[64] '. . . a place which makes arrangements for the individual student to pursue any course in which he is interested and has the ability to achieve, without regard either to grade level or sequence.'
>
> Dufay:[65] 'A philosophy of education that includes the notion of continuous pupil progress, which promotes flexibility in grouping by the device of removing grade labels, which is designed to facilitate the teacher's role in providing for pupils' individual differences, and which is intended to eliminate or lessen the problems of retention and acceleration.'
>
> Howard and Bradwell:[66] 'Nongradedness refers to any effort on the part of a faculty or administration to take into account factors other than age when the grouping of students is being considered.'

The statements given, and others that could be quoted, are somewhat vague.

They refer to an intention to secure certain results, such as individualization of instruction and independent study, rather than to definitive organizational plans. Perhaps a concept which takes its meaning from the negation of another is inevitably vague until it is elaborated in more positive terms.

Goodlad's analysis,[67] which puts non-grading into perspective when related to other forms of school organization, gives to the concept the positive meaning that it needs. He classifies school organization into three models, each being delineated by reference to five features — (i) school function, (ii) means of fulfilling function, (iii) organizational structure, (iv) individual differences, (v) pupil progress.

The advantage of looking at the concept of nongradedness within such a conceptual scheme is that it brings out the interdependence of organization and other associated features such as objectives, curriculum, method, etc.

The model that deals with organizational structure as *graded* has the following associated features:

School function: to inculcate a specific body of subject matter.

Means of fulfilling function: prescribed curricula.

Individual differences: recognized as a factor determining a child's chances in the race to cover prescribed material, but not as one to be taken account of in planning the programme.

Pupil progress: non-promotion the primary mechanism for dealing with slow-moving students.

The model that deals with organizational structure as *non-graded* has the following associated features:

School function: to develop the pupil as an individual and as a member of society.

Means of fulfilling function: by concentrating on the ways of knowing and thinking of individuals.

Individual differences: recognized in many aspects of development and used in planning highly individualized programmes.

Pupil progress: provision is made both for differentiated rates of progress and variations in kinds of programme according to individual needs and abilities.

The third model lies in between these two. It is multi-graded* in organization, and has the following features:

School function: (as in the first) to inculcate a body of knowledge.

Means of fulfilling function: (as in the first) prescribed curricula.

Individual differences: differences in ability and accomplishment are recognized, with an attempt to differentiate progress accordingly.

Pupil progress: non-promotion is not used, but the time allowed for

* The term 'multi-graded' is used to describe a class in which a number of grades within the class are identified.

completion of the course is decreased for bright students, and increased for less able students.

It can be seen from these models that any consideration of gradedness or nongradedness brings up the larger questions of the school's purposes, the methods of teaching, and the way in which differences among children are dealt with. As Goodlad says:[68]

'Take grades away then; have done with them. The result is non-graded structure. All this appears rather simple, but it is only a beginning. Since school structure is but a shell, dropping the grades and adding or changing nothing else leaves curriculum and instruction — the heart of the educative process — as they were before. *Non-grading is a significant factor in school improvement only as it is seen and used by teachers as means to significant ends they wish to achieve.'*

A 'full-fledged' non-graded school, according to Anderson,[69] would be able to claim that all the following statements apply to it.

(i) Suitable provision is made in all aspects of the curriculum for each unique child by such means as (a) flexible grouping and subgrouping of pupils, (b) an adaptable, flexible curriculum, (c) a great range of materials and instructional approaches.

(ii) The successive learning experiences of each pupil are pertinent and appropriate to his needs.

(iii) Each child is constantly under just the right amount of pressure. Slow learners are not subjected to too much pressure, as they are in a graded school, nor are talented learners exposed to too little.

(iv) Success, with appropriate rewards, is assured for all kinds of learners so long as they attend to their tasks with reasonable diligence and effort. Such success spurs the child to a conviction of his own worth and to further achievement.

(v) Grade labels and the related machinery of promotion and failure are non-existent.

(vi) The reporting system reflects the conviction that each child is a unique individual.

(vii) The teachers show sophistication in their curriculum planning, evaluation, and record keeping.

(viii) For certain purposes, pupils enjoy regular social and intellectual contacts with other pupils of like mind and talent; for other purposes, their contacts are with pupils of different minds and talents.

(ix) The school's horizontal organization pattern allows for flexibility in grouping pupils, and in using the school's resources. *It is possible* to have a non-graded, self-contained classroom pattern, for example; although it is also possible to have a more flexible horizontal arrangement such as the Dual Progress Plan,* informal cooperative teaching, or full-fledged team teaching, in combination with the non-graded arrangement.

It might appear from Anderson's inventory that a non-graded school is equivalent to a good school. Not all agree with this. Below are set out some of the common criticisms culled from two sources:[71]

The effect on the teacher: (i) it places an impossible burden on the teacher; (ii) it lacks fixed standards and leads to 'soft pedagogy'.

The effect on the curriculum: (i) it replaces grade requirements by some other requirement, e.g. reading levels; (ii) the curriculum sequence tends to lack specificity and order.

The effect on parents: it makes it difficult to report adequately to parents.

Concluding comment on non-grading The three headings used above – what non-grading means in terms of demand on teachers, what significance it has for what is taught at school, and how pupils' success is made known to parents – are the main ideas around which discussion on non-grading will centre.

As teachers increasingly accept the challenge of guiding the learning of a heterogeneous class of students as a normal teaching task, and adjust to the fact that personal development takes surprisingly different forms, and as the community becomes less competitive and more disposed to judge achievement on a variety of criteria rather than on the few that lead obviously to preferred vocations, the need for talking about non-grading will disappear.

It is a concept that expresses a protest against grading, rather than a substantive one in its own right. Positive ideas, like teaching for personal development, will probably make its use necessary.

IX. Team Teaching

Shaplin and Olds[72] define team teaching in the following way:

> 'Team teaching is a type of instructional organization, involving teaching personnel and the students assigned to them, in which two or more teachers are given responsibility, working together, for all or a significant part of the instruction of the same group of students.'

It has leapt into prominence in America. As Anderson[73] states,

> 'Even the most casual examination of state and national convention programmes shows that team teaching is among the most prominent

* The Dual Progress Plan as proposed by Stoddard[70] is a semi-departmentalized approach for grades 4, 5, and 6. Half the day is spent with a home teacher responsible for reading studies and a physical education specialist; the other half is devoted to mathematics, science, art, and music taught by specialists.

topics for discussion and debate. Almost every national magazine in education has already given the topic signal attention, and the research agencies of the NEA, the U.S. Office of Education, and affiliated groups have in some cases been swamped with appeals for information and help . . . . It may well be wondered whether any other arrangement has created so much excitment in so short a space of time.'

An examination of the case for it, and a more detailed description, are made in the following sections.

The case for team teaching (i) The first point is the advantage to *children* that is likely to accrue from being taught by a number of teachers. Not all elementary-school teachers are equally good at each field of school work, particularly at present when the demands being made on teachers by the new curricula are so great. Though most elementary-school teachers in America have a substantial background in English and social studies, relatively few have a thorough understanding of mathematics, science, music, art, or foreign languages. Even under conditions where the modern training of elementary-school teachers is likely to produce an improvement in scholarship in these subjects, special competence and preferences in them will remain. The question of how the special strengths of staff members are best used is a practical matter of great importance, and will be taken up in describing team teaching in a later section.

(ii)The second point is the advantage that *teachers* are likely to derive from working as a team. Under ordinary conditions, when teachers are responsible for the work of a single class, they see surprisingly little of their fellow teachers' work, nor do they have the experience of having their own teaching observed by others. Team teaching brings them together in a way that enables them to become more aware of teaching styles, more aware of their own approach, and more disposed to examine alternative approaches.

Teachers vary not only in their teaching styles, but also in their experience. A newly appointed teacher is feeling his way; a senior teacher has much to give; a teacher's aide has limited responsibility, and requires direction; a student-teacher (who is so often to be found in schools) requires help and encouragement. In separate classrooms every teacher (apart from the aide and the student) is expected to assume much the same responsibilities. In a team they contribute according to their capacities and responsibilities and receive assistance as they require it. It is the different purposes that a teaching team can serve for different teachers that makes it such an appealing idea to Conant.[74] He writes:

'The long-standing notion of a self-contained classroom of 30 pupils taught by one teacher is giving way to alternative proposals. One of these proposals is team teaching, which ... has advantages in orienting new teachers.

If the idea of team teaching becomes widely accepted – and many elementary-school principals predict that it will – there will be places in classrooms for a wide range of instructional talent. How such schemes will work out over the years in practice remains to be seen, but team teaching seems to many the answer to the questions of how to attract more of the ablest college students into elementary-school teaching. The possibility of a teacher's having an opportunity to take advantage of her special field of interest is exciting.'

(iii) The third point is the advantage that comes from the more flexible grouping of students that is possible when compared with the ordinary arrangement of single-teacher classes. Teachers use intra-class grouping for various purposes in teaching, but team teaching makes it possible to use any form of grouping within the larger group over which the team presides.

In the secondary-school version of team teaching a common arrangement is to group all the children for some mass teaching, e.g. for lectures, films, or TV. For many people this is a *sine qua non* of team teaching, and provision for it is increasingly being made in the newer school buildings. Anderson[75] gives the following three reasons in support of it:

(i) in certain circumstances it may be a more efficient manner of working because of the spur of a large group to the teacher, and the availability of a wide range of audio-visual devices;

(ii) it is economical because of its size, and seems capable of giving results equivalent to the results in smaller groups;

(iii) even assuming that the results obtained are somewhat inferior to those from smaller groups, they may be adequate to justify the use of such groups in view of the economy of staff time involved.

For many elementary-school teachers for whom any regular use of mass teaching is hardly compatible with the objectives of teaching at this level, these arguments do not appear to be very compelling, and it is more comforting to read Anderson's[76] comment on this in another place:

'Although it is true that most teams do a good deal of teaching in large groups, it is theoretically legitimate and possible to have scarcely any large group lessons in team teaching.'

(iv) Fourth, there is the advantage that team teaching has in stimulating thought and discussion among teachers who are jointly responsible for a group of children. Professional behaviour is likely to develop best where there is a strong sense of involvement and responsibility. A school which is run dictatorially, with all the important decisions about curriculum and organization being made by the principal, is not likely to engender this sense of responsibility. A team-teaching arrangement which is allowed to operate responsibly and with reasonable freedom within the school organization is considered to be a most productive one for encouraging teachers to act professionally. The situation imposes specific demands needing thought and imagination. The processes of deliberation heighten involvement, and involvement intensifies the search for worthwhile solutions to problems.

Practical issues in team teaching The theoretical case for team teaching is a strong one, but its success will rest on the way it works in practice. Indeed its full meaning will only emerge as teachers in different settings work it out in their own way. A few procedures have emerged for the composition of teams and their method of working, the grouping of students, special school facilities, evaluation procedures, and the like, and there has been a tendency to identify team teaching with these procedures. What is needed are widespread trials of the idea, and detailed case studies of actual practices. One might predict that it will prove to be a productive idea, not only in fulfilling its own special purposes, but in influencing other aspects of the work of the school as well.

The points used in the preceding section to put the case for team teaching are convenient ones for discussing the practical aspects; these are dealt with now.

Using the special talents of teachers The obvious plan for making use of the different qualifications of teachers is some form of specialist teaching, but there is little enthusiasm for this at the elementary-school level. The slogan adopted by the elementary school in Lexington, Massachusetts, which pioneered team teaching – 'most of the teachers in the teams will teach most of the subjects most of the time' – is widely accepted. The case for multi-disciplinary teams at elementary-school level is not that each teacher will teach only those subjects in which he is competent. It is rather that he will make a specialist contribution to the team in planning the teaching of the subject, in accepting a special responsibility for studying new developments in the subject and bringing them to notice, in acquiring appropriate books and equipment, and from time to time in making a specialist contribution to all the groups on topics which the other teachers could not manage. He will, in short, act as consultant within the team for a particular subject.

The success of a plan like this depends on having a balanced team in which all the major subjects of the elementary-school curriculum are provided for. As teachers with strong qualifications in mathematics, science, and foreign languages are likely to be in short supply for some time, and as it is unlikely to be possible in each school where team teaching is attempted to form well-balanced teams, it will be necessary for some teachers to assume special responsibilities for developing competence by their own reading and attendance at in-service courses where weaknesses exist.

The composition and structure of teams Depending on the number of children it is considered convenient to put together as a group, the teams are likely to consist of two or more teachers, together with auxiliary staff as these become available. Such staff may include teacher's aides, a clerk, a library assistant (perhaps part-time) and student-teachers where these are regularly attached to the school. In structure they may be formal, with well-defined positions for each person, or informal with a democratic form of functioning.

Goodlad's[77] use of the term 'team teaching' implies a hierarchy of personnel as well as a differentiation of staff functions based on differences in qualifications or personal interests. The hierarchy involves a team leader, assistant teacher, teacher's aide, intern teacher, and clerk, or some other array of resources. So-called team teaching that does not have such a hierarchy is more properly called cooperative teaching. Anderson,[78] another authority in this field, regards hierarchical structure as a very logical and attractive arrangement, but not as an absolute requirement in the definition of team organization. He sees the team leader selected for his position because of his talent as a teacher, his special qualifications in a particular subject, his organizing ability, his understanding of the curriculum, and his skill in diagnosing and evaluating pupil behaviour, together of course with his willingness to take on the additional responsibility. It has been argued that a position of such responsibility should be rewarded by a higher salary, and that to do so would increase the career prospects of good teachers in the classroom and make it less likely that they would seek promotion by leaving teaching for administrative positions. The hierarchical model for a team may also contain the position of 'senior teacher', who occupies a rank next to the leader, and whose qualifications would be more pedagogical than administrative.

One view of the bureaucratically structured team is that it affords a means of providing adequate leadership and supervision of staff throughout a school. In a large school it is obviously impossible for the principal to give all the supervision and leadership that would be desirable. Team teaching offers a solution to this problem by dividing staffs into small units.

Such an arrangement could produce a very tight form of control in which the policies of top administration could flow through principals and team leaders to classroom teachers. So far as the classroom teacher is concerned the consequences of this could conceivably be the opposite of that claimed for team teaching, at least in the stimulation of teachers' professional interest. As Lortie[79] points out:

'. . . it probably would result in a routinization of task and subordination of status, especially where team leaders were closely coordinated through the school system. Levels of output could be more closely controlled than under current arrangements . . . . Teaching style and content could come under the control of a dominant leader . . . . Educational objectives would become more specific and standard throughout the system . . . . The range of choices made by the classroom teacher would contract . . . '

The alternative to the bureaucratically structured team is what Lortie[80] calls the collegial type. In this there is a strong emphasis on internal equality and close harmonious relationships among members. Such an arrangement is not inconsistent with some differentiation of role within the team, such as leadership in particular activities, or responsibility for specific tasks, but these arise from within the group itself rather than being imposed from without.

The difference of opinion over the nature of the structure of groups is generally debated with fully qualified teachers in mind. Clearly, so far as student-teachers and para-professional staff are concerned, the need for clearly stated roles exists. If the collegial team arrangement is used, it must be sufficiently formal to provide for these.

The grouping of students It has been pointed out that the full meaning of team teaching will only emerge as evidence of it in practice accumulates, and the details of these practices are made known. This is particularly true in relation to the grouping plans used. There has been something of a tendency for grouping practices to be routinized, and for a uniform pattern to be followed (or described), consisting of large group instruction followed by the normal class group plus a tutorial period in a group half or one-third the size of the class. But the criteria for forming groups are many and varied – a common interest, a common difficulty, the use of some special facility, a common need for remedial work, etc., and the size of the groups could vary according to the need. The greater flexibility in grouping that is so frequently put forward as one of the advantages of team teaching is achieved in some degree by balancing large groups against small ones, but above all by balancing teaching time against private study. An effective team-teaching situation provides both the opportunity in time, and the materials, for independent study by pupils. Once it is accepted that the pupils do not have to be directly taught all the time, flexibility in grouping becomes possible.

The professional stimulation to teachers afforded by team teaching The central problem in securing professional growth among teachers is to get them to relate effectively the practical realities of day-to-day teaching to a developing body of educational theory. The usual means employed to do this is by the offering of in-service courses of various kinds. Such courses are of course necessary, but in themselves they have only limited success. Team teaching offers a unique setting for professional involvement by teachers that can contribute significantly towards professional development. The teachers are in a situation where they are interacting with each other, while dealing with problems and pupils that are a matter of direct personal concern. As one American teacher[81] is quoted as saying:

> 'In the old kind of school you could close the classroom door at the semester's start and not come out until the semester was over, and you could be teaching the telephone book for all anybody knew. As a member of a team, the job churns with stimulating variety . . . . Once, teachers had little to share with each other but gossip. Now they are constantly exchanging ideas and making decisions with team mates.'

A common problem reported by teachers who have become involved in team teaching is that there is inadequate time for all the meetings and discussion that are desirable for planning work, discussing individual students, considering evaluation measures, and so on. But this kind of problem inevitably arises when interest in an activity increases. Not being able to find time for all the things one wants to do in a job is a sure indication of deep involvement.

Team teaching is not a panacea for education. Like other organizational steps it does not solve problems, unless other factors are favourable. As stated by Bair and Woodward[82] in their general assessment of team teaching:

> 'The desperate need for curriculum revision, the tragic neglect of the individual pupil, and the urgent need for better-trained personnel with time to plan, teach, and evaluate are all brought into sharp forms by this type of programme. Team teaching does offer an effective vehicle for identifying these problems, for studying them, and for seeking solutions to them.'

Concluding Comment

In concluding this account of innovation in elementary education in America it is appropriate to repeat that no assessment has been attempted of the degree to which ideas have been adopted in practice. Whether the ideas are in the schools or not, they certainly are in the conferences, the journals, books, and popular magazines, and in the research bodies. There is tremendous traffic in them as they move through the different communication networks. To a visitor the almost obsessive concern with innovation is a little bewildering, but it is also stimulating. Undoubtedly many of the ideas currently being explored will have an enduring effect on practice both in America and elsewhere.

REFERENCES

1. Paul H. Hirst, 'Educational theory', in *The Study of Education* (Ed. J. W. Tibble), Routledge & Kegan Paul, London, 1966.
2. Paul H. Hirst, *ibid.*, p.44.
3. J. S. Bruner, *The Process of Education*, Vintage Books, New York, 1960, p. 31.
4. Donald McNasser, *This Frantic Pace in Education*, March 1967 (mimeographed).
5. Donald McNasser, *ibid.*
6. James B. McDonald, 'The person in the curriculum', in *Precedents and Promise in the Curriculum Field* (Ed. Helen F. Robinson), Teachers' College, Columbia University, 1966, p. 47.
7. R. S. Peters, 'Education as Initiation', in *Philosophical Analysis and Education*, The Humanities Press, New York, 1965, p. 107.
8. Robert B. Davis, *Discovery in Mathematics: A Text for Teachers.* The Madison Project, 1964, p. 21.
9. Franz Hohn, 'teaching creativity in mathematics', *Arithmetic Teacher*, March 1961, p. 112.
10. University of Illinois Arithmetic Project, *General Information* (mimeographed).
11. Robert B. Davis, *Discovery in Mathematics*, 1964, p. 8.
12. Patrick Suppes, *Sets and Numbers*, Institute for Mathematical Studies in the Social Sciences, Stanford University, 1960 (mimeographed).
13. Introduction to Elementary Science Study (ESS) by Educational Services Incorporated (E.S.I.), 1966.
14. Robert Karplus, *Theoretical Background of the Science Curriculum Improvement Study*, Berkeley, California, 1966, p. 4.
15. Emma M. Birkmaier, 'Foreign languages' in *Using Current Curriculum Development*, Association for Supervision and Curriculum Development, Washington, D.C., 1963, p. 25.
16. The Report of the President's Commission on National Goals, *Goals for Americans by the American Assembly*, Prentice-Hall, New York, 1960, p. 9.
17. Robert F. Hogan 'English' in *New Curriculum Developments*, Association for Supervision and Curriculum Development, Washington. D.C., 1965, p. 16.
18. Roger Barker and H. F. Wright, *Midwest and its Children*, Row & Peterson, Evanston, Ill., 1965.
19. J. S. Bruner, Introduction to *Revolution in Teaching* (Ed. Alfred de Grazia and David A. Sohn), Bantam Books, New York, 1964, p. 54.
20. J. Dewey, *Democracy and Education*, Macmillan, New York, 1961, p. 257.
21. J. Dewey, *ibid.*, p. 258.
22. Paul H. Hirst, 'The logical and psychological aspects of teaching a subject', in *The Concept of Education* (Ed. R. S. Peters), Routledge & Kegan Paul, London, 1967, p. 55.
23. B. S. Bloom, *Taxonomy of Educational Objectives, Handbook 1: The Cognitive Domain*, Longmans, New York, 1956.
24. Donald Snygg, 'A learning theory for curricular change', in *Using Current Curriculum Developments*, Association for Supervision and Curriculum Development, N.E.A., Washington, D.C., 1963, p. 110.
25. J. S. Bruner, 'Theorems for Theory of Instruction', in *Learning about Learning* (Ed. J. S. Bruner), U.S. Department of Health, Education and Welfare, Washington, D.C., 1966, p. 208.

26. Albert J. Caron, 'Impact of motivation variables on knowledge-seeking behaviour', in *Productive Thinking in Education* (Ed. M. J. Aschner and C. E. Bish), N.E.A. and Carnegie Corporation of New York, 1965, p. 132.
27. D. E. Berlyne, *Conflict, Arousal and Curiosity*, McGraw-Hill, New York, 1960.
28. D. C. McClelland and others, *The Achievement Motive*, Appleton-Century-Crofts, New York, 1953.
29. Robert Glaser, Variables in discovery learning', in *Learning by Discovery* (Ed. Lee S. Shulman and Evan R. Keisler), Rand McNally, Chicago, 1966, p. 25.
30. D. E. Berlyne, 'Notes on intrinsic motivation and intrinsic reward in relation to instruction', in *Learning about Learning*, 1966, p. 106.
31. Richard Alpert, 'Motivation to achieve', in *Productive Thinking in Education*, 1965, p. 113.
32. J. S. Bruner, 'The act of discovery', *Harvard Educ. Rev.*, 1961, p. 26.
33. J. S. Bruner, 'Some elements of discovery', in *Learning by Discovery*, 1966, p. 101.
34. Lee J. Cronbach, 'The logic of experiments on discovery', in *Learning by Discovery*, 1966, p. 76.
35. Howard H. Kendler, Reflections on the conference', in *Learning by Discovery*, 1966, p. 176.
36. M. C. Wittrock, 'The learning-by-discovery hypothesis', in *Learning by Discovery*, 1966, pp. 42-44.
37. *Ibid.*, p. 35.
38. Lee J. Cronbach, 'The logic of experiments on discovery', in *Learning by Discovery*, 1966, p. 90.
39. Robert M. Gagné, 'Varieties of learning and the concept of discovery', in *Learning by Discovery*, 1966, p. 149.
40. *Ibid.*, p. 150.
41. E. R. Keisler and L. S. Shulman, 'The problem of discovery: conference in retrospect', in *Learning by Discovery*, 1966, pp. 181-199.
42. J. S. Bruner, 'Some elements of discovery', in *Learning by Discovery*, 1966, chap. 7.
43. *Ibid.*, p. 107.
44. *Ibid.*, p. 107.
45. Lee J. Cronbach, 'The logic of experiments on discovery', in *Learning by Discovery*, 1966, p. 77.
46. J. S. Bruner, 'Theorems for a theory of instruction', in *Learning about Learning*, 1966, pp. 197-211.
47. *Ibid.*, p. 211.
48. Donald Ely, 'Facts and fallacies about new media in education', in *Revolution in Teaching* (Ed. Alfred de Grazia and David A. Sohn), Bantam Books, New York, 1964, p. 42.
49. P. H. Rossi and B. J. Biddle, *The New Media in Education*, Aldine Publishing Co., Chicago, 1966, P. 126.
50. Philip Lewis, 'Emerging instructional technology', in *Using Current Curriculum Developments*, Association for Supervision and Curriculum Development, N.E.A., Washington, D.C., 1963, p. 102.
51. Donald Ely, 'Facts and fallacies about new media in education', in *Revolution in Teaching*, 1964, p.45.
52. Lawrence M. Stolurow, 'Programmed instruction and teaching machines', in *The New Media and Education*, 1966, p. 129.
53. R. C. Atkinson and D. N. Hansen, *Computer-Assisted Instruction in Initial Reading:*

The Stanford Project, Technical Report No. 93, Institute for Mathematical Studies in the Social Sciences, Stanford University, 1966, p. 8.

54.   E. N. Adams, *Computers and Automation*, March 1966.

55.   R. Glaser, W. Ramage, and J. Lipson, *The Interface Between Student and Subject-Matter*, Technical Report No. 5, Learning R & D Center, University of Pittsburgh, 1964, reedited 1966, pp. 23-60.

56.   R. C. Atkinson and D. N. Hansen, *Computer-Assisted Instruction in Initial Reading: The Stanford Project*, 1966.

57.   *Ibid.*, p. 29.

58.   D. D. Bushnell, 'The automated classroom', in 'The role of the computer in future instructional systems', monograph 2, *A.V. Communication Review*, March-April 1963, Chap. 5.

59.   *Ibid.*, p. 56.

60.   *Ibid.*, p. 60.

61.   S. Senshu, 'The Penultimate Teaching Machine', *IRE Transactions on Education*, September 1960.

62.   John I. Goodlad and Robert H. Anderson, *The Nongraded Elementary School*, Harcourt, Brace & World, New York, 1959, Revised 1963.

63.   R. H. Anderson, *Teaching in a World of Change*, Harcourt, Brace & World, New York, 1966, p. 54.

64.   B. Frank Brown, *The Nongraded High School*, Prentice-Hall, Englewood Cliffs, N.J., 1963, p. 43.

65.   Frank R. Dufay, *Ungrading the Elementary School*, Parker Publishing Co., West Nyack, N.Y., 1966, p. 24.

66.   Eugene R. Howard and Roger W. Bardwell, *How to Organize a Nongraded School*, Prentice-Hall, Englewood Cliffs, N.J., 1966, p. 13.

67.   John I. Goodlad, *Planning and Organizing for Teaching*, N.E.A., Washington, D.C., 1966, pp. 54-56.

68.   John I. Goodlad, *School Curriculum and the Individual*, Blaisdell Publishing Co., Waltham, Mass., 1966, p. 42.

69.   R. H. Anderson, *Teaching in a World of Change*, 1966, p. 68.

70.   George Stoddard, *The Dual Progress Plan*, Harper & Row, New York, 1961.

71.   Adapted from the following: Stuart E. Dean, 'The nongraded school: is there magic in it?' *School Life*, 1964, pp. 22-23; *Change and Innovation in Elementary School Organization: Selected Readings*, (Ed. Maurie Hillson), Holt, Rinehart & Winston, New York, 1965, pp. 296-297.

72.   J. T. Shaplin and H. F. Olds, Eds., *Team Teaching*, Harper & Row, New York, 1964, p. 15.

73.   R. H. Anderson, 'Team teaching in the elementary and secondary schools', in *Revolution in Teaching*, 1964, p. 121.

74.   James Bryant Conant, *The Education of American Teachers*, McGraw-Hill, New York, 1963, p. 147.

75.   R. H. Anderson, in *Team Teaching*, (Ed. J. T. Shaplin and H. F. Olds), 1964, pp. 210-211.

76.   R. H. Anderson, in *Revolution in Teaching*, 1964, p. 122.

77.   John I. Goodlad, *Planning and Organizing for Teaching*, National Education Association, Washington, D.C., 1963, p. 82.

78.   R. H. Anderson, *Teaching in a World of Change*, 1966, p. 89.

79.   Dan C. Lortie, 'The teacher and team teaching', in *Team Teaching,* (Ed. J. T. Shaplin and H. F. Olds), 1964, p. 281.
80.   *Ibid.*, p. 283.
81.   Raymond A. Hettler, 'Team Teaching', in *Modern Education*, Nov.-Dec. 1967.
82.   M. Bair and R. G. Woodward, *Team Teaching in Action*, Houghton Mifflin, Boston, 1964, p. 215.

Part III

THE PROCESS OF INNOVATION

Chapter 6

Factors Influencing Change

New ideas in education arise in a communication network involving both transmission and response. The communicating and responding persons will be teachers, principals, administrators, researchers, professors, politicians, parents, publishers, and others. They may communicate directly by teaching, conferring, or conversing, or indirectly through some such medium as print. The communication network may be efficient in parts, and inefficient in other parts.

The meaning of an innovation is likely to vary according to the response made to it by the recipient. The response is partly a personal one, and partly an institutional one. For example, a teacher may react to an idea transmitted to him by someone in authority in terms of his personal outlook on teaching, his previous ideas of a related kind, and the personal appeal of the idea. He is likely to react to it also in terms of his responsibility as a teacher, that is as one who has to use the idea in a practical situation, and as one who feels obliged to take seriously ideas coming from supervisors. A professor may react to the same idea in personal terms also, but his principal reaction is likely to be in terms of his institutional role as theoretician, seeking as comprehensive an explanatory framework of ideas as possible. A politician's interpretation may be coloured by the implications it may contain of additional expense, or of political reaction. The publisher will be concerned among other matters with the commercial possibilities involved. All the above interpretations are legitimate, as also are those by which ideas transmitted from abroad are modified in the receiving country.

Once an idea gets well established in the communication network, those involved with it are usually not aware of, or concerned about, its origin, or the actual pathway it has taken through the network. If, however, it is desired to introduce some change, or to accelerate a change that is lagging, then the relative strategic significance of agents in the change process, and the pattern of movement through the communication network, acquire great significance, and an understanding of them becomes essential. It is the purpose of this chapter to examine some of the main agents or instruments involved; in succeeding chapters the process of innovation as it appears to be occurring in Britain and the U.S.A. will be described.

Centralized and decentralized structure and function

In different countries it is likely that similar institutions and groups of people — teachers, principals, administrative personnel, teacher-education institutions, research bodies, etc. — will be involved in innovation, but it is to be expected that differences in the structure and function of systems, and in the role played by different elements, will influence the process significantly.

In some systems that are highly centralized, and in which clearly defined authority gradients exist, it can be assumed that any new idea must be accepted at higher levels of the system before it is at all widely taken up at the lower ones. This is likely to be true even if the idea arises at a lower level, for example through the initiative of a teacher. It may also be assumed that in such a system a change can be diffused throughout the whole system fairly rapidly because of the closely integrated structure and the hierarchical relationships. In systems that are divided into autonomous sections, innovations may occur in one part without necessarily affecting, or being affected by, another part. Within each section the authority gradient may of course exist, producing for the section concerned the same general characteristics as would be found in a whole centralized system.

An education system may be described in functional terms as well as in structural ones, and in terms of informal functioning as well as of formal functioning. A system may have the structural characteristics of centralization (the subordination of part to part with central coordination or direction, the existence of officials to exercise checks to ensure that uniform policies are observed, explicit role definition for those working at the different levels of the system, etc.) and yet be so permeated with a liberal spirit that it functions in a democratic rather than a bureaucratic way. Another may have the structural characteristics of decentralization (diversification from part to part, few significant 'line' relationships, few officials charged with coordination, etc.) but be permeated with a rigid and dictatorial spirit.

To say this is not to imply that the effect of structure on function is unimportant. On the contrary, some modes of operation in a system are facilitated by the structure, others are possible only in spite of the structure. For example, a centralized system is more conducive to a bureaucratic mode of operation than is a decentralized one.

The structure of education systems is determined by a variety of factors relevant at the time in history when the system was established. It is usually not possible to alter this easily when changing conceptions of function make the existing structure less effective; and a system undergoing such transformation is faced with the problem of having to use its structure in a new way until modifications can be made. For example, while few changes have been made in the state-based systems of education in Australia since they were established towards the end of the 19th century, new demands of cooperation at a national level, decentralized functioning within the state structure, and a changing attitude to the responsibility of teachers, have all exerted pressure towards newer patterns of function. While it appears unlikely that additional jurisdictions for education will be created in Australia, other than by the creation of new states, modes of operation more likely to arise in a decentralized system will have to be made to work in the existing system if programmes of modernization are to succeed.

One of the most significant indications of the way in which an education system functions, whatever appearance it gives through its structure, is the role assigned to its teachers. Correspondingly, one of the central issues in the process of innovation is the role played in it by teachers, since, whatever the source of the ideas, it is the teachers who have to make most of them effective at a practical level. This role will be very different if they carry out this work with a high degree of professional responsibility from that if, at the other extreme, they act merely as functionaries under close supervision or direction. In the first case they will be expected to cooperate with other change agents, or even to take the initiative; in the second, they will be expected only to adopt the new procedure as required. This question of the responsibility of the teacher is now taken up in some detail.

The freedom and responsibility of the teacher

In some countries it is commonly accepted that the work of teachers should be directed and supervised by someone external to the classroom. The justification usually given for this is that teachers are insufficiently trained for it to be reasonable to expect them to use freedom efficiently. They need guidance and direction from more experienced and expert members of the profession to keep them working effectively. In developing countries where there is an inadequate number of well-trained teachers, the use of closely prescribed syllabuses, teaching schemes, inspection, and external tests is supported with this argument. In passing it might also be said that in some highly developed countries with greatly varied and expanded job opportunities in science, technology, and commerce, there is also an inadequate number of able and properly qualified teachers. This situation has accelerated the development of technological aids such as computerized equipment and television in an attempt to offset the shortage of teachers. This movement could easily reintroduce into teaching a formalism which the advances in methodology of recent decades have greatly reduced, and could be as damaging to the professional development of teaching as earlier limitations were on the teacher's responsibility.

An argument of a different kind is that, in any system of education that offers reasonable career opportunities for teachers, it is necessary for the work of teachers to be known by those who make or influence appointments to higher positions, so that just and suitable selections are made. External assessors, it is claimed, can do this task of evaluation more equitably than internal ones, in that their judgment is not based on the standard of work in a single institution.

One influence on the teacher's work that can be very powerful is the external examination. In the case of the primary school, this examination is designed to assist selection for secondary education, and its impact on the primary school depends on the requirements for this selection procedure. Theoretically, an examination may be of a kind that allows the teacher to work with great freedom, and indeed rewards him for working in this way. In practice, as the history of such examinations amply reveals, examinations give prominence to formal and prescribed elements, and tend to encourage forms of teaching that lead to stereotyped learning. Furthermore, a sense of urgency and strain is created in children preparing for these examinations, and in the teachers (and parents) concerned. The more critical the selection procedure involved, the greater is the sense of strain, and the more empty the idea of the freedom of the teacher.

Another group of people external to the classroom which may influence the teacher's work is the parents. A fruitful partnership between home and school can greatly strengthen the objectives of each. Except in special cases the main responsibility for the upbringing of children must rest with their parents. School is a powerful supplementary influence, but it is subordinate. It provides a different kind of social setting for the purpose of learning, and addresses itself to aspects of the child's development which are not systematically dealt with by the home. Nevertheless, if it does accept a broad view of its function, embracing the child's social, emotional, and moral, as well as his cognitive development, the modern primary school's general objectives are very close to those of the home. In spite of this, the relationship has not been an easy or productive one in most societies. The reasons for this no doubt are many and complex. Schools may have identified themselves with values which are alien to many homes; parents may have interpreted their financial support of the school through fees or taxes as qualifying them to interfere in professional matters, or have interpreted the teacher's expertness as justification for their own non-involvement; and busy teachers may have found the task of cooperating with parents too great an additional burden to bother about, except for the occasional special event. For a teacher to be free of parental interference in what he does at school may be another way of saying that he is cut off from the group most concerned with what he is doing, and the group which, in many cases at least, is in the best position to reinforce it. When the teacher is engaged in an innovative activity, the need for this understanding and support is even more apparent.

The question of the teacher's responsibility, however, is a very much wider one than his freedom from arbitrary control by people outside the classroom, important as this is. His capacity to exercise a large measure of control over his own teaching programme, and to be responsive to new ideas and critical of them, is dependent on his grasp of the ideas and issues involved, and his professional freedom must be tested in terms of this mastery as well. The main ideas and issues with which he must be concerned are those dealing with the curriculum, and with method and organization. Both of these make rigorous demands on the teacher.

The primary-school curriculum has traditionally been a simple one, consisting of rudimentary instruction in the literature of the mother tongue, arithmetic, social studies, science (particularly nature study), music, art and handicraft, health, and in some schools religious knowledge. In addition skills such as reading, competence at arithmetical computations of various kinds, writing, spelling, speaking, were assiduously cultivated. The demands on the scholarship of the teacher were slight. Whatever professional challenge the work may have had was in the pedagogy involved, not in the level of knowledge taught.

Today this view of the curriculum has changed out of all recognition. Whether the curriculum is viewed as a unified whole in which little or no separation into subjects is made, or in the more usual subject form, the objective is to bring out the nature of various forms of knowledge, and to increase the child's capacity to acquire and use knowledge. What are dealt with are the important concepts on which the subject is based and characteristic methods which it uses, rather than a number of predetermined facts or results in the subject. The treatment of subjects like mathematics and science in this way has transformed them to such a degree that many teachers who have been educated in a different tradition find them almost unrecognizable. To their astonishment they discover that they do not understand the subjects, even though they have been teaching them for years. The same is likely to be true of social studies and language, and to add to the teachers' surprise, if not dismay, they are expected to command and teach a foreign language. Now the modern primary-school teacher is expected to think like a mathematician, scientist, linguist, social scientist, artist, musician, and man of letters.

But, more than this, he must be able to assist children to do so as well. This will require of him an intelligent understanding of curriculum construction, and of the pupils' growth and development. What this involves is considered in more detail later when the training of the teacher is discussed, but unquestionably it is a crucial element in guaranteeing his freedom as a professional worker.

It would be anomalous if pressures towards educational reform had the effect of weakening the freedom of the teacher. In England, for example, where the freedom of the teacher is well established, in-service courses confront him on all sides, many of them, such as 'How to use programmed learning', with a hint of omniscience in their titles. Reports on the teaching of various subjects and other memoranda are being published under authoritative auspices, and are being disseminated widely. Advisers and other experts are being appointed in increasing numbers, and, along with the inspectors, are enthusiastically encouraging teachers to change their ways. Confronted by such a cloud of witnesses, there is a danger that the teacher will lose some confidence in his own professional skill, and adopt uncritically the various schemes placed before him. The mere following of educational fads is a travesty of any real expertise, and a denial of professional freedom. It is important that this danger of a servile attitude on the part of the teacher should be seen, and actively combated. Putting this in more positive terms, it should be recognized that to strengthen the professional freedom of the teacher is the surest way to guarantee a continuing concern for progressive ideas, and that all steps taken to introduce or accelerate change should promote, or at least be in accord with, this professional freedom. One obvious way to do this is to secure the participation of teachers in the study of proposed innovations, either in a study group, or by action research in their own schools. In doing this the special knowledge of the adviser or research worker is being made use of, but it is made available in a way that is likely to assist teachers most. Didactic courses which simply tell the teacher what ought to be done are usually unsuccessful in achieving any effective change.

Teachers ought to work in an atmosphere which encourages continuous reappraisal and self-renewal. New procedures for accelerating change can assist the growth of such an atmosphere, provided they are seen as ways of working with the teacher, and not as ways of controlling his work. Teachers should be hospitable to new ideas, and expose themselves to them through reading and lectures, but they should judge them with caution. All too often extreme reactions occur, such as the rejection of ideas without proper examination of them, or their adoption with almost fanatical zeal. Devotees of 'Cuisenaire', or 'i.t.a.', or other new ideas, can become as rigid in their thinking as the staunchest conservative who rejects all 'new-fangled' notions. A readiness to consider new ideas, and a careful appraisal of them, usually result in an enrichment and invigoration of the teacher's knowledge. A teacher may for example be forced to reinterpret his understanding of certain mathematical concepts in an attempt to see the nature of a set of structured materials such as that prepared by Professor Dienes. Having done this he may decide to use that material to assist children to understand the idea of a number base, or he may decide to do so in another way. But, in either case, the main value of the new material to the teacher has been successfully exploited: it has forced him to rethink the point involved.

Educational material of one sort and another is pouring from the manufacturers and publishing houses. Much of it can be adopted by teachers, and put to good use. But its chief value is in assisting teachers to test and clarify their own ideas, and in helping them to provide a suitable programme for the particular children whom *they* know, and for whom *they* are responsible. Without a well-understood body of principles to guide them they will be overwhelmed by the flood of materials, and the innovative steps represented by the production of these materials will be self-defeating.

The pre-service education of teachers

The view of the responsibility of teachers expressed in the preceding sections leads naturally to a consideration of the training they receive before appointment, and the assistance they get after appointment. The question of their pre-service training is taken up in this section, that of their in-service training in the next. The main question that needs examination is whether the programmes that prepare teachers for employment should be innovative in orientation, or carried through more conservatively so as to leave the work of innovation to in-service courses.

When education is in a state of transition, those who prepare teachers for employment find themselves in a position of conflict. Traditional schools seek traditional teachers, and are critical of those with advanced notions. Progressive schools seek progressive teachers, and are critical of those who have only the old-fashioned skills. Even when the training institution does explicitly declare itself to be on one side or the other, it is likely to encounter difficulties in providing appropriate practical experiences in schools for all its students, some of whom will inevitably find themselves in an environment that is not in harmony with the objectives of the training programme.

In suggesting an answer to this general question, it seems reasonable to hold that the main influence of a teacher-education programme ought to be towards innovation. Any profession is entitled to expect that its new members should be familiar with modern thought and practice. This is not to say that these members will be able to perform the newer practices expertly. Some period of initiation or internship to allow for this skill to develop is essential. But less sophisticated methods should not be allowed to prevail simply because they are easier for novices to use. The young teacher ought to be encouraged to be oriented towards experimentation; with a focus on the learning process. He should be taught to take pride in using and evaluating methods that are effective in producing desired pupil behaviour.

Further, in support of the answer being given, it should be stressed that the staff of a training institution is likely to be recruited on the basis of their academic standing and professional leadership. It would be strange indeed if their teaching were not oriented towards progressive practices. Yet, as will be pointed out later with specific instances, the training institution is often a target for criticism by the profession, on the ground either that it is advocating ideas that have been largely superseded in practice, or that it is advocating ones that will not work in practice. Certainly, the fact that staff members have high academic standing and leadership at the time of their appointment does not alone guarantee the continuing influence and reputation of a training institution. Its relations with the profession, and its own internal life in teaching and research, must be such as to create and maintain it as a vigorous centre. Training institutions ought to play a significant part in assisting newer and better practices to prevail more widely, but they will do so only if they recruit good staff, and then provide favourable conditions for them to work at a high level. The institution must also give continuing attention to its relations with the profession to ensure that it retains its influence and effectiveness.

The in-service education of teachers
It may be assumed without question, whatever strategy may be used for promoting innovation, that a vigorous programme of education for practising teachers is essential. What is not so clear is who should provide it. In England, where in-service education is well developed, one is surprised at the great profusion of bodies undertaking this work. Courses, conferences, study groups, and displays are arranged by The Department of Education and Science, the Institutes of Education and affiliated Colleges of Education, and many of the local education authorities. In addition, although usually on a more modest scale, courses are offered by teachers' organizations and groups, and by other specialist groups. The inspectorate of the Department of Education and Science, and the administrative and advisory staff used by many local education authorities, work personally with teachers in the schools as well as acting as lecturers and group leaders in various courses.

In specific centres some coordination exists among these courses, but it is more common for each body to act independently. It could be argued that the need for in-service education is so great that no harm can come from having it provided by so many authorities. On the other hand it seems unnecessary that there should be overlapping and even competitive offerings, which could be confusing to teachers. The question arises whether an effective rationalization could be worked out so that authorities could contribute best according to their facilities and responsibilities. In pursuing this question, it will be appropriate to concentrate attention on two types of authority, the academic institution (institute, college, university) with its teaching function, and the employing authority with its responsibility for efficiency among its teachers. These two types of authority will be involved in any of the countries under consideration.

If a clear basis for rationalizing the function of these two types can be stated, it should not be difficult to see the role of other bodies in the field.

The most obvious contribution that the academic institution can make to the continuing education of teachers is the provision of high-level courses which allow the teacher to review his theoretical formulations in the light of new research evidence and new theorizing. It was stressed in a preceding section that the teacher needs a sound basis in theory for his practice, and it is the university course which can provide this best. Some of these courses will be 'for credit' in that they form part of a degree or diploma course, but courses of a similar type could appropriately be offered without being for award purposes.

The most obvious contributions that the employing authority can make to the development of teachers are to provide a stimulating professional environment for them, to encourage them to improve educational practice, and to assist them to do so by bringing to their notice new ideas, methods, and materials, and then helping them to explore these by means of demonstrations, personal discussions, study groups, and conferences. The most effective point of contact between supervisory staff and teachers is in the school itself, not in the lecture room. It is assumed in saying this that an earlier authoritarian relationship that existed, in some countries at least, between supervisory staff and teachers is quite out of place in the programme envisaged. Inspectors and advisers are now expected to give educational leadership to teachers, not to try to standardize what they are doing. Where the old authoritarian tradition was strong, the subservient attitude of teachers may linger on, but it is out of place in a modern education system.

Between these two types of contribution there is likely to be some common ground. Academic institutions may from time to time arrange shorter courses or conferences with a more immediately practical reference point (perhaps because of the special strengths of members of staff); and employing authorities may from time to time arrange longer courses or conferences with a more theoretical orientation (also, perhaps, because of the special strengths of members of staff). But with close cooperation, and with some interchange of staff, these overlapping functions should present no difficulty.

A development that will put this cooperation to the test in a quite critical way is that of teachers' centres. The English conception of these will be described in the appropriate section. At this stage we need only a brief sketch of them sufficient to enable us to pursue the point raised. A teachers' centre is an institution catering for the needs of teachers who want to meet for courses, groups, and demonstrations, and to become familiar with new curriculum materials. An alternative name for it might be a curriculum laboratory, in which the various books, equipment, and aids now being developed in such profusion for the different subjects are on display, and where there are a number of associated rooms for lectures, discussion, recreation, etc. Who should take the initiative in providing these centres – the teaching institutions or the employing authorities? Both actually do so in Britain. At present these centres can be found in universities, in colleges of education, and in buildings either specially built for the purpose by education authorities or adapted by them from existing buildings. It may be claimed by a teaching institution that its teachers' centre will be used for the type of sustained course referred to earlier, and by an education authority that its teachers' centre will be used for the shorter type of familiarization course or conference. But whether there is need for two types of teachers' centre is dubious.

Probably the best answer to questions of this kind can be given by teachers themselves. Whether one authority or another is more appropriate for providing services to teachers ought to be decided by them. A mature teaching force would recognize the need for in-service courses, and make known any specific requests. Clearly teachers' centres, as a facility, are needed, and the most obvious people to provide them are teachers. If they have not the financial resources to do this themselves, it seems most appropriate that the education authorities should provide them for the teachers. But in the use made of them, teachers ought to have a good deal of influence. With an arrangement like this, the question whether courses for them should be given by the universities or the education authorities becomes less of an alternative. Such differences would be merged, and the people most appropriate for the purpose would be used. It is hoped, and expected, that some of these would be teachers themselves.

The role of national bodies

It is an emerging characteristic of education today that major financial and administrative issues are being discussed in a national context. The expanding scope and cost of education services have left smaller bodies such as states and local authorities inadequate in discharging their responsibilities without additional assistance. Furthermore, increasing recognition of the national significance of educational programmes, combined with greater mobility of populations, have focussed attention on national solutions. In their programmes of financial assistance, national governments have expressed priorities, tending to favour institutions of higher learning and vocational education. But there is an increasing awareness of the importance nationally of more general cultural objectives as well.

The problems of expressing education in national terms differ from country to country because of the particular administrative traditions that exist, the typical non-governmental units of the U.S.A. presenting one sort of problem, the local government authorities of England another, and the states of Australia yet a third. They are different also because of the cultural traditions that exist in the country. These problems will be considered in some detail in succeeding chapters.

A fear commonly expressed about the increased influence of national bodies in education is that it will lead to an undesirable uniformity, particularly in respect of the curriculum. Many are prepared to recognize the need for national participation in the sense that local authorities and other bodies should be assisted from national funds; but they are opposed to a direct national influence on educational programmes. Probably the fear underlying this opposition relates most to social and personal beliefs and prejudices to do with political, religious, class, and racial matters. These, it is felt, can be managed in the freest way by having a multiplicity of authorities, each with its own control over curriculum. Undoubtedly, for some time, moves toward curriculum development at a national level are more likely to be accepted in such subjects as mathematics and science than in social studies or the humanities, in spite of the fact that a disciplined and comprehensive study of social values within the broad context of the nation as a whole is undoubtedly of critical importance for national development.

National intervention in education, however, whether through existing bodies or through new ones designed specially to promote change, ought not to mean an imposed uniformity. Statements about school curricula, and about matters of method and evaluation, which are formulated by bodies external to the school, should be in a form that permits interpretation and development by individual schools and teachers, rather than in prescriptive form. This should be so whether the authority be national or local. The statement in the Foreword to Book 1 of the Nuffield Foundation's new French course already referred to, *En Avant* expresses this spirit well.

'The suggestions made for the guidance of teachers in this volume, and in its numerous successors, represent ideas which have stood the test of widespread practice in classroom trials, but they should certainly not on that account cease to be regarded as suggestions. Each teacher planning to embark on the programme must (and no doubt will) feel free to adapt the materials to meet the needs of his or her own pupils, and it is to be hoped that each will see significant ways of improving on the new ideas developed here.'

The Nuffield Mathematics Teaching Project is another example of a highly influential body of ideas which is stimulating rather than stereotyping the work of teachers. It is conceived and presented in such a way that teachers are encouraged to make authentic interpretations of their own, and there is substantial evidence that this in fact is happening. The process need not be one of invention – communication – acceptance – imitation. Rather it can be one of invention – communication – stimulation – adaptation and further invention.

Assuming that objections to nationally based development schemes can be adequately met, it is clear that they have a number of positive advantages. They focus attention on matters of national importance, be they mathematics, science, or social studies; they exert greater leverage than lesser schemes; they mobilize funds and human resources more effectively. Curriculum development today is expensive. It requires the full-time services of highly paid educational experts, it needs to commission expensive research and to prepare expensive materials. The budgets of the Nuffield Foundation projects and of the Schools Council in England, and of the Research and Development Centers and the big Foundation-sponsored projects in the U.S.A., are striking illustrations of this. Moreover the supply of these experts is by no means unlimited. They need to be effectively concentrated, and their efforts coordinated rather than dispersed.

To advocate the national-level body as a powerful instrument in the strategy for promoting development does not imply that bodies and individuals at other levels are unimportant. On the contrary, they are quite essential. The work of innovation needs its intimate phase, close to the classroom, as well as its more remote phase dealing only with ideas. Goodlad[1] has pointed out that the single school, with its principal, teachers, students, parents, and community setting, might well provide the most strategic unit for educational change, particularly if it is supported by good ideas and assistance from outside. The work of national committees does not make redundant the work of other groups. Rather, these provide a richer range of ideas within which to move.

The influence of educational publications

The stream of educational publications is at present running very strongly; indeed it might be considered to have reached flood proportions. No doubt many a promising educationist has gone under in it.

Yet we cannot say with any assurance what effect all this print has in influencing the course of academic endeavour. One suspects that it is considerable, as print makes up in ubiquity and the cloak of authority what it lacks of the more intimate appeal of the spoken work. One suspects also that it exerts its influence differentially, as groups of readers become attuned to special kinds of publications, and also obliquely, as ideas are caught up by some readers and used by them to influence others, often being reinterpreted and restated in the process. Undoubtedly also some of the most potentially influential writers need their interpreters and popularizers to enable them to make their maximum impact. It is a vast and highly significant element in the innovative process, almost untouched by research.

We may conveniently classify educational literature into four categories which refer, in the main, to the principal consumers. These categories, together with some examples of the types of publications in each, and the consumers involved, are set out in tabular form on the following page.

Among the official type of literature is listed the major report of a governmental or other high-level committee of inquiry. This has special features which, in a table of this kind, could perhaps best be catered for by making it a category by itself. In this writer's view it stands out among the various kinds of educational writing as being specifically oriented towards innovation; it appears also to be an instrument of quite extraordinary influence.

The type of report referred to may be found in one form or another in various countries, but it has come to assume a specific form and spirit in England, and in this form it may be regarded as uniquely English.

Australia has made use of a somewhat similar type of report. Recent influential reports that have appeared are the *Wyndham Report,*[2] dealing with the reorganization of secondary education in New South Wales, and the *Martin Report,*[3] dealing with the whole field of tertiary education in Australia. It does not appear to be very much in vogue in the U.S.A. There the nearest comparable documents are perhaps those of bodies like the National Society for the Study of Education, and the Educational Policies Commission, those of the White House Conferences in Education, and reports of influential individuals, like J. B. Conant[4] — but in fact all these differ from the reports of English committees of inquiry in quite significant ways. A full description of the type of document referred to is given in the next chapter, which deals with innovation in England.

We may conclude this section by a brief reference to the other three categories of educational literature. Professional literature undoubtedly plays an important part in influencing educational practice. Of all educational literature it is closest to the day-to-day work of the classroom. Whereas other types of literature may put ideas into the teacher's head, this literature puts tools into his hand. It gives him the reading material he needs, the workbooks, guidebooks, programmed material, films, and other educational material. Increasingly, too, as publishers and manufacturers of equipment join forces, these publications tend to assume more the scope of teaching schemes, or teaching systems. No effective changes can occur without high-quality publications of a professional kind. They make possible now patterns of teacher behaviour that were impossible before, and increase the prospects of greater efficiency. The publishers of these books and materials must be accorded a definite place among the educational innovators. Presumably their motive is a commercial one, and this has its dangers,* but their judgment on what type of publication to support must also

---

* This point is elaborated in discussing publishing in America in Chapter 8.

Category	Examples of types of publications	Likely consumers
Official	Statistical reports of governments, and other educational bodies; reviews of educational practices, legal provisions, etc; major reports of governmental or other high-level committees of inquiry	Politicians, officials, but also others for special purposes Major reports would have a wide appeal (see text)
Professional	Curriculum documents, courses, teaching schemes, school texts, readers, programmed texts, structured materials	Teachers, professional administrators and other specialists, and (to a lesser degree) academics
Academic	Educational journals, technical reports, monographs, texts	Academics (lecturers, research workers, students), professional administrators and other specialists
Popular	Non-technical books of general educational interest (often paperbacks) aimed at the 'intelligent layman', politicians, etc; general press and magazine articles	General readers, politicians, teachers

be an educational one. In one case, that of Pitman's i.t.a. in England, the original idea, as well as its promotion through research and publication, came from a publisher.

The remaining two categories can be dismissed in a few words. Popular educational literature is rare indeed. The educationist, perhaps because he tends to take himself too seriously, lacks the common touch in writing. He fails to bring home to ordinary people the great possibilities that education has in influencing the quality of society, and its potential for increasing the richness and variety of individual human lives. He often fails to do these things even with his own pupils. Some writers, taking a tougher line, are having more success in convincing businessmen and industrialists, who devote most of their attention to creating wealth, of the economic significance of preparing the rising generation through education to assist them in their task; and for this we may be moderately grateful.

Those who publish research articles in learned journals and books communicate with others of their own kind on a private communication network. It is an immensely important network, and, appropriately monitored, it is potentially a very powerful instrument of change. Its relation to innovation is taken up in the next section.

Research and Innovation

Research generates new knowledge, and tests old knowlege. Obviously it is the keystone of the arch so far as innovation is concerned, assuming we want to change from something that we have to something that we believe to be better. If we think of change as being good in itself, of course, the support of research is less important.

Silberman,[5] speaking of the scene in the U.S.A., laments the separation of research and innovation:

'If the effectiveness of instruction were proportional to the volume and rate of research papers, there would not be an instructional problem, but unfortunately research and educational innovation are far from synonymous.'

And in England, Michael Young[6] makes a plea that they should be brought together:

'The mother of innovation will remain what it has always been: more new things will be tried because necessity calls. But research? You can easily have innovation without research — the fashions which periodically sweep through the educational world are witness to that. You can, and almost always do, have research without innovation. This book urges – it is the principal theme – that the two should be brought together.'

Yet it is not surprising that the two have developed apart. The researcher and the innovator are usually different people with different responsibilities in education. Not uncommonly they are critical of each other, or at least a little suspicious. The researcher, in order to get a tight design for his study, moves away from a practical teaching situation which is fraught with unknown and uncontrolled variables. The innovator is concerned with getting something that works under normal conditions. He is also impatient to change what is to him patently unsatisfactory for something better. He cannot wait for research's slow and piecemeal conquest of truth. Educational practice is a notoriously difficult field in which to carry out definitive research. Results are hard to express in quantitative terms, particularly those involving some of the more elusive qualities. Results may be short-term or long-term, and hard to relate unequivocally to specific variables where, as is usual, a cluster of variables exists. If educational progress were made only on the basis of unquestioned research results, it would be very slow indeed. The researcher may be able to afford to wait (provided he is not doing a thesis for a degree); the educational reformer cannot. The researcher is usually in the university, or the research institute, and interprets his obligation as being to produce a paper, or a book. What might be done with it practically is for others to be concerned about. To translate it into practical terms may involve the preparation of a text or some other educational material, or the devising of a method or facility. The researcher feels that this practical step is not within his sphere of interest or competence. It is one of the important advances in our understanding of the change process in education to realize that innovation is not likely to follow from research unless development is also undertaken.

Some research of course is practically oriented, and is close to the development phase; some is more remote. Some responsible educationists in America have expressed serious concern about what they regard as an excessive concentration on applied research. Cronbach[7] for example writes in alarm about the emphasis placed on development and dissemination activity by the Office of Education.

> ' . . . I am concerned lest the movement may cause the universities, and particularly their schools of education, to neglect their true and unique function. If those whose first calling is the study of education now put off the robe of the scholar and don the armour of the crusader, they will betray the public by leaving the scholar's badly needed work undone.'

Kerlinger[8] writes in much the same vein.

'I am not saying that practical research never has any value. On the contrary, significant scientific hypotheses and discoveries are sometimes turned up in the course of research oriented towards the solution of practical problems. I am saying that major concern with practical ends impedes the advance of scientific discoveries and growth in education.'

For a contrary view we turn to Ebel.[9] In a spirited attack on the view that basic research in education is what is needed, he writes:

'They [the defenders of basic research] greatly overestimate the scope and versatility of nomothetic, experimental science. They greatly underestimate the variety and power of other techniques of gathering data and solving problems .... Seldom if ever do the findings of basic scientific research have significant impact on the decision reached. The alternative to basic scientific research is not just traditionalism or mysticism or speculation. There are also empiricism (i.e. experience) and discussion and reasoned decision.'

To lament the paucity of educational reform that comes from a large volume of published research, as Silberman does, and to urge that the two move together, as Young does, are perhaps to assume too readily that the researcher must be first in the field, or at least be in the field from the beginning, of any modification of practice. The sequence, idea − research − development − innovation appears to be a rational one, but in fact it is not one that is usual, or even common, in the history of education. Innovations have more usually been realized by creative practitioners, or suggested by scholars, without there being substantial theoretical or empirical support for them. Research usually follows − and it may support, modify, or discredit them.

An increase in research in education need not be at the expense of spontaneity in educational change. Indeed it is to be expected that the conditions which support greater research activity will also support more adventures in practice. These conditions arise when the need for change on many fronts is widely accepted. Innovators and researchers, even though acting differently, are often responding to the same general ideas. These ideas often have a considerable history, and are fulfilled at different times and in many ways. Some of these ways rest on intuitive judgment, some on deduction from assumed principles, some on research, and some on the fruitful interaction of these. Progress in education is likely to continue to need this varied kind of background.

A marriage of innovation and research, as Michael Young proposes, could be a happy and fruitful union, but only if each member of the partnership is given a large measure of freedom of action. If research in education is done only in the service of some planned innovation, or if innovations are expected to be made only after a course of action has been established by research, both innovation and research may suffer.

Strategies for change

How can the pace and direction of change in education be controlled? This question raises many issues, and few of them are understood fully. An education system is the product of external influences as well as internal ones, and the interaction of these is very complex indeed. Effective strategies for change will have to await further clarification of the change process itself as it occurs in education.

A useful classification of change strategies is that given by Robert Chin.[10] He distinguishes three general types of strategy for bringing about change in education which he calls (i) empirical-rational, (ii) normative-reeducative, and (iii) power with compliance. Each is elaborated below.

(i) *The 'empirical-rational' approach* The assumption underlying this approach is that existing educational practice will change as more valid ideas displace less valid ones, provided of course that there is an adequate communication system so that the new knowledge will be known to those who have to make use of it. It is an affirmation of belief in a science of education.

To anyone committed to this strategy the emphasis is put on research, development, and dissemination of ideas. It is a major part of the strategy for change being used in America today, as will be shown in chapter 8. The emphasis on research there, with the setting up of the research and development centres, the regional laboratories, the National Science Foundation, etc., has shifted educational research from the edge of educational endeavour to a central position. It has also by its actions provided strong support for the view that research is more productive when it is organized in a centre, with a balanced team of experts, rather than left to the initiative of individuals in universities. It has also reinforced the view that research needs to be followed by development, and, as Schutz[11] says, made 'user-oriented' rather than 'knowledge-oriented'.

According to Clark,[12] educational research and development is coming of age in America. He states,

> 'It is now central to the enterprise of educational practice, and the crude fledgling regional laboratories are the first evidence of its organizational form.'

But it is on trial, and the proof of its success will be sought in the classrooms, not in the laboratory.

(ii) *The 'normative-reeducative' approach* The history of education coulc be written as a record of lost opportunities, of failure to use the knowledge that does exist. It is optimistic indeed to believe that a concentrated effort to create new education knowledge by mounting a massive national applied research programme will alter educational practice significantly, even if it is successful in the laboratory. The following comment by James[13] may be satirical in tone, but it does express a realistic view of the fact that there can be a gap between knowledge and acceptance.

'Supervisors and helping teachers, resource specialists, curriculum consultants, and other experts are kept busy proposing or explaining changes and getting promoted to administrative jobs that are opening up everywhere. But when teachers get out of their meetings and close the doors to their classrooms, things will go on pretty much as they have for decades in most schools.'

The Elementary and Secondary Education Act (1965) in the U.S.A. stressed the importance of dissemination of knowledge, and of course, it is obvious that new ideas will only affect educational practice when they are known and understood by the teachers who have to apply them. But it is also a fact that the teachers have to *accept* them, and this means that they must change habits of action. This is often quite difficult. What we have learned to do habitually has a functional autonomy which tends to perpetuate the action. McPhee[14] points out that

'our individual enthusiasm for a specific change is usually inversely proportional to how much we ourselves must change. We desire it greatly in and for others. We praise change for others, but seldom value changes for ourselves.'

To quote in similar vein from *Punch*,[15] a less likely source for a reference for education:

'The facts of life are conservative. We don't like change, especially when change involves us individually in any reconstruction of our private plans, hopes, and expectations. We enjoy occasional bouts of theorizing, but we are in rooted opposition to all who would translate theory into fact.'

To use reeducation as a strategy means tackling the tasks of changing the ideas, skills, and values of those directly concerned with practice. It is the teacher whom we usually see in this category, but he is by no means the only one. Principals, superintendents, board members, specialists of all kinds, and indeed any who by their position can facilitate or block change, are all concerned. One of the serious errors that is commonly made about educational reform is that it is only a particular group of practitioners, for example teachers, that falls behind.

The nature of the reeducative process is by no means clear. Experience suggests that it occurs most effectively when people are brought into active participation in a project as collaborators. Much of the literature dealing with innovation, however, uses terms like 'adoption', 'dissemination', 'packages', as though a new idea passes from one person to another or from one place to another like an object.[16] Correspondingly, the person to whom the idea is disseminated is called a 'client' or 'target'. This notion of innovations as having a discrete quality, and of being transmitted (and dealt with in other ways) as objects or products can be seen in the schema on the next page. This schema has been prepared by two writers well known in this field, Clark and Guba.[17]

The analysis of the diffusion process (items 8–11 in the Clark-Guba schema) appears to assume that the innovation is like a manufactured object, a 'package' which passes unchanged from developer to user. No doubt there are educational objects of this kind, and for them the process of diffusion as described is probably appropriate. But it should not be assumed that this is an adequate paradigm for the diffusion of all educational innovations. If it were it would describe the educative process itself, rather than a business-type promotional process. The term 'package' is only a metaphor when applied to some educational innovations, and to treat it literally leads to serious error.

An idea like team teaching, for example, may be described in conceptual terms, but essentially it is a description of an educational practice (a description of what teachers do), and it has to be validated in terms of successful practice. In these existential terms it is expressed in unique forms, worked out by particular people working in particular settings. A teacher, 'adopting' team teaching in this sense, is involved quite deeply. He has to understand and accept the objectives of the method, to know its general features, to revise a number of deeply habituated modes of teaching and firmly held attitudes to such matters as privacy and relations with pupils, and to practise new skills. The meaning of a complex set of processes like this would be better conveyed by words like 'reconstructing' and 'interpreting', than by 'adopting'. The change is a comprehensive behavioural one, and is more likely to be brought about by actual participation in planning and action than by statements and demonstrations.

(iii) *The 'power' approach* Common forms that the exercise of power takes in effecting changes in education are legislation, court decisions, the provision of

	FUNCTION	PURPOSE

R
E
S
E
A
R
C
H

(1) Conducting scientific inquiry

(2) Investigating educationally oriented problems

(3) Gathering operational and planning data

(1) To advance knowledge

(2) To advance knowledge about the social-process field of education.

(3) To provide a basis for long-range planning

D
E
V
E
L
O
P
M
E
N
T

(4) Gathering operations and planning data

(5) Inventing solutions to operating problems

(6) Engineering packages and programmes for operational use

(7) Testing and evaluating packages and programmes

(4) To identify operational problems

(5) To solve operational problems

(6) To operationalize solutions

(7) To assess the effectiveness and efficiency of the packages and programmes

(8) Informing target systems about packages and programmes

D
I
F
F
U
S
I
O
N

(9) Demonstrating the effectiveness of the packages and programmes

(10) Training target systems in the use of the packages and programmes

(11) Servicing and nurturing installed innovations

(8) To make potential adopters awar of the existence of packages and programmes

(9) To convince the adopter of the efficacy of the packages and programmes

(10) To develop a level of user competence with the packages and programmes

(11) To complete the institutionalization of the invention

funds subject to conditions,* and the use of authority in administrative relationships.

England has made some limited use of this approach, as is shown in the next chapter – particularly in the setting up of the new body, the Schools Council; but it is America which furnishes the most striking examples of the power strategy. The prominent feature of the last decade has been the volume of educational legislation, particularly in the federal sphere. This legislation is described in some detail in a succeeding chapter. It touches American education at many levels, and in many specific ways, aiding existing institutions as well as creating new ones. The main force of this legislation is applied through the offer of funds. It specifies the direction in which it expects change to occur; and, by the system of approval of proposals made to it, it remains very much the arbiter, if not the director, of the national effort.

To a foreign observer, the use of detailed comprehensive legislation by the United States to effect changes in the system seems curiously out of character. The system of decentralized education was created to put education closely in touch with community needs, and at the same time to divorce it from party politics. At the state level the boards of education were designed to achieve much the same purpose, although in fact in many states the dominance of the districts has tended to weaken the role of state boards as policy-making bodies. A major feature in the structure of educational administration in America is the trust placed in policy making by lay boards specifically charged to think about educational matters and to reach decisions on them. Under such a system it might be imagined that legislation would be used sparingly, and only to authorize necessary financial procedures and to determine broad features of public policy (such as the statutory age of attendance, the powers and responsibilities of the bodies to whom authority is delegated, and so on). In fact, governments appear to act as super-boards of education, dealing with educational minutiae, and embodying them in legislation. State governments, for example, prescribe many details of the curriculum in acts of parliament. By contrast the national government in Britain makes no prescription regarding curricula except that there be a form of religious observance in the schools. The curriculum is considered to be a matter for educationists to determine in the light of social needs.

The recent spate of American federal legislation about education is even more remarkable. At the state level it may be considered that the legislation is taken on the advice of the state board of education, but at the federal level there is no comparable non-political body to give such advice. What has been done at the federal level presumably arose out of views expressed at high-level conferences,

---

* 'Policy made possible by continuous bribery', as Conant calls it.

the deliberations of special committees, and the advice of influential spokesmen from the Department of Health, Education and Welfare and the Office of Education. In a country in which the non-political, democratic character of educational policy making has been hailed as a vital feature, it is surprising that the major recent steps to change education should have been taken in such a different way.

When innovation is considered on a long-range basis, it is apparent that new machinery is needed by means of which rational educational policy may be considered, and appropriate legislation prompted. Action taken by parliament in a spirit of crisis is not likely to be a satisfactory continuing solution. Most of the federal legislation of the last decade has short-range objectives, and deals with symptoms. The discovery of more significant and lasting solutions will require sustained deliberation by a body specially charged with this responsibility. This may prove to be a national board of education, or some kind of federal body to bring the state authorities together.

Conant[18] has drawn attention to constitutional difficulties involved in setting up a national body, but he believes a *nationwide* policy could be achieved by the creation of a compact between the states, thus forming an 'Interstate Commission for Planning a Nationwide Educational Policy'.* The idea of course is not new, as some regional compacts of states already exist. What is new is the nationwide scope of the commission proposed, and the extension of the major concern with higher education to all aspects of education.

The chief sanctions that the Federal Government can apply are financial ones, and undoubtedly these are powerful. But they cannot compel progress. As in other fields of human endeavour, there are limits to what money can buy.

Concluding Comment

The three strategies proposed by Chin provide a useful guide to the account of the role played by different institutions and groups in England and America given in the following chapters. Clearly, all three — improving knowledge, reeducating those responsible for change, and encouragement or coercion — are likely to have a place in a country's plans for reform. What is of interest is the balance of these three.

The United States is making use of them all, but the greatest emphasis appears to be on the campaign to extend and improve educational knowledge, and on encouragement and compulsion by the Federal Government. In England, by contrast, the greatest emphasis seems to be laid on the spread of new knowledge, and on securing the acceptance and cooperation of the teachers in making it a reality in the classrooms.

* In fact, this has been established.

This difference is explained partly no doubt by the different administrative problems that each country has. The greater size of the American population, the greater diversity of its educational and governmental authorities and of its regional traditions, present it with a more difficult task in acting nationally than England has.

The difference in emphases is partly explained by the greater acceptance that there appears to be in America of bureaucratic methods; and by a greater consciousness of status in different levels of the bureaucratic structure, in spite of an easy informality in personal relationships. This status factor may be related to the insecurity that many teachers, principals, and superintendents feel. The system of appointment, promotion, and tenure seems to make them more vulnerable than is the case in England and Australia.

Mainly, however, it may be explained by the different way in which teachers are regarded vis-a-vis administrators and other specialist personnel as change agents. In spite of the vast increase in public spending on education in America, little of the money seems to have been devoted directly to improving the teacher in the classroom, or to raising his professional status. Activity among the educational middlemen offering the school system various expert services has increased sharply. Because of the large amount of money available for such services, rates have soared. Consulting has become a profitable activity. This strange development — that education, at least for some, has become a highly remunerative profession — is of course well known to the teachers of America. It is also well known to them that they have little share in this new-found affluence.

There are those outside the ranks of teachers who put their trust in the technological revolution's making the teacher virtually redundant. Influential academics like Cremin[19] protest against this attitude, as is shown in the following quotation, but it is nevertheless a significant, it not dominant, view.

> 'Education is too significant and dynamic an enterprise to be left to mere technicians; and we might as well begin now the prodigious task of preparing men and women who understand not only the substance of what they are teaching, but also the theories behind the particular strategies they employ to convey that substance. A society committed to the continuing intellectual, aesthetic, and moral growth of all its members can ill afford less on the part of those who undertake to teach.'

McPhee,[20] an experienced American administrator, comments on the role of the teacher as a change agent in this way:

> 'As a source of innovation the classroom teacher seldom plays a

major role . . . . it appears that teachers are more likely to be acted upon than to be actors in the beginning of the improvement process.'

An English observer, Elvin,[21] who is Director of the University of London Institute of Education and who knows both Britain and the U.S.A. well, recently wrote to Americans as follows:

'But I suspect that in this matter [i.e. of curriculum] there is more freedom, and therefore more responsibility, for the teacher in the English school than is general with you.'

This freedom of the English teacher, referred to by Elvin, is the source of his influence as a change agent. If we can trust the judgment expressed in the Plowden Report,[22] this influence has been considerable.

'The willingness of the teachers to experiment, to innovate, and to change has been one of the mainsprings of progress in the primary schools.'

The three strategies discussed in the last section are not necessarily the only ones by which change may be brought about, nor can one say with assurance that one is more appropriate than another. What is effective at one time or place may well not be at another. But, since it is concerned with primary education, and with what is done in primary-school rooms, this book has laid greatest stress on the role of teachers, and success and progress in education have been expressed in terms of their success and their progress. The same emphasis will be apparent in the examination of the change factors at work in England and America in the following chapters.

REFERENCES

1. John I. Goodlad, The League of Cooperating Schools, Paper prepared for *California Journal of Instructional Improvement.*
2. *Report of the Committee appointed to survey Secondary Education in New South Wales,* (Wyndham Report), Sydney, 1957.
3. *Tertiary Education in Australia,* (Martin Report), Vol.I, Commonwealth of Australia, Melbourne, 1964.
4. J. B. Conant, *Shaping Educational Policy,* McGraw-Hill, New York, 1964.
5. Harry F. Silberman, 'The effect of educational research on classroom instruction', *Harvard Educ. Rev.,* Summer 1966.
6. Michael Young, *Innovation and Research in Education,* Routledge & Kegan Paul, London, 1965, p. 8.

7.   Lee J. Cronbach, 'The role of the university in improving education', *Phi Delta Kappan*, June 1966, p. 589.

8.   F. N. Kerlinger, 'Practicality and educational research', *School Review*, Autumn 1959, p. 290.

9.   Robert L. Ebel, 'Some limitations on basic research in Education', *Phi Delta Kappan*, Oct. 1967, p. 83.

10. Robert Chin, 'Basic strategies and procedures in effecting change', in *Planning and Effecting Needed Changes in Education*, An Eight-State Project, Denver, Colo., 1967.

11. R. E. Schultz 'Developing the "D" in educational R and D', *Theory and Practice*, April 1967. Dr. Schultz is Director of the South West Regional Laboratory, Los Angeles.

12. David L. Clark, 'Educational research and development', in *Implications for Education of Prospective Changes in Society*, An Eight-State Project, Denver, Colo., 1967, p. 172.

13. H. Thomas James, *School and Society*, 2293, Summer 1967.

14. Roderick F. McPhee, 'Planning and effecting needed changes in local school systems', in *Planning and Effecting Needed Changes in Education*, 1967, p. 183.

15. Bernard Hollowood, Editorial in *Punch*, May 24, 1967, p. 741.

16. See R. O. Carlson, *Adoption of Educational Innovations*, Center for the Advanced Study of Educational Administration, Eugene, Oregon, 1965.

17. David L. Clark and Egon G. Guba, 'Effecting change in institutions of higher education', address to the International Intervisitation Project of the University Council for Educational Administration, Oct. 1966 (mimeographed), p. 3.

18. J. B. Conant, *Shaping Educational Policy*, McGraw-Hill, New York, 1964, chap. 5.

19. Laurence A. Cremin, *The Genius of American Education*, University of Pittsburgh Press, 1965, p. 59.

20. Roderick F. McPhee, 'Planning and effecting needed changes in local school systems' in *Planning and Effecting Needed Changes in Education*, 1967, p. 187.

21. H. L. Elvin, *The Transatlantic Dialogue in Education*, 29th Annual Sir John Adams Lecture, University of California, Los Angeles, 1962.

22. Central Advisory Council for Education (England), *Children and their Primary Schools*, Vol. 1, H.M.S.O., London, 1967, p. 423.

Chapter 7

Agents in the Innovative Process in England

The preceding chapter was concerned in a general way with the forces of change in education. We turn now to examine the main agents in the innovative process in England. Our concern is with the primary school, but of course the authorities and institutions are concerned with the whole school system, and the strategies for change being used are directed at other sections of the system as well.

As a first step we will identify those bodies which influence or control primary education, which have a stake in the changes that occur in it, and which have a role to play in effecting change.

(i) *The local governing bodies* (county councils and county borough councils) which control it. These authorities, 146 in all, through their education committees, provide the schools, employ the teachers, are responsible for their efficiency, and meet a large share of the expenses involved from general council revenue. These bodies discharge their administrative responsibility through three main groups: the members of the education committee, the administrative and professional officers (the Chief Education Officer and his professional staff), and the headmasters and teachers in the schools.

(ii) *The Department of Education and Science*, a national ministry, which is responsible in a general way for the efficiency of education in England, but does not itself maintain any schools. Its responsibility for education is discharged through·other institutions, through its inspectorate, its publications, and its financial assistance to local authorities and other bodies. It is assisted in its deliberative function by two advisory councils, one concerned with education in England and one with education in Wales.

(iii) *The universities*, which in most centres are responsible, through their institutes of education, for the academic and professional standards of the colleges of education in which primary teachers are trained, and for in-service courses provided. In addition their departments of education undertake teaching and research, issue publications which influence primary education, and in some cases offer graduate training for primary teaching in courses parallel to those they more characteristically offer for secondary teaching.

In some universities the department and the institute have become integrated into a single school or faculty of education.

The universities are independent bodies, their autonomy being protected by legislation. Most of them are substantially assisted by public funds, and this assistance is increasing. To this extent their autonomy is dependent on the liberal outlook of governments, because financial control can be virtually complete control.

(iv) *The National Foundation for Educational Research*, which was established as an independent research body to work closely with all sections of the education service which support it (by corporate membership and in other ways). It conducts research into primary education (not exclusively, of course), and finances it either from its own slender resources or from funds provided when research is commissioned. It publishes an educational journal (The Journal of Educational Research), and in other ways acts as a clearing house for research information.

The progress of the N.F.E.R. was until recently only moderate, owing to the lack of any sense of urgency in the profession about intensifying educational effort, and to the lack of support for educational research generally. More recently it has undergone a great and sudden expansion as its services have been called on to provide answers to questions on which critical action was needed, and as financial support has increased. The part it is playing in providing authoritative data is considerable, and it is clear that it will continue to play an important part as further change occurs. It has developed considerable expertise in test construction and evaluation, and it is possible that in studies involving the evaluation of new practices it will make one of its distinctive contributions.

(v) *The Nuffield Foundation*, a private body, which has collaborated with the Schools Council, and provided substantial funds for research and development in primary education in recent years. Its projects in mathematics, French, and other subjects represent a major contribution to the development of English education.

(vi) *The publishing houses*, which publish materials for the schools and educational literature generally. These provide an essential service to teachers, and the special knowledge that they have of forms of presentation may fairly be regarded as an important element in the total scene. Attractive books, well printed pictures, and specialized materials are an asset to the teacher. Without doubt there has been great development in this field.

(vii) *The public*, who express their interest through a number of channels — (a) in membership of bodies of managers appointed to supervise the affairs of individual schools, (b) in association with their children's school, and more generally (c) through the exercise of their franchise at local and national elections.

Those who serve on committees may be assumed to play an active part in education. What their actual role is in educational change it is more difficult to say. The close contact that they establish with teachers, together with their interest and involvement in education, are at least promising indications.

It is difficult to know whether there are promising signs among the great majority who control education only in an indirect way — through their votes at election time. The problems about the public, so far as educationists are concerned, are how to recognize their attitudes, and how to communicate with them. Making speeches, writing articles in the press, making public appearances on T.V., etc., presumably result in some kind of communication, but it is not unlike trying to communicate during a seance. Usually the feedback is not good.

When educational processes are fairly stable, there seems to be little to be concerned about. When substantial and rapid educational changes are needed, often requiring considerable public funds, the task of moving public opinion takes on a new and urgent character. Communicating effectively with the public, and interpreting educational ideas to it, is something the educationist needs to cultivate. At present he seems to know little about it.

Among the agencies listed, three of them have a direct and major responsibility for primary education. These are the local education authorities, the Department of Education and Science, and the universities. It will repay us to give something of the recent history of these institutions, and show what contribution each has made to the progress of education in England, what special resources each has, and what contribution each seems best fitted to make to an accelerated programme.

This will help to explain the special steps recently taken to increase the pace of change by the creation of the Schools Council.

The local education authorities

Among the advantages claimed for a decentralized scheme of education we may distinguish these three major ones:

(i) that a multiplicity of authorities (rather than just one, or a few) increases the prospect that progressive policies will be followed;

(ii) that public interest and support are more likely to be engendered, because of the more intimate nature of a local system as compared with a national or state system; and

(iii) that local needs are more likely to be met, and distinctive cultural features respected.

To an observer from abroad, with a background of educational systems that are more centralized, it would appear that the English local authorities, in their provision of education through more than half a century have, in the main, justified these claims.

Among the educational officials needed to staff so many local authorities there have been men of great ability and vision, who were able to make substantial, and often distinctive, progress in education in their areas. Nor has there been great inequality, as the forces of competition and emulation have ensured that less ambitious authorities have been encouraged, if not coerced, to follow the lead of the more adventurous ones. Inequality arising from differences in financial strength has been negligible.

In the most progressive authorities, often sustained by the leadership of an outstanding educator for one or two decades, modern thinking in education has been translated into effective practice, and considerable responsible experimenting has been done. Two achievements of major significance may be mentioned: (i) the liberal concept of administration that has been developed, and is so obvious at present, and (ii) the admirable system of infant education.

It is common to depict large and monopolistic organizations as impersonal and bureaucratic, and smaller organizations as personal and liberal. This of course is not necessarily true. Petty tyrannies are common enough, and destructive because their influence is so direct and intimate. It is one of the admirable features of the administration of education in England that it has generally been suffused with a liberal spirit, and has expressed in practice the idea that it is a means to an end, and should not be allowed to become exalted over the end.

The spirit has encouraged the idea that the work of the schools (that of the head and the teachers) should be given pride of place. The freedom of the headmaster and of his teachers to be allowed to create a good school according to their vision of it has been adhered to by enlightened administrators, who have regarded it as their particular responsibility to create the best possible conditions for schools to do their most effective work. They have used administration *educatively* to stimulate, guide, and lead, rather than to prescribe and regulate.

This attitude is one of the most significant features of English education today; it is likely also to be one of its greatest assets in the present national effort to increase the tempo of educational change. For any country needing to innovate which lacks this professional attitude in its teachers, a major transformation of attitudes is needed as a first difficult step; for a country which has it, there are still problems, but their chances of solution are better.

A second major achievement of English schools in the primary field has been the creation of a system of infant schools that is a model of modern thinking about the nurture and development of the young child, and the establishment of a corps of teachers enthusiastic about infant education, and imbued with its principles. The educative use of play, the idea of free discipline, the fruitful use of the environment, and adventurous school architecture, have all been developed to an advanced degree. The influence of the infant school on the junior classes above it has been one of the factors in the transformation of the primary school that is taking place.

The local authorities have undergone change as the demands on them have changed. In the two decades before the war they were faced with many problems arising out of the growth of secondary education. The growing acceptance of secondary education as a normal second stage in education, and the increasing public demand for it, brought about an enormous expansion of facilities and an increase in costs. It also produced perplexing problems about the differentiated forms that secondary education ought to take to meet the needs of a total age group. The growing need for technical education added to the problems of expansion, a need that was critically shown up by the inadequate supply of trained people at the outbreak of World War II.

With the dramatic growth in education services by 1939, it was apparent that only the larger of the local authorities (the councils of the counties and the county boroughs) had the financial strength and administrative resources to cope with the post-war developments, and a drastic elimination of the smaller ones was written into the 1944 Education Act, a major piece of legislation which shaped education in the post-war period. The local authorities were reduced from 315 to 146, and these 146 were welded under a Ministry of Education more closely into a national education system. Their authority has not been weakened in the process, nor have they suffered in importance as innovative agencies.

With adaptations, the local education authorities have been able to cope with the evolutionary progress of education during the first half of this century. The quickening social changes since the war have made it apparent that this process of growth and adaptation is not in itself sufficient, and that special steps are needed to provide the additional stimulus. As we shall see, this has been done without detracting from the authorities' key influence and power.

Indeed these appear to be enhanced.

The Department of Education and Science

The power of the central government in education has increased greatly since the war. This change reflects increased governmental awareness of the national significance of education services, of the necessity to plan educational development with the needs of the nation as a whole in mind, and of the need to stimulate and assist development by financial assistance. The 1944 Education Act replaced the Board of Education (which was charged with the vague task of superintending education) by an Education Ministry with much greater authority.

The Department of Education and Science plays an important role in promoting the efficiency of education services in the country at all levels, but it does not do this by usurping the authority of other bodies. The responsibility of the local education authorities is quite plainly acknowledged.

The influence of the Department is exercised through its financial support to local authorities and other bodies, its publications, and its inspectorate. One of the special features of the central authority for decades has been its use of a deliberative committee to consider educational issues, and to provide an authoritative review of them for general consumption. The Consultative Committee, which served the Board of Education until its dissolution with the passing of the 1944 Education Act, gave very distinguished service to education. Under such chairmen as Sir Henry Hadow, it published major statements on educational issues. With the setting up of a Ministry of Education, two advisory councils (one for England and one for Wales), were established, and these have performed a similar function. The work of these committees may be regarded as an important element in England's strategy in assisting educational progress. A fuller account of them is reserved for the section dealing specifically with strategies of change.

The professional staff of the central authority have played an important part in the development of education. They have been selected for their scholarship* and leadership in education, and have been placed in a position of great influence. They play a role of supervision and leadership, but the emphasis is on leadership. By personal influence in the schools, by lecturing in Ministry courses, by publications, and by serving on committees, they make a substantial contribution to educational progress.

The strategic role of the Department in initiating, facilitating, and supporting national movements in education is very significant. Not the least of these actions were those in connexion with the setting up of the Schools Council.

The universities

In the period since 1945, the universities have had an influence on the development of primary education in two fairly distinct ways: (i) through the institutes of education, and (ii) through the departments of education. The first of these has been the more direct and effective; the second has been indirect in most cases, and, until quite recently, slight.

From an uncertain beginning in 1945, when the McNair Committee[1] was divided on the issue whether training colleges should be brought within the orbit of the universities, the institutes of education have developed with undoubted success.[2] The curriculum of the colleges has undergone a major reconstruction, academic standards have been raised, and the basic course of training has been

* Among many distinguished people the name of Matthew Arnold may be mentioned.

increased from two to three years.* The colleges have been transformed from small, sometimes parochial institutions with immature professional standards and an underdeveloped tertiary spirit, into major institutions. To match their new-found stature they have changed their name from training colleges to colleges of education.

Perhaps the most striking indication of the development of the colleges is the part they are playing in the newly introduced Bachelor of Education degree. The need for such a degree has been felt for some time. The higher standards of work being achieved in the colleges, the recognition of the need to increase the length of the training course (at least for some) from three to four years, and the increasing number of students enrolling who are of university calibre but who have not achieved university entrance, all have combined to strengthen the case for the setting up of the degree. In fact, it has been set up, and students are already working towards it. The highly significant thing is that in most institutes the teaching for the degree is being done in the colleges of education. Two decades ago this idea would have seemed absurd.

Nevertheless the preparation of teachers in the colleges is not without its critics. In schools and education authorities, particularly in those where innovative practices are found, it is the retraining of teachers that is the problem most frequently mentioned in reply to the inquiry about the difficulties of introducing new ideas — including that of the teachers fresh from training. The young teachers themselves, when questioned about the newer practices they are using, quite frequently claim they have learned them on the job, although they admit that 'they may have been mentioned in college.'

Colleges, on the contrary, assume, and declare, that they are preparing students for the world of change outside. Clearly there is a gap in this matter between the perception of the college and that of the schools. One does not doubt the intention of the training authorities, nor their expertise. Indeed, the in-service courses offered by them are accepted eagerly by teachers unfamiliar with new ideas. A personal reminiscence is relevant at this point. The headmistress of a school who was eagerly involved in a particular innovation was (under duress of questioning) bemoaning the fact that her young teachers, fresh from training in a particular college, had not heard of it. In reply to a rather indelicate question as to where she had heard of it, she replied, 'at an in-service course at —— college.' It was the same college.

It would be a mistake to conclude that the training institutions are not oriented towards innovation, or that the criticisms of the experienced administrators and teachers are malicious. It may fairly be concluded that the colleges are saying things to their students that they do not hear or understand, or that they are not able to deal with operationally.

* in 1961.

One form in which the criticism of the colleges was put was that they had become too 'academic', and were apeing the universities in their attempt to increase their acceptability in the academic world. The influence of the new B.Ed. degree, it is claimed by these critics, is to accelerate the flight from reality. Whatever substance there is in this criticism should be carefully heeded by the colleges; if there is any substitution of irrelevant academic study for essential professional study, it is a grievous fault. It is, however, a distressing state of affairs when the word 'academic' in the training of teachers is used as a term of reproach.

The problem is how to study the intensely practical things that teachers do in the classroom with the academic approach that they do in fact require in order to be properly understood, and yet ensure that the practical bearing is not lost. It is a problem common to most forms of professional training. It is one which the colleges must solve if they are going to contribute as they should to the spread of new practices. Their training must be explicitly geared to change. The innovations outside must be orthodoxies of college training. The new degree course will be the severest test of all. It could, if academic responsibility is falsely interpreted, bring the university preparation of teachers into discredit; or it could bring the training of teachers, particularly of primary teachers, to a new level of success.

The success of the institutes in upgrading the training of primary-school teachers has been matched by their programmes of in-service training for teachers already practising. It was one of the original conceptions of the institutes of education that they should provide a variety of services for practising teachers, using their resources of staff and their buildings to assist them in the study of new ideas. The institutes have varied in their emphasis on this work, and in their success in it, but on the whole it has been a stimulating chapter in the history of teacher education.

It is sobering to reflect on why, as in the case of the pre-service training of teachers, the effort of the institutes has proved to be inadequate, and why a new strategy, involving stimulation from outside the universities, should have to be adopted. Even so, in the new deployment of forces, it is clear that the institutes have an important part to play.

The departments of education have been concerned mainly with the training of secondary teachers, and have reflected a good deal of the rigidity that has, until recently, characterized secondary education. A few of them did engage in the training of primary teachers as well, but this was a small part of their responsibility. One might have expected that the limited activity of the departments in the training of teachers would be accounted, perhaps compensated for, by concentration on post-graduate studies, research and publication, thus influencing primary education in an important, if oblique way. This does not appear to be so. There are notable exceptions, but on the whole the departments have pursued a fairly unenterprising course.

There has been an important strand of scholarly writing in education, but mainly of a philosophical and historical kind; much less has been written in educational psychology and sociology, and less still which has been focussed directly on the curriculum and methods of teaching. Method was something you 'learnt' during periods of practice and observations in the schools. Recently the scene has undergone a quite remarkable transformation. Departments have been strengthened, chairs of education have multiplied and been devoted to new studies such as curriculum and sociology of education and to research, and a great upsurge of effort is evident. Books have suddenly appeared purporting to say what education is, and what its study entails.[3] The response to this new source of wisdom by bodies like the Schools Council is evident. The new additions to staff in the behavioural sciences, as well as others, have added enormously to the research potential of the university departments, and a good deal of research concerned with curriculum innovation and other projected changes in education is already based there. Undoubtedly in the period ahead the universities will have a very important part to play.

Accelerating Innovation

Three strategies for accelerating innovation were discussed in the preceding chapter: increasing and spreading educational knowledge, reeducating teachers and others concerned with innovation, and coercing or assisting change.

In England all three are in evidence. There is much stronger support being given to educational research in the universities, the colleges of education, and the N.F.E.R., and there is a stress on in-service courses, on opportunities for discussion among teachers, and on involvement of them in new ventures. There is also a widespread canvassing of professional and public opinion on specific educational issues; evidence about them is sifted, and policies or objectives formulated to stimulate further discussion or guide future action. The notable example of this kind of activity in the field of primary education is the recent work of the Advisory Council on Education, and its publication, the Plowden Report.

The use of the 'power strategy' has resulted in the formation of the Schools Council, a new body specifically charged with the task of innovation in the field of curriculum and evaluation. By its membership, its prestige, its specific mandate, and its financial strength, it exercises both power and encouragement. But it works mainly by seeking to increase knowledge in the curriculum field, by the dissemination of this knowledge, and by providing, particularly through the use of teachers' centres, opportunities for reeducation.

Undoubtedly the work of the Schools Council is the major new force for innovation in England today, and a somewhat detailed account of it is warranted. Before this is undertaken, however, it is intended to describe more fully the type of committee action which produces publications like the Plowden Report. This is not new in English practice, but it appears to the writer to be so important in the innovative process as to merit closer study. Few nations have used it so effectively as has England, and all have a great deal to learn from England in this respect.

The report on education as an agent of innovation

One might cite a dozen reports of the kind being brought to notice here which have described the progress of education in England, and which, to a significant degree, have charted this progress. They deal with the education of teachers (the McNair Report[4]), the Public Schools (the Fleming Report[5]), non-academic secondary students (the Newsom Report[6]), and so on. The one we have most immediately in mind in the discussion that follows, since this book is about primary education, is the Plowden Report, *Children and their Primary Schools* (1967).

The characteristics of the procedure, culminating in the production of a report, may be described conveniently in three phases: launching the investigation, pursuing the investigation, and ensuring the impact of the report. Each of these is taken up in turn.

Launching the investigation

(i) An undertaking of this kind is begun usually when the time is judged to be propitious. This state of readiness is expressed in, and no doubt assisted by, publications of various kinds, including research reports, popular articles, discussions, and perhaps public criticism.

(ii) The decision to set up a committee is made at a high level (usually ministerial), and a distinguished chairman and members are appointed. (In the case of the Plowden Committee, it was the Central Advisory Council for Education (England).) Thus the launching of the investigation is seen as being an important public event.

(iii) Care is taken to see that the committee adequately represents the range of opinion involved and of institutions or interests affected. This is to assure both comprehensiveness and objectivity. The objectivity is further secured by having an independent chairman (that of the Plowden Committee (Lady Plowden) was not a professional educationist at all).

(iv) Adequate finance and expert secretarial assistance are provided (the estimated cost of the Plowden Report was £120,699, of which the greater part was spent in commissioning research).

Pursuing the investigation

(v) The scope of the inquiry is contained in the terms of reference given to the committee. The objective is straightforward and practically oriented, even though interpretation of the task is usually needed. (The terms of reference to the Plowden Committee were as follows: 'To consider primary education in all its aspects, and the transition to secondary education'.)

(vi) The task is analysed by the committee to permit treatment of it topic by topic, and to provide a convenient structure for purposes of publication.

(vii) The committee uses resources other than the knowledge and experience of its own members by:

(a) obtaining evidence in written form, or by interview, from persons approached, or accepting it from persons who voluntarily provide it;

(b) commissioning research on particular issues;

(c) using authoritative publications;

(d) observing relevant practice at home or abroad (the Plowden Committee, or some members of it, visited six countries abroad including the U.S.A. and the U.S.S.R.).

(viii) The committee works towards the production of a report which has the following features.

(a) It is readable, with a wide audience in mind. (Statistics, technical reports, etc., are usually placed in appendices. The Appendices to the Plowden Report amount to 633 pages, and constitute a separate volume.)

(b) It is authoritative.

(c) It is comprehensive, in bringing together material from widely different sources and from a wide range of types of literature.

(d) It is interpretative and evaluative. The committee does not merely place evidence before the reader, but evaluates it, and relates it to practice. These evaluations are recorded as recommendations. They usually appear in the section of the report to which they are related, but they are also conveniently brought together at the end of the report. (In the Plowden Report there are 197 recommendations, and the institution or authority concerned with implementing them is indicated.)

Lack of agreement among members of the committee on any particular point is recorded, and the nature of the disagreement set out in a supplementary statement.

Ensuring the impact of the report

(ix) The committee's method of working in commissioning research, visiting schools, and contacting witnesses generates a wide measure of interest and expectation. The publication of the report is awaited with interest, and is regarded as an event of importance.

(x) The report is widely publicized. It is published by a government authority, and is relatively inexpensive (Volume 1 of the Plowden Report, 556 pages long, is published by H.M.S.O. and is priced at 25/6).

Because it is easily available and widely read, and is discussed in the mass media, there is a great amount of feedback of public and professional reaction to the recommendations. If legislation is necessary to give effect to any of the recommendations, it can be undertaken on the basis of good insight into public opinion.

(xi) Because the report is transmitted to the responsible minister, it is likely to be tabled in the House, debated in parliament, and read by politicians, as well as by academics, administrators, and teachers.

All in all, this type of publication seems to occupy a unique position among publications as an instrument for facilitating change. It brings together relevant information from a variety of other publications; it is undertaken in an atmosphere conducive to change; and it speaks directly to all the people who have to be convinced that change is needed and who are seeking an authoritative statement about the form it should take.

Accelerating innovation by the creation of the Schools Council

When responsibility is divided among a number of specialized institutions and authorities, as is the case in England, the task of accelerating innovation can be approached in a number of ways.

(i) One way is to create new authorities with a special responsibility for innovation.

(ii) Another is to strengthen the central authority, and bring the existing institutions into its sphere of influence in a bureaucratic framework.

(iii) A third is to create machinery which will more effectively mobilize the existing agencies, and bring them into new relationships, so that in combination they will each be capable of much more effective action.

England's main solution is the third one. It is to create new machinery which makes use of the existing agencies. Its action on these is as a catalyst, stimulating them to new achievement. This machinery is the Schools Council. The establishing of the Schools Council, and the conception underlying it, may best be described by reference to official documents.

In 1963 a representative meeting of educators took place in London to discuss the need for new cooperative machinery in the fields of school curricula and examinations. It appointed a working party under the chairmanship of Sir John Lockwood to examine the lines on which action might be taken. The working party reported to the Minister of Education in March 1964, and recommended the setting up of a new body to be called the Schools Council for the Curriculum and Examinations (since abbreviated to the Schools Council). The conception of the new body is very clearly set out in the working party's report.[7] Two of the vital recommendations are quoted below in abbreviated form.

(i) The control of the machinery should be vested in a body *fully representative of all those principally concerned*.

(ii) The character of the new body should be that of *a free association of equal partners*, who would combine to promote the pursuit of common objectives. The Schools Council would not, in other words, be advisory to all its member interests.

The Council was created, and met for the first time, in October 1964, under the chairmanship of Sir John Maud, G.C.B., C.B.E., Master of University College, Oxford. As he rather racily put it,[8] when contemplating the task ahead:

> 'We are no bunch of stooges. We have our own headquarters, our nameplate on the door, our own budget, and our own full-time staff. It is our own fault if we fail!'

The conception of the Schools Council is such an important one, and so admirable, that a more detailed statement of its objects and responsibility is merited.

Its objectives[9] are to uphold and interpret the principle that each school should have the fullest possible measure of responsibility for its own work, with its own curriculum and teaching methods based on the needs of its own pupils, and evolved by its own staff; and to seek, through cooperative study of common problems, to assist all who have individual or joint responsibilities for, or in connexion with, the school's curricula and examinations to coordinate their actions in harmony with this principle.

In order to promote these objectives, the Council proposes to keep under review curricula, teaching methods, and examinations in primary and secondary schools, and also aspects of school organization so far as they affect the curriculum, and to draw attention to difficulties arising in those fields which appear to merit consideration by the appropriate authorities.

In particular, the Council plans to:

(a) discuss with the schools ways in which, through research and development, and by other means, the Council can assist the schools to meet both the individual needs of their pupils and the educational needs of the community as a whole;

(b) ascertain the views and interests of the schools on all matters falling within the Council's terms of reference, and represent those views and interests in discussion of such matters with any bodies or persons concerned directly or indirectly with education in all its aspects (it will be free to publish its findings and recommendations at its own discretion);

(c) carry out the functions hitherto undertaken by the Secondary School Examinations Council; and

(d) offer advice on request to any member interested and, so far as practicable, to any bodies and persons concerned with the work of the schools.

The governing body of the Council consists of about 80 members, of whom the majority represent the schools, but all the major educational interests are represented — local authorities, central authority, universities (through both their vice-chancellors and their education staff), colleges of advanced technology — and there are a substantial number of members coopted by the Council itself. In addition three Curriculum Steering Committees are provided for in the constitution — one concerned with the 2–13 age group, a second with the 11–16 age group, and a third with the 13–18 age group. The age ranges selected are deliberately overlapping, so as to prevent unnecessary divisions from occuring in the system as a whole, and to prevent Council policy from becoming separated into compartments. These committees are also representative, but teachers predominate in them. Below these are thirteen subject committees. With the governing body and the committees, the membership of the Council is of the order of 400, a number large enough to give the Schools Council a substantial degree of visibility in many institutions in the land.

The staffing policy of the Council emphasizes that it is not separated functionally from the institutions that it serves. The working party considered that a career secretariat and study-team organization were not needed, but rather that staff should be drawn from a variety of sources — such as schools, local education authorities, universities, Her Majesty's inspectorate — and should serve the Council only for a short time. During this period of service they are given the temporary status of civil servants, and are paid by the Ministry. It should be stressed, however, that the bulk of the Council's income for the pursuit of its work comes from the local authorities, not from the central government. Politically and financially the Council is independent of the central government.

The activity of the Schools Council since its formation in 1964 has been prodigious. In describing its tactics it would, however, be more valuable to indicate not so much what it has achieved as the type of objective it has set itself. These objectives may be stated as follows; they will then be elaborated below.

(i) Determining priorities for its programme;

(ii) stimulating interest by the profession in problems being dealt with by the Council;

(iii) commissioning relevant research;

(iv) mounting national curriculum-development projects;

(v) administering national projects; and

(vi) working with teachers at the local level.

(i) *Determining priorities*. In its first outline, setting out tasks needing urgent attention, the Council decided that the following should be given priority: the projected raising of the school-leaving age to 16 years in 1970,* sixth-form curricula and examinations, the teaching of English throughout the whole age range, and the curriculum for primary schools.

(ii) *Arousing interest throughout the profession in Council projects.* The procedure followed in doing this is to publish a broad description of the problem, stating what is already being done, and what needs to be done both locally and nationally. These initial ideas are prepared by a working party (usually small) that produces the document for publication. These are some of the working papers already published:

No. 1,	1965,	Science for the Young School Leaver;
No. 2,	1965,	Raising the School leaving Age;
No. 3,	1965,	English: A programme for research and development in English teaching,
No. 4,	1966,	Science in the Sixth Form;
No. 5,	1966,	Sixth Form, Curriculum and Examinations;
No. 6,	1966,	1965 C.S.E.† Monitoring Experiment: Parts I and II.
No. 7,	1966,	Closer links between Teachers and Industry and Commerce,
No. 8,	1966,	French in the Primary School,
No. 9,	1967,	Standards in C.S.E. and G.C.E.‡;
No. 10,	1967,	Curriculum Development: Teachers' Groups and Centres.

(iii) *Commissioning relevant research.* The Council is not a research agency, but it is a consumer of educational research, and within its financial resources it sponsors research in connexion with its own projects. The following research studies are given, with the centres at which they are being undertaken, as examples of Council-sponsored research.

(a) Teaching English as a second language, at the University of Leeds;
(b) Linguistics and English teaching at the Communications Research Centre, University College, London;
(c) Various projects in connexion with the proposal to raise the school-leaving age, at the Manchester University School of Education, and the National Foundation for Educational Research.

---

* Since deferred
† Certificate of Secondary Education — an alternative examination at the end of Secondary Schooling for non-academic students.
‡ General Certificate of Education, the examinations taken at the end of secondary schooling.

(d) Modern language projects at the National Foundation for Educational Research.

(iv) *Mounting national curriculum-development projects*. National curriculum-development projects, engaging the full-time services of a number of well qualified people over a period of years, are expensive. To date the Schools Council has been fortunate in being able to collaborate with the Nuffield Foundation. This has been important for the Council, not only in increasing its capacity to undertake work, but also in establishing its image as an independent body, which early financial reliance on governmental authorities might have affected.

(v) *Administering national projects*. The method of working adopted by Nuffield teams has been very successful, and is likely to be an influential model for further activities. It involves these steps:

(a) Careful study of the objectives of the particular subject. All sources of knowledge and competent opinion are tapped in this phase of the study. Groups of teachers who are to be associated with the project study the question in local centres, and make a statement of their deliberations. Out of this comes the statement of objectives which guides the project in its first phase.

(b) Development of materials which seem likely to assist a teacher in reaching these objectives. Supporting statements explaining them to teachers are also prepared.

(c) Field trials of the materials in schools which have agreed to cooperate. Discussion and study by teachers concerned continue in local centres during this period.

(d) Assessment of the success of the materials in achieving the objectives.

(e) Review, and if necessary revision, in the light of the information gained.

(f) Preparation of materials in 'final' form for wider dissemination. The cooperation of a commercial publishing house is secured.

(g) Further development work, as feedback from a greater number of users accumulates.

(h) Further evaluation, by objective criteria if these can be developed.

(vi) *Working with teachers at the local level*. Great stress is laid by the Schools Council on local work in curriculum development. This is expressed well in the following quotation.[10]

'The essence of curricular review and development is new thinking by the teachers themselves, as well as their appraisal of the thinking of others. This means that teachers should have regular opportunities to meet together, and that they should look upon the initiation of thought, as well as the trial and assessment of new ideas and procedures drawn from other sources, as an integral part of their professional service to society.'

An essential step in implementing the strategy for change envisaged is the setting up of teachers' centres, where teachers may come together to become familiar with new material, hear lectures, conduct study groups, and compare experiences. It appears to be assumed that most commonly these centres will be provided by, or associated most closely with, the local education authorities, rather than with colleges of education or the universities, although assistance from these institutions is regarded as desirable. As mentioned at the beginning of this section, teachers' centres could be a sensitive part of the cooperation net-work.

Concluding comment

Any action taken to accelerate change in education is an act of faith, since there is little that is positively known about the change process. It is based on assumptions; or perhaps they may be called calculated risks.

The assumptions involved in the movement that has brought the Schools Council into being appear to be as follows:

(i) that the existing educational institutions — local education authorities, universities, etc. (suitably strengthened or adapted where necessary) — are adequate to provide the education services that England needs, provided that the processes of research and development and the professional development of teachers are intensified, and communication is improved;

(ii) that the best kind of structure within which to relate the various agencies in education is a cooperative, not a hierarchical one (it is, of course, assumed that the institutions will cooperate);

(iii) that suitable enabling administrative machinery can be devised to mobilize or manoeuvre the existing institutions into an effective combination of forces;

(iv) that it is possible for effort in curriculum development to become more organized and institutionalized without detracting from the sense of initiative and responsibility which teachers now have and which is valued by them and by others;

(v) that curriculum is a matter entirely (or mainly) for the 'education community',

(vi) that curriculum-development work is best carried out by staff who engage in it temporarily, not by 'professional developers'.

Assumptions of course may be incorrect, or inadequate. There are questions that come to mind. There are probably good answers to them, or good answers will come in time, but they are perhaps worth asking.

(i) Is it possible that a 'Hawthorne' effect is at work in producing the enthusiasm, effort, and success to date, which is independent of the strategy employed?

(ii) Are the strategy and tactics geared closely enough to public opinion? No doubt the determination of what is taught *is* a matter for the 'education community', but not exclusively so. Although the Council is concerned with curriculum *development*, it cannot help but be concerned with curriculum objectives, and this is not exclusively a matter for the 'education community'.

(iii) Is the organization in its structure and function a little too heavily weighted towards the teachers and the local education authorities, and not enough towards the universities and colleges and the public?

(iv) Will the Council's efforts gradually weaken initiative and responsibility on the part of teachers, in spite of its frequent affirmation of the need for the schools to be independent? Is it possible that the habit could develop of leaving curriculum matters to the Schools Council?

Will it have a damping effect on fundamental research, because of the development of a pattern of funding that principally encourages applied research?

It is not possible to say yet how effective the strategy is that England is employing. It promises success, but the period is short so far. What is appealing is that it makes use of the most liberal elements of English education, and endeavours to strengthen them rather than to override them with new authorities that promise quicker results.

To an Australian observer the volume, variety, and impact of the Council's work are very impressive. If its 'presence' or 'visibility' is any indication, it is being very successful. In one sense it is an organization in London; in another, and more important, sense, it consists of individuals and groups in schools, universities, colleges, and education offices up and down the country, who talk of what the Schools Council is doing, and mean by it the work of their own group in their own building.

REFERENCES

1. Great Britain Board of Education, *Teachers and Youth Leaders* (Chairman, Sir Arnold McNair) H.M.S.O., London, 1944.
2. M.V.C. Jeffreys, *Revolution in Teacher Training*, Pitman, London, 1961.
3. For example: R. S. Peters (Ed.), *The Concept of Education*, Routledge & Kegan Paul, London, 1967; and J. W. Tibble (Ed.), *The Study of Education*, Routledge & Kegan Paul, London, 1966.
4. Great Britain Board of Education, *Teachers and Youth Leaders* (Chairman, Sir Arnold McNair) H.M.S.O., London, 1944.
5. Great Britain Board of Education, *The Public Schools and the General Educational System* (Chairman, Lord Fleming) H.M.S.O., London, 1944.

6. Central Advisory Council for Education (England), *Half Our Future*, H.M.S.O., London, 1963.
7. Central Advisory Council for Education (England), *Report of the Working Party on the Schools' Curricula and Examinations*, H.M.S.O., London, 1964.
8. The Schools Council, *Change and Response*, H.M.S.O., London, 1965, Foreword.
9. *ibid.*, p. 34.
10. The Schools Council, *Curriculum Development: Teachers' Groups and Centres*, Working Paper No. 10, H.M.S.O., London, 1967.

Chapter 8

Agents in the Innovative Process in the U.S.A.

Introduction

The American scene in education is so vast, and is such a mosaic, that it is difficult to see it as a whole. It is easy to grasp the idea of innovation in particular activities such as teacher education, or the teaching of mathematics, or in particular places such as California or Mississippi; but it is hard to grasp the idea of the whole system being changed. Yet this is the spirit of the present movement towards reform. It is education as a whole that is the target; the nation is committed to educational reform at its top levels of power. The scale of the effort being expended is enormous, the difficulties faced numerous. Because of the unprecedented pressures at the national level, the system is being called upon to change according to a national pattern, when in fact it has never worked as a national system.

A brief sketch of some of the prominent features of this mosaic may show up the problems more clearly.

(i) There are fifty separate state systems of education in states with differing demographic, economic, political, religious, and ethnic features. They differ in the amount and quality of the education they provide, the types of institutions they have developed, and the educational problems encountered.

Within most of these states there is a multiplicity of local school districts, differing in type from state to state, and differing in their relationship to each other and to superior authorities. They also cover areas that are often significantly different in demographic, economic, political, religious, and ethnic features.

(ii) Control and financial support come from authorities at three levels – the local board of education, the state board of education and state government, and the federal government. The interrelations of these three levels are very complex and take different forms in different states. In some states the major responsibility rests with the local authorities, in others there is virtually a state centralized system.

In addition to problems arising from different administrative traditions and

167

financial arrangements, the local—state—federal partnership in education is complicated by political differences, particularly on the issues of civil rights, religious schools, and states' rights. The racial and religious issues are quite central to the question of federal intervention in education, and the question of sovereignty of state government underlies both, as well as being an issue in itself. In any negotiations between the federal government and the states all these issues are likely to be involved. Thus, what may be put forward in congress as an educational proposal may well be judged by some to infringe states' rights, by others to support (or fail to support) parochial schools, and by others to interfere in the racial situation. When federal and state political philosophies are not congruent, it is hard for educational policies to be so. The complexity, variety, and strength of these social issues make it seem remarkable that any federal legislation on education at all has been achieved, and particularly legislation such as the 1965 Elementary and Secondary School Act which affects the general school system.

(iii) There is a large and varied higher education system, part under state control, part independent, and increasingly dependent financially on the federal government. The role of this system in influencing innovation at the school level is quite vital, because of the general and professional training that it provides, the research that it undertakes, and its influence on the development of knowledge. Mobilizing it to serve national ends more directly, however, is no easy task.

The foci of authority, responsibility, and influence in so varied a structure are many; and the lines of force from them intersect in a highly complex manner. In these circumstances it is by no means clear how change is brought about, nor whether the exigencies of a particular time, the force of an historical tradition with its body of beliefs and stereotypes, or the influence of individuals in positions of power, affect the outcome most.

In the account that follows only institutions are described, not because it is assumed that the influence of particular people is expressed only through institutions, or that an institution is the same no matter who speaks for it, but because in a contemporary study of this kind it is manifestly premature, if not impossible, to account for social changes in terms of persons. The most obvious institution to examine is the Federal Government. Others that are looked at, less closely, are the school districts, the state governments and state boards of education, the universities and colleges, the philanthropic foundations, the educational business houses and the teachers' organizations. The three strategies for innovation referred to earlier form a background to the discussion.

The role of the Federal Government in innovation in education

The Federal Constitution gives the Federal Government no direct control over education, but there are constitutional provisions which when invoked and interpreted by the courts prove to have quite significant relevance. A number of recent decisions by the Federal Supreme Court involving the First and the Fourteenth Amendments to the Constitution* have had quite dramatic effects on those states where separate schools systems were maintained.

But the Federal Government has power to legislate for individuals as citizens of the United States, and it has been through this more general power that it has intervened in education. Whether all that has been done is constitutional is not known. As most of the legislation has conferred financial benefits on the states and other bodies, it is not likely to be challenged.

In American education since World War II, the most striking new factor concerned with reforming and intensifying educational effort has unquestionably been the Federal Government. While its share of the nation's expenses on education is not yet large† compared with that provided by the central government in Britain, the new financial aid is, nevertheless, considered as an additional amount, a massive stimulus.

The scale of the Federal Government's financial assistance is one measure of its influence. Another is the specific way in which it has expressed its authority. It is thus acting not only to increase financial support to the existing education authorities, but as an independent education authority. Through its legislation, it is by implication expressing policies for change in such matters as teaching children in impoverished districts, educational research and development, creative activities in education, the curriculum, teacher training, technical training, and so on.

None of this action on the part of the Federal Government is quite new, but in view of the scale of the current assistance, and the nature of the specified activities, it may be regarded as being new. In Campbell's words 'The year 1965 will probably go down in history as a major turning point in the relations of the Federal Government to education.'

It may be argued that the specific, or categorical, form in which federal legislation is cast is not intended to express detailed federal policies, but is adopted rather on grounds of political expediency to secure the passage of the legislation. There has been long-standing opposition to general federal aid to public education, and any such proposal is still likely to fall foul of those, on the one hand, who fear federal control, and on the other, of those who are seeking its extension to private and parochial schools. President Kennedy's 1961 bill to

* The First Amendment deals with the separation of church and state, the Fourteenth with civil rights.

† It is roughly one-fifth. Expenditure of Federal funds on Education and related activities was $10·583 billion in 1966. This figure includes $3 billion for specific expenses related to training Federal personnel and professional and technical training of the military. (Source: *Statistical Abstract of the United States*, 88th annual ed. 1967, Table 207, p. 145.)

aid education – particularly to raise teachers' salaries, speed up the building programme, and give special assistance to schools in depressed areas – left it to the states to determine how the money was to be spent, with the one proviso that church schools were excluded. It failed. Another proposal in 1963, even more ambitious, was, in his own words*, 'a comprehensive, balanced programme to enlarge the Federal Government's investment in the education of its citizens'. Kennedy's argument for its necessity was eloquent and disarming: 'Fundamentally, education is, and must always be, a local responsibility, for it thrives best when nurtured on the grass roots of our democracy. But in our present era of economic expansion, population growth, and technological advance, state, local, and private effort are insufficient. These efforts must be reinforced by national support, if American education is to yield a maximum of individual development and national well-being. The programme here proposed is reasonable and yet far-reaching. It offers federal assistance without federal control.' It also failed; although sections were extracted from it which were subsequently passed.

However, there is a long history of successful federal legislation for special aid which avoids the sensitive spots. This dates from the Northwest Ordinance of 1787, in which provision was made for the sale of federal lands for the support of public education. It continues through the Morrill Act of 1862, which gave land for the establishment of colleges, to the Smith–Hughes Act in 1917 to foster vocational education for high-school students, the Lanham Act of 1941 and the Impact Laws of 1950, reimbursing local districts for education expenses arising out of the siting of military establishments and war factories, the Service Man's Readjustment Act of 1944, and to the current legislation.

If present federal assistance to education has been given on a specific basis, rather than by general aid, in order to avoid the threat of federal control of education, the outcome is a curious one. The forms of specific aid are now so numerous that, taken together, they fall only just short of general aid. Yet, because they are specific, many require administration procedures involving separate approvals at the federal level, which is a very detailed form of federal supervision. In an information statement issued recently by the U.S. Office of Education,[2] there are set out in four groups – (i) for construction, (ii) for programmes, instruction and administration, (iii) for teacher training and student assistance, and (iv) for research – no less than 112 types of assistance for education, with the purpose of the assistance stated, the total amount of money appropriated for each, who is eligible to apply, and where application should be made. Those who are eligible to apply (some of whom are supposed to make educational policy) would be less than human if they did not let their own policies go along with the 'purpose of the assistance'.

---

* In his special message to Congress on education in support of the bill.

There appears to be no doubt in the mind of the present* U.S. Commissioner of Education, Harold Howe II, that the Federal Government is acting with specific objectives in mind, and that the authority of the Federal Government is needed. He states,[3] 'The Federal Government has gone beyond offering sporadic financial aid to taking an active, constructive part in improving American education. Towards this end, the Congress has enacted 24 major pieces of education legislation in the past three years. These new laws are channels through which billions of Federal tax dollars will go into our elementary schools, high schools, vocational schools, colleges and universities.

But this money is not simply handed out in the pious hope that it will be put to good use. Each of the education laws — the Elementary and Secondary Act, the Higher Education Act, and the rest, old and new, is quite specific. Categories and conditions of aid have been established to ensure that these funds are spent in an efficient and prudent manner.'

We may get a more complete picture of the Federal Government's participation in educational innovation by surveying briefly the major recent legislation, as embodied in the following acts:

(i) The National Science Foundation Act (1950);

(ii) The National Defense Education Act (1958, amended 1964) (NDEA);

(iii) The Elementary and Secondary Education Act (1965) (ESEA);

(iv) The National Foundation for the Arts and Humanities Act (1965);

(v) The Higher Education Act (1965).

The National Science Foundation Act The National Science Foundation was established by statute in 1950 to help America cope with the era of science that had burst upon the world. It was given a broad mandate to strengthen basic research and education in the sciences, and a generous budget and considerable autonomy to follow it. In 1963 it spent $100 million on such activities as supplementary teacher training, curriculum improvements, and fellowship grants. Like so much of federal legislation in education, it was done in the name of national development and security, replacing the dominant idea of education for consumption by that of education as investment. The official purposes given for founding it were 'to promote the progress of science, to advance the national health, prosperity and welfare; to secure the national defense; and for other purposes'.

By the early 1960s the Foundation was supporting extensive programmes in the following:

(i) financial aid for graduate students, advanced scholars, and teachers;

(ii) supplementary training of teachers of science, mathematics, and engineering through a system of institutes;

* 1967

(iii) improvement in the subject matter of science and mathematics teaching, particularly at secondary level; and

(iv) identification and motivation of able high-school and undergraduate science students through a variety of special programmes.

The training of teachers of science and mathematics has been very successful. The courses were conducted by institutions of higher education, and most of the costs were met by the Foundation. It is estimated that in the years following Sputnik 10 to 20 per cent. of the nation's high-school teachers of science and mathematics had attended institutes sponsored by the National Science Foundation.

The updating of courses in science and mathematics has also been a feature of the Foundation's programme, and it has met with great success. The procedure has been to encourage committees of research and teaching scholars in the subject to undertake projects of curriculum revision. The major projects are the well known Physical Sciences Study Committee (PSSC), the School Mathematics Study Group (SMSG), and the Biological Science Curriculum Study (BSCS); but there were in addition a number of less extensive studies in other curricular fields, and the production of supplementary teaching aids such as laboratory equipment, educational film, and television programmes. Important studies were also sponsored in the field of elementary-school science. Teachers are involved in their courses as they are developed, publicity is given them, and institute programmes are arranged, so that by the time they are ready for general use, they have obtained some recognition and a measure of acceptance.

Further activities of the Foundation in support of science are seen in the aid given in various ways to high-school students for the study of science and in the granting of fellowships to secondary-school teachers for them to pursue advanced degree requirements.

Without doubt the National Science Foundation has been a powerful agent for change in a specific field.

The National Defense Education Act The National Defense Education Act consists of the following ten sections or titles:

Title I   — General provisions, purpose and definition;
Title II   — Loans to students in institutions of higher education;
Title III   — Financial assistance for strengthening science, mathematics, and modern language instruction;
Title IV   — National Defense fellowships;
Title V   — Guidance, counseling, and testing; identification and encourage-ment of able students; counseling and guidance training;
Title VI — Language development centers for research, language institutes;
Title VII — Research and experimentation in more effective utilization of

television, radio, motion pictures, and related media for educa-
al purposes;

Title VIII — Area vocational educational programs;
Title IX — Science information service;
Title X — Improvement of statistical services of state educational agencies.
Specifically, it provides for the following;

(i) Matching grants to state authorities to enable them to improve the
teaching of science, mathematics, and modern languages in schools, and
low-interest loans to non-profit-making private schools for the same purpose (in
a later amendment, the list of subjects was extended to include history, civics,
geography, English and reading):
(ii) (a) Loans to students to assist them through colleges and universities —
with special provision for teachers: whereas the ordinary loan had to be repaid
within ten years, that for teachers could be cancelled up to 50 per cent. in return
for five years' service, and up to 100 per cent. for service in certain specified
unfavourable areas;
(b) Fellowships to graduate teachers to encourage them to prepare for
college teaching, and to work towards the Ph.D. degree;
(c) Grants to universities and colleges to establish modern language
centers, provide post-doctoral and graduate fellowships, and undergraduate
stipends, and undertake research in language teaching, with the emphasis on
modern languages not previously offered (the most common out of the 70 being
studied are Arabic, Chinese, Hindu-Urdu, Japanese, Portuguese, Russian, and
Latin-American Spanish);
(iii) Grants to public and private agencies, organizations, and individuals (or
contracts with them) for undertaking media research and utilization for teaching
purposes.
The Act can fairly be described as an expression of concern, if not alarm, by
the Federal Government about the state of education in the country in a number
of critical subjects, following Russia's successful launching of its first satellite.
Congressman Carl Elliott, Chairman of the Special Education Sub-Committee,
expressed this quite clearly: 'There is a real good reason for each title in the
bill . . . . each has its place . . . and will serve a very worthy purpose in doing
what we want to do for America, namely to answer the Soviet threat to gain
supremacy over us in science.'
The Elementary and Secondary Education Act The Elementary and Secondary Act (ESEA) deals with the following five matters:

Title I — Financial assistance to local educational agencies for the education
of children of low-income families;

Title II – School library resources (including audio-visual materials), text-
        books and other instuctional materials;
Title III – Supplementary educational centers and services;
Title IV – Educational research and training;
Title V – Strengthening state departments of education.

The major emphasis of the Act is in Title I, nearly three-quarters of the total
funds available being devoted to the special needs of educationally deprived
children. Obliquely, the act is an attempt to improve educational conditions for
Negroes. How the money will be used to improve education in these schools has
of course to be worked out. It is the intention of the proposed legislation not to
prescribe types of programmes: these are left to the discretion of local public
school agencies. The hope of Congress in passing the legislation is that the tasks
of compensatory education will be approached in new ways, as well as by
obvious measures such as remedying deficiencies in books and equipment and
improving the staffing position.

The funds may be used for children attending private schools in activities
which can appropriately include them, such as educational radio and television,
and mobile educational services. Stress is laid also on involvement in other
community resources aimed at improving the lot of the deprived. The value of
this is obvious, as the school alone is unlikely to solve the problems of cultural
deprivation.

The Title III provision is of particular interest. This is called PACE (Projects
to Advance Creativity in Education), and is officially described as a programme
for making grants for supplementary educational centres and services, to
stimulate and assist in the provision of vitally needed educational services not
available in sufficient quantity or quality, and to stimulate and assist in the
development of exemplary elementary and secondary school educational
programmes to serve as models for regular school programmes. Stress is laid on
cooperation with other community organizations in setting up the centres –
with libraries, museums, artistic and musical organizations, etc.

The U.S. Office of Education[4] makes the following suggestions for projects,
but points out that in planning them school districts will be held back only by
the limits of their own inventiveness and creativity:

(i) educational parks, to offer a variety of educational services;
(ii) mobile units with displays of various arts and crafts;
(iii) counselling centres for drop-outs;
(iv) visits by outstanding citizens to stimulate the children, e.g. by an
astronaut,
(v) mobile planetariums, zoos, aquariums;
(vi) science-teaching museums;

(vii) multi-purpose youth centres;

(viii) community-based industrial exhibits;

(ix) performing arts centres, with permanent staff;

(x) demonstration curriculum programmes;

(xi) model demonstration schools;

(xii) a centralized teaching faculty perhaps providing for the gifted, handicapped, or retarded.

(xiii) summer or year-round camp;

(xiv) learning resources centres providing modern equipment to area schools;

(xv) after-school study areas;

(xvi) educational television;

(xvii) a mathematics learning centre, featuring innovations in teaching methods;

(xviii) expansion of the services of art galleries and museums by special programmes in cooperation with public schools.

It is of interest to review briefly what actually happened under the PACE[5] programme in its first year of operation.

Submissions were made for 2,706 projects, requesting $249,624,955. Of these 1,030 costing $75,251,637, were approved.

The initial response to the title was one of 'riding off in all directions'. Nevertheless all the twenty special consultants employed to evaluate it were quite laudatory about the overall picture of accomplishments during its first year, and they were confident of even greater accomplishments in the future. They comment on some of the best of the proposals as follows:[6]

'Among the many outstanding Title III programmes are an under-water classroom to study marine biology in Sarasota, Fla., a life-simulator laboratory in Medford, Mass; a computerized instruction system in Boulder, Colo; a team-teaching project in Ogden, Utah; an electronic classroom in Block Island, New Shoreham, R.I.; and a non-graded organization in Guthrie, Okla.'

Being inventive and creative is hard work, but clearly under Title III of ESEA the rewards are great for those who succeed.

Title IV of ESEA extends the educational research and development facilities in the country. Ten university research and development centres had been set up,* under the Cooperative Research Act (1954) each specializing in one field, and two by provisions of the Vocational Education Acts. The universities involved, the year of establishment, and the special research interests of these centres are listed below:

* One at Harvard University has been abandoned.

1966	University of California, Berkeley	American higher education
1966	University of Georgia	Children's interests, 3–12 years
1966	University of California, Los Angeles	Evaluation processes and techniques
1966	Stanford University	Teacher education
1966	University of Texas	Teacher education
1967	Johns Hopkins University	Social organization of schools and the learning process

Under the new law leglisation, programmes of research are more widely based, being open to state educational agencies, professional associations, and private non-profit-making organizations and individuals, as well as to colleges and universities. A research training function has also been added.

In addition, a system of regional educational laboratories for research development has been established. Twenty of these laboratories are already in operation. They are putting most of their effort into development, that is into producing materials which can be used in schools. This development is based on research findings, and may involve further research, but it is not on research that the major emphasis is laid, as it is in the R & D Centres. These regional laboratories also propose to give research training, and to disseminate their products to regional schools. At present there is little to disseminate, as the laboratories have only recently been established; but it is not altogether clear how the vital dissemination process will take place. The U.S. Office of Education has ruled that the products of these laboratories will be in the public domain. But there is the dilemma of choosing between a public form of publishing, which will bring the laboratories into competition with the educational business houses, and the formation of arrangements with commercial firms. If the latter way is chosen, salaried officers of the laboratories may find their ideas being exploited profitably by a commercial firm without any return to them. Enterprising business houses can of course resolve this dilemma to their own advantage by making the decision to publish the material. Because it is public, no law would be infringed by their doing this. A firm that is anxious to be first in the field with some new product of the laboratory could in fact publish before the laboratory is completely satisfied with field trials.

The concept of a combined operation of research, development, training, and dissemination is obviously an important one, and one in which the Federal Government has great faith — but, as can be seen, it is not without its problems.

Finally, in considering this important legislation, the provisions of Title V, aimed at strengthening state education departments, should be noted, particularly in view of the obvious criticism that the Federal Government's action is likely to weaken them by detracting from their authority. The funds provided for this purpose are intended to assist the departments in improving their administrative machinery. As examples of the use of these funds, it may be mentioned that the grant to California is to be used in surveying the state education board's role in community college administration, and to assist the work of the state Committee on Public Education; while that to West Virginia is to be used in educational planning, research and data processing.

The National Foundation for the Arts and Humanities According to the U. S. Office of Education, the United States has been almost alone among the free nations of the West in its lack of national support for the arts and humanities. The Act establishing the National Foundation for the Arts and Humanities is designed to remedy this.

The foundation is governed by a chairman and a 28-member council appointed by the President of the United States. It has power to receive and spend both private and public funds. It will function in two branches: one for the arts, assisting in such fields as theatre, film, dance, opera, ballet, and song, and one for the humanities, aiding the study of language, literature, aesthetics, philosophy, archaeology, history, and anthropology and other social sciences. It may assist individuals as well as organizations and groups.

The Higher Education Act (1965) The purpose of this Act is to enlist the services of institutions of higher education in special programmes of community services and continuing education, particularly in urban areas; to improve library resources, train librarians and conduct research in the library sciences; to give special assistance to the small and developing institution; and to extend the student assistance programme. The Act supplements the 1963 legislation which was designed to improve higher education facilities to cope with the vastly increasing demands being made on them.

The role of the school districts and state departments of education The actions of the Federal Government have dominated the educational scene in the last decade, but the front-line tasks of maintenance, if not innovation, have been undertaken by the school districts and other agencies. In this section a (necessarily brief) description is given of the local school districts and the state education departments, and an assessment of their present role in the system is made.

It will be convenient to deal with the state and local education authorities together because of their close interdependence. The state is the major authority, in that it is legally responsible for education. By tradition, however, in most states, the school districts, acting with delegated authority, have played the greater part administratively. It is they* who have provided most of the funds

---

* Even in 1965–66 the average public-school revenue was 53 per cent. from local sources, 39 per cent. from the state, and 8 per cent. from the Federal Government.

for education by an ad hoc tax on property; it is they who have built the schools, employed the teachers and provided education within the broad requirements laid down by the state; it is they who have given the professional and lay leadership needed to keep education responsive to local needs and, to a degree, anticipatory of changing needs.

The clearest image of American education abroad (certainly in Australia) is of the great variety within the country caused by the decentralized administration, and of the progress made by many districts when stimulated by personal contact with parents and citizens and by community pride and initiative. A fainter image, but persistent, is one in which the idea of variety is interpreted as inequality. Australians have often drawn comfort from this, because their own state centralized systems have made equality of opportunity a major goal, placing teachers and facilities in areas remote from the cities and towns far in excess of the local community's capacity to provide them. Critics of the Australian system admire the attempt made through one-teacher schools, correspondence education, schools of the air, and the scheme for transferring teachers to provide education in remote areas, but they claim that the equality has been pitched at a fairly low level, and that the bureaucratic nature of the systems has prevented what Brickell calls 'a broken-front line of progress', by which he believes the[7] American nation has been well served.

During this century the local system in America has undergone considerable transformation, as with far-reaching social changes the self-sufficient local community has become less and less of a reality. Campbell[8] describes the changes in these words:

> 'Free land is gone, the rural predominance has vanished, industrialization has taken over, cities have spawned, mass media bring immediately every world altercation to all eyes and ears, man circles the globe in hours, and competitors have placed a rocket on the moon. These technological changes have made their social, economic, and political repercussions. Complete local government in today's world is an anachronism.'

The transformation of education during this century has been on an extraordinary scale, and it is not surprising that administrative units created to deal with education in an earlier day have been put to unbearable strain. The demand for education, the extension of it is beyond the elementary school, the growth of special educational knowledge as pedagogy became established, the greater concern with non-local objectives as the vocational pattern changed and populations became more mobile, have all required major adjustments to the district system. The smallest units have been quite unable to manage, and have been either abolished or absorbed into larger ones. In 1932 there were still approximately 127,000 school districts in America. In 1967 there are only approximately 25,000.

The ferment of the period after World War II, and particularly of the last decade, has been associated mainly with action taken by the Federal Government, as has been described in the preceding section. With the strengthening of national sentiment in education, the local system has been under close scrutiny. Many think it is in danger from Federal encroachments, in spite of assertions to the contary emanating from the highest levels in Washington. Other major influences shaping American policy are national, or at least non-local in spirit – the professional organizations, the regional accrediting agencies, philanthropic foundations, the leading graduate schools of education, textbook publishers, and Supreme Court judgements. What is then the substance in the local system in the face of so many powerful influences outside it? A great deal, according to President Kennedy:[9]

'The control and operation of education in America must remain the responsibility of state and local governments and private institutions. This tradition assures our educational system of the freedom, the diversity, and the vitality in support of public elementary and secondary education.'

Is this kind of statement merely a national stereotype, an incantation with emotional overtones, which is far removed from the practical realities of the actual power? Are the local authorities like so many stage puppets, giving in their movement the illusion of self-determination because the wires that control them are undetected?

Writing in 1961, Bailey[10] gives this assessment of the autonomy of the local authorities:

'But what is local control today? Those who think that such control involves the absolute right of local persons to make decisions without reference to higher authority have accepted folklore as fact, for local control of this type is non-existent today.'

James,[11] in discussing the impact of the new federal programmes and the problems of implementing them creatively and efficiently, claims that under the restrictions the legislature has placed in recent years on the powers of school boards they lack the power to be creative, and they may not have even the power to be efficient. He argues that, if under state policy the local boards are to be continued, they must be given sufficient authority to allow them to function effectively.

The powerful American Association of School Administrators[12] has thrown its weight in on the side of the state-local system. In 1962 it published the following resolution, after a careful study of the current movements.

'The Executive Committee of AASA reaffirms its belief in the principle long held in the United States that education is a state function, and that the principle works exceedingly well when the responsibility of the state is delegated in large measure to local boards of education who operate with close sensitivity to needs of developing young people and adults in a given community. Although the record is never perfect, and not even good in some instances, the Executive Committee holds to the concept that on the whole the educational needs of the local community, the state, and indeed the nation can best be served when the control of education rests at the state and local levels rather than at the national level.'

One of the critical features about the local authorities is their size; and this is likely to become an important issue. Earlier the dramatic reduction was noted in the number of school districts from approximately 127,000 to 25,000 in about three decades. Even so, according to Johns,[13] most school districts in the United States are still too small to be efficient. He recommends that 85 to 90 per cent. of them should be reorganized and enlarged. Benson[14] recommends that the total number should be about 600. He bases this figure on a minimum population per district of 250,000 except in areas of very low density, and uses criteria such as financial competence and administrative responsibility.

There appears to be a serious dilemma over the idea of growth by the local authorities to match their growing responsibilities. Among the values of localism are close identification of administrative aims with local aspirations (with a correspondingly small number of mediated, official relationships), a powerful incentive system based on the well-being of one's own family and friends and community, and a strong sense of accountability. Such a system of course has the defects of its qualities. Local aspirations may be selfish and exclusive; the well-being of one's family and friends may only be a euphemism for exploitation. It would be very easy for the school system to become in a particular community an expression of local selfishness and local prejudice, a power weapon in the hands of the illiberal. Fear of the misuse of the local system in this way in America does not appear to be strong. On the contrary, it is the opposite view that is more commonly heard: that the local system is a protection against the possibility of domination by the Federal Government, if by some mischance this fell into the wrong hands.

The dilemma is how to grow in size while at the same time retaining the values associated with intimacy. Goldhammer expresses this dilemma well in the following statement:[15]

> 'But the larger the school organization becomes the greater is the tendency to bureaucratize procedures and apply general rules for program and material allocations rather than remain responsive to localized needs. The more remote the government is from the people, the more frustrated the people are in being effectively heard and individually served. The fear of bureaucracy and its indifference to local requirements arises. Public relations become more difficult; operations become more political. The public is inclined to become less responsive to organizational needs. Somehow the public school administrators must work out the means for maintaining public concern and support for the educational enterprise as they develop mechanisms for total organizational responsiveness to the human needs, values, and aspirations of the many subcommunities and neighborhoods the centralized school district will serve.'

The dilemma is clear, but not the solution. Goldhammer's pathetic adverb 'somehow' underlines where the problem lies, but hardly points the way to a solution. In the kind of impersonal mass society which appears to be developing, the nation that can 'develop mechanisms for total organizational responsiveness to the human needs, values, and aspirations of subcommunities and neighborhoods' will hold the key to the future. If the local education authorities in the U.S.A. are allowed to grow beyond the point where they can do it, the country's most likely institution for this purpose will have been abandoned. Since money is a much easier resource to come by than mechanisms for responding to human needs, one would imagine that it would pay the country to provide the funds for local authorities from some other treasury so that they could grow rich (or rich enough) without having to grow large.*

In passing, it is of interest to point out that in England the local authorities have for a long time been too large to deal with education on an intimate basis, and that in Australia there have never been any. England appears to be solving this problem successfully by making the individual school functionally more important — by increasing the authority of the head of the school and delegating many administrative tasks. There are some signs in parts of Australia that this is

---

* It should be pointed out that Richard Netzer, who has made detailed projections of educational expenditure and revenue, concludes surprisingly that state and local governments would be able to raise the additional $50 billion that will be needed in 1970 above the 1960 figure *without* any large new programmes of Federal grants-in-aid.

(Quoted by Otto Eckstein, State and local investment in education', in *Challenge and Change in American Education* (Ed. Seymour E. Harris), McCutchan, Berkeley, Calif., 1965, p. 192.

beginning to happen too, as the inspector's role changes from that of assessor to that of an advisory colleague.

The values of intimacy, accountability, personal involvement and the rest that might be claimed for education at a local level are perhaps more closely aligned to the idea of a community functioning in a normal way than to one undergoing rapid change. Yet it appears likely, whatever the source of new ideas, and whatever the authority that is sponsoring them, that they will only be effectively introduced by an efficient local system. Whatever educational revolution there is going to be will be brought about by *teachers* working with *children*, whether it is in the name of national development, the great society, or military security, and irrespective of whether the money is raised at federal, state, or local level. Without doubt the local system has failed to do what the Federal Government is attempting to do. But it may be just as certain that the Federal Government cannot be successful without the local system.

The dependence of one level or sphere of administration on another is brought out by Brickell, writing of local organization as it will be needed in 1980. He states[16] that 'what is needed is not simply bigger administrative units, but instead a series of units arranged in concentric circles round each group of students, with function being passed back and forth among the units as circumstances change'. An idea proposed by Johns[17] is similar in that it rejects the obvious Weberian bureaucratic model for relating administrative levels. He calls it *creative federalism*, an idea based on the assumption that increase in power at one level of government to deal with a particular educational problem does not reduce the power of another level of government to deal with this too. Thus the local authorities need not necessarily diminish in importance as the state and Federal Government intervene more directly in education. Johns envisages a model 'with a strong, well-staffed, capable federal agency interacting with strong, well-staffed, capable state educational agencies in interaction with strong, well-staffed, capable local education agencies'.

At the present time in most states, because the local education authorities have been the major agencies for education, the state departments have been relatively weak. Brickell[18] describes the state department as 'an agency utterly trapped in its 19th-century habit of regulating things'. 'No other agency, public or non-public,' he claims, 'is so trapped by its past. It is a picture of frozen power.' Miller[19] is equally derogatory:

'States today operate, in general, less as practically autonomous units than as administrative districts for centrally established policies. They are not quite hollow political shells, but their once great power has been vitiated by the movement of history. They have "housekeeping" duties, but little real concern with important decisions. When new problems arise, eyes turn to Washington, not to the state capital.'

Allen[20] who is Commissioner of Education for New York State, is also critical, but in gentler vein:

'I believe that state departments of education have in the past been a constructive force, but it would be naive not to recognize that they all need to improve — some, of course, more than others. Even today, most of them are not able to offer the type of leadership which they should be providing.'

But he believes that America's greatest hope for meeting the challenges of education lies within the individual states, provided they can accept the task of identifying and solving educational problems, clarify their own legal power, accept the task of coordinating all the educational activity within the state, and improve the quality of the members of state boards of education.

Allen's sentiments are in tune with Conant's,[21] who argues for a strengthening of state education departments, overriding sectional views in the process:

'What is needed according to my view is to discredit the accrediting agencies, increase the effectiveness of the state educational authorities, and see to it that the state brings about an integration of the views of the state teacher association, the professors of education, the academic professors, and the layman.'

Conant's prescription is difficult to achieve, if not illiberal. Certainly not all would agree with so authoritarian a role for state departments. Many influential institutions, particularly private ones who may benefit from Federal aid, do not want to deal with the Federal Government through a state department of education, and would oppose any requirement to do so.

Allen's argument for strengthening the state department, particularly by improving the calibre of the board members and by having an appointed* superintendent, would be widely accepted. At present the volume of legislation at the state level, regulating such details of school procedure as the curriculum, is excessive, or so it seems to a foreign observer. The separation of education from politics may be, as Lenin claimed it to be, a lie and an hypocrisy. But the political decisions which must be taken should be based on detached and comprehensive deliberations conducted within a universe of educational discourse, completely apart from political expediency. Only a strong committee, not in any way dependent on political patronage, can do this. Such a body can tackle the important tasks of stating educational policy in broad terms and developing a strategy for implementing them; and, if it is secure enough to be administratively wise, it can lend its strength to local committees to ensure that they tackle their task at least with integrity, and possibly with imagination as well.

---

* At present in many states the State Superintendent is elected.

The role of the universities and colleges

In considering the role of the universities and colleges* in bringing about change in school practices we are confronted with a most intriguing paradox. Quite obviously the universities in America play a more substantial role in relation to the schools, through in-service and pre-service courses for teachers and in other ways, than do their counterparts in England and Australia, yet they are more severely criticized both within and outside the profession. This curious fact is elaborated and commented on below.

Compared with the development of teacher education in England and Australia, that in the U.S.A. has been markedly precocious. Normal schools were established in the latter part of the 19th century, and by the end of the first decade of the 20th century their upgrading into teachers' colleges had already begun. Between 1920 and 1940, 103 normal schools were transformed into teachers' colleges, and most of them had increased their course from two to four years, bringing themselves into line with the liberal arts colleges and universities in becoming degree-granting institutions. Development beyond this point is even more startling. Many of them ceased to be single-purpose institutions, and have added general liberal arts courses and vocational courses other than teaching to their curricula. To complete the metamorphosis, they have dropped the word 'teachers' from their title, and become state colleges. To blur the one distinction that might be invoked in trying to distinguish them from universities, many have been allowed to introduce graduate courses, even including the doctorate.

Compared with Australia and England, there is also a striking difference in America in the development of Education as a subject, and in the staffing of it. In the U.S.A. by 1900, according to Conant[22] the field of Education had so developed that doctoral degrees were being awarded, and shortly thereafter one could specialize on the doctoral level in such fields as educational psychology, school administration, curriculum and instruction, and the history and philosophy of education. In 1960† there were only six professors of Education in the whole of Australia, and not a great many more in England. In most Australian university departments of Education there is a modest number of options, with provision for sequential years of study; but there are no separate departments for subdivisions of the subject such as Educational Administration and Educational Psychology. In America faculties of Education usually are divided into departments, and into a considerable array of course offerings, including

---

* For the rest of this section the term 'universities', unless obviously used to exclude colleges, may be deemed to include colleges as well.

† The comparison with the full professorship in the U.S.A. is the most accurate. The term 'Associate Professor' is used in only some universities in Australia, and 'Assistant Professor' not at all. Staff in teachers' colleges are not called professors. Since 1960 there has been an increase in some universities in the number of professors in a department.

post-graduate courses associated with the master's and doctoral degrees.*
Graduate courses and research often claim the attention of the senior members
of the staff, and the courses for prospective teachers and the supervision of
practice teaching are left in less experienced hands.

The volume of books and periodicals published by these American professors
is prodigious, and even alarming to anyone who has a conscience about keeping
abreast of it. Some of it is first rate, and is regularly used as textbook or
reference in Education courses abroad. Some of it is ephemeral and repetitious.
The worst of it has a studied incomprehensibility, presumably to impress the
unwary. The task of sorting it out is quite exhausting.

University professors are the undisputed authorities of the world of education
in America. They are the names that are associated with the newest innovations;
they are the major consultants called in for advice by the school systems,
government departments, business firms, and private foundations. They produce
the textbooks for the schools, and develop the new curricula and teaching
materials. The Education professor in Australia plays a much more modest role.
He may seek his satisfactions from fellow academics in other university
departments†, or identify himself more with the schools. If the latter, he has to
work hard to establish a leadership role, often against the suspicion that as an
academic he can scarcely have a realistic grasp of the problems of practical
teaching.

The American universities also have a virtual monopoly of the continuing
education of the teacher. In the evenings, or in the summer term, teachers flock
to take courses of all kinds. Increased salary increments and promotion are
usually tied to increased academic and professional qualifications, a fact that
must surely account in large part for the support of these courses. Conant[23]
suggests that attending courses is akin to an occupational disease.‡ 'Discussing
this subject in a summer school with more than one group of teachers,' he said
he felt as if he were 'talking to opium smokers who were praising the habit of
which they had long since become the victims.'

Taking all these facts together — the substantial development of the training
of teachers in universities and university-type institutions, the extensive

---

* According to Koerner, there are 1,500 doctorates a year awarded by about 100
institutions. This is the largest number from any field, and constitutes 18 per cent. of the
total number given. He does not state the year; presumably it was 1964. (James D.
Koerner, *The Miseducation of American Teachers*, Penguin Books, London, 1965.)

† In a number of Australian universities the subject Education is in the Faculty of Arts and
may be taken as a major subject (including honours) for an Arts degree. In other
universities, where there is a separate faculty of Education, some reciprocity between
Education and Arts degrees usually exists.

‡ He also reports that one New York private institution lists no fewer than 600 courses open
to teachers.

provision of courses for them in-service to meet the requirements of a higher degree or for credit on a salary scale, the impressive array of professors, departments, and courses within faculties of education, and the pervasive influence of the professors throughout the educational world on conference platforms, on the title pages of books, and in positions of influence in educational publishing houses — it is clear that we are dealing with a major, if not determinative, force in American education. Here surely one would think is the major source of innovation, and also the main channel through which innovation reaches both the novitiate and the experienced teacher.

Yet these same professors and the training they provide are the object of severe, sometimes bitter criticism. To a foreign observer the battle raging round teacher education, like Disneyland, is hard to take in during a short visit. The main criticism seems to come from the liberal arts professors and journalists, but there are critics within as well, including some of the professors, and many teachers who with curious ambivalence are highly critical of the course that they have chosen to attend.

Undoubtedly part of the criticism is linked to the more general dissatisfaction with the education system which was felt after World War II; part of it is the culmination of a long-standing hostility on the part of some liberal arts professors to the large Education empires within the university;* and part of it (the criticism of the teachers) is a reaction to the system of gaining extra salary by taking courses whether they are useful or not. Finding a scapegoat is a familiar exercise in all countries, but the Americans seem to go about it with more than ordinary thoroughness and vehemence.

How much of the criticism is just it is difficult to assess. We hear moderate criticisms like this:[24] 'What about our colleges and universities as communication components? Certainly there have been some lighthouses among colleges and universities, but these have been in the minority. For decades, most colleges and universities have neglected to communicate their discoveries and pertinent information to educators on the local level. There does not appear to be much prospect of any significant change of attitude and behaviour on their part in the future.' Or this:[25] 'It appears doubtful whether college and university faculties in education have had much direct influence on school practice. As teachers of teachers they would appear to have a strategic position to influence future developments in the schools, but I do not see much evidence that they have used their leverage well.'

---

* The following witticism is an amusing, if somewhat indelicate, indication of the psychological warfare among the professors. Some educationists accuse liberal arts professors of cramming students with subject matter which on examination day they only regurgitate. The stock rejoinder of the liberal arts professors is that Education students have nothing to regurgitate. On examination day, they retort, their students can only 'burp'.

James Koerner,[26] in a more severe indictment, claims that Education has 'grown too large, too fast, on too slippery a foundation.' He claims that it now has 'an established market of such size and diversity that it spends 95 per cent. of its energies and resources supplying that market, instead of shoring the foundations of the field, producing important research to verify its own assumptions and to improve its programs, and raising its standards all round.' He claims that there is lack of congruence between the actual performance of its graduates and the training programmes through which they are put, and an appalling lack of evidence to support the wisdom of this or that kind of professional training for teachers.

Perhaps the best known and most thorough recent assessment of the education of American teachers was that undertaken by Conant[27]. During the course of his study he visited 77 institutions, including widely different types, in 22 states. Some of his conclusions that are pertinent to this study are summarized below.

(i)   To improve the effectiveness of the teachers' preparation,

(a) there should be an 'all-university' approach, ensuring that, in the planning and conduct of courses for teaching, the resources of departments of the university other than the Education Department should be available, and that the voices of these departments should be heard.

(b) the arrangements for practice teaching should be improved.* 'Clinical' professors, who are skilled teachers and who are able to help students to bridge theory and practice, should be appointed to supervise the work of the students. The state should regulate the arrangements for practice teaching to ensure that only teachers who are competent to do so should be appointed as cooperating teachers in the schools. These teachers should have their work load reduced and their salary raised.

(ii) to improve the effectiveness of teachers' in-service education, school authorities should contract with an educational institution to provide short term seminars during the school year so that all the teachers (without cost to them) may benefit from the instruction. No credit towards salary increases should be given.

In addition school authorities should provide leave of absence with salary for a full-time semester residence at a university to enable teachers to study towards a master's programme, provided that this programme is designed to increase the competence of the teacher.

During the probationary period of employment the new teacher should be given limited responsibility, and receive aid from experienced teachers whose

* This matter is also well treated by Boyan in his paper to the White House Conference: Norman J. Boyan, 'Improving the quality of education', in *Consultants Papers: The White House Conference on Education*, Vol. 1, 1965, pp. 30–31.

own work load is reduced so that they can work with the teacher in the classroom.

(iii) The certification of the teacher by the state should be based only on

(a) the possession of an approved bachelor's degree,

(b) proof of successful practice teaching, and

(c) proof that the institution responsible for the training considers him to be adequately prepared to teach.

Conant's hope in publishing this book was that a matter of such vital importance to the quality of American education as the education of teachers should cease to be the subject of prolonged and acrimonious debate, and should be reformed as a matter of urgency. There appears to be little evidence to date that the hatchet has been buried, or that a new approach to teacher education is being developed.

Goodlad,[28] in his recent recommendations to the State Committee on Public Education in California, stresses that a complete overhaul of the training of the teacher is needed if instruction in the schools is to become efficient. His proposals include the following three features:

(i) a seven-year training course – embracing a four-year bachelor's degree, emphasizing course work with a modicum of paid clinical experience as aide and intern, a three-year period emphasizing clinical experience with a modicum of related course work, the whole culminating in formal acceptance into the teaching profession;

(ii) analyses of films showing actual teaching and video-tapes of the students' own teaching, and experience as an aide or intern as a member of a team of cooperating teachers in a neighbouring school;

(iii) rotating term opportunities as clinical personnel to be given to teachers within the teaching teams in which the students are placed.

In these proposals Goodlad is tackling the hard core of the problem of making training effective – namely, how to bring home to students how educational ideas and practice are related. The old way of listening to formal lectures followed (often considerably later) by practical teaching in a setting quite divorced from the original lectures, and often suffused with different objectives, has been tried all round the world, and found wanting.

His scheme requires considerable changes in the cooperating schools* as well as in the training institutions, and the lesson is also being learned (sometimes quite painfully) that a school system cannot be improved through the new recruits alone. Rather it is necessary to improve the system as a whole so that the objectives of the training institutions in teaching contemporary ideas are reinforced from the larger and more influential system – the schools themselves.

---

* Because of the large number of student teachers being trained at any one time, the number of cooperating schools also has to be large. This problem cannot be solved merely by having a few picked schools.

The spirit of these suggestions for training teachers should also, it is hoped, enliven the provision of in-service courses. An important objective, in the writer's opinion, should be to involve teachers as participants and discussion leaders, and to improve their own self-assurance. At present the taking of courses dominates the scene. The teacher is relatively passive as he sits at the feet of some expert. Experts abound. There is no mystery to which some expert does not hold the key. The adverse criticism that teachers make of these experts, often in private, does not seem to make them less willing to listen to the next. For every fallen idol, a dozen promising new ones spring up. The sense of the omniscience and omnipresence of the expert depresses the confidence that teachers should have in their own powers. Many seem to be fearful of acting lest they do something foolish.

Under these circumstances innovation is hardly attempted at all – or, if it is, it becomes a process of copying a model, rather than of using one to stimulate one's own thinking. A few sentences from a recent publication of the Center for Coordinated Education[29] express this thought well, even though they have a patronizing touch about them:

'It cannot be assumed that the nation's teachers are expectantly awaiting an opportunity to engage in a long arduous struggle to upgrade their professional talents. Reasonably, however, we can assume that, given an authentic opportunity to explore ideas in which they are genuinely interested, and in which their efforts are subsidized in necessary ways, teachers will respond to the challenge posed by the enigmas of their craft. A necessary condition, therefore, is that the teacher be allowed to work on things which he regards as important, that he be allowed to work in ways which make sense to him, and that he have at his disposal means both abundant and convenient.'

A similar point is made in an earlier publication by the *Commission on Teacher Education* set up by the American Council on Education:[30]

'Tasks growing out of teaching situations provide the starting point for in-service programmes. The teacher's personal and professional concerns become the focus for attention, as they should be. Helping the teacher to do better what he sees as his job, and to see better what his job might be, becomes the goal . . . . Teachers who are able to help form policies and encouraged to act responsibly and freely in implementing them find new satisfaction in the profession.'

Words like these point the way to effective in-service practice for a system that wants to innovate. But it is difficult to do, much harder than setting up a new laboratory, working out a new course, or purchasing a lot of audio-visual aids.

The role of the philanthropic foundations

Philanthropic foundations, according to the *Encyclopedia of Educational Research*,[31] are 'non-profit legal entities used for channelling private wealth to educational, cultural, religious, and other charitable general welfare purposes'. While they are not a unique American institution, they have flourished in the U.S.A. because of the great build-up of private and company wealth, and the political policy of allowing tax exemption on funds applied to public welfare purposes.

There are more than 15,000 such foundations in America, with total assets of approximately $12 billion, and with an annual expenditure of approximately $700 million. The earlier ones, established in the 19th century by individuals like George Peabody and Andrew Carnegie, were created out of private fortunes, but more recent ones have been established by corporations, which have been able thereby to reduce taxable income, and avoid or reduce estate and gifts taxes. The six largest are the Kellogg Foundation, the Carnegie Corporation of New York, the Hartford Foundation, the Duke Endowment, the Rockefeller Foundation, and the Ford Foundation. The assets of the largest one, the Ford Foundation, are $3,316,000,000. Some foundations only disburse funds and do not engage in welfare activity themselves. Others use their funds to carry out projects of their own devising and with their own staff; some assist others, and also engage in projects of their own.

In the context of discussion on innovation in American education, we are obviously interested to know what role the foundations play. Quite clearly their role has been positive. No more arresting proof of this can be adduced than the fact that they have been the subject of no less than three governmental inquiries in less than 40 years. In 1915 they were investigated[32] as the tools of big business exercising undesirable conservative and reactionary influences. In 1952[33] an investigation was made as to whether they were a corruptive influence – in particular, 'whether they supported or assisted persons or projects which, if not subversive, at least tended to weaken or discredit American economic and cultural life, and to favour Marxist Socialism and Communism'. This was followed in 1953 by a further inquiry by a Special Committee into charges of 'diabolical conspiracy'. Commenting on the latest inquiry at the time, Hollis[34] enigmatically writes as follows: 'It is too early to assess either the positive or negative effects of the work of the committee, but it is not unreasonable to expect that some of its findings will have a salutary effect on foundation policies and procedures.'

Leaving these rather extraodinary events, we now take up the question of the influence of the foundations as based on more normal criteria. Although the amount of money spent by them annually is not large in relation to total educational expenditures, they have, by concentrating on specific projects, undoubtedly had a substantial influence on educational development in the country.

Among notable innovations sponsored by them may be instanced the following:

(i) the National Merit Scholarship Program, instituted in 1955, by Ford, Carnegie, and others providing college scholarships for high-school students of unusual academic promise;

(ii) Carnegie's Commonwealth Program with its focus on higher education in Africa, its support of studies by Flexner on medical education and by Conant on teacher education, and various studies in the improvement of teaching;

(iii) Kellogg's special support for the University Council on Educational Administration, and for research and teaching in the field of education administration;

(iv) Ford's multi-million-dollar programme with the liberal arts colleges to improve educational leadership, and its teacher-education assistance scheme in Oregon;

(v) Rockefeller's assistance to medical, agricultural, natural, and social sciences, and the humanities.

Not all educationists have approved of the policy decisions made by the foundations, or agreed with the actual projects supported. The Arkansas project in teacher education, supported by the Fund for the Advancement of Education, is an example of a highly controversial project, being condemned by no less a body than the American Association of Colleges for Teacher Education. According to critics it was an example of promoting an idea about teacher education rather than testing an hypothesis, and taking advantage of an impoverished state school system without due concern for the risk of wrecking the established pattern of Arkansas teacher education.

The unpopularity of particular decisions made by a foundation does not by any means condemn it, as the committee of the American Association of School Administrators pointed out:[35] 'Individual perceptions of foundations vary greatly — some see them as benign and useful examples of private action for the public good; some see them as a dangerous and unregulated nexus of economic power; some see them as determiners of social ends; some see them as accelerators of the public hopes and aspirations.'

The recent flow of federal funds to education has significantly altered the position of the foundations. Public funds are now becoming avaliable for purposes which previously were available only from the foundations. Undoubtedly this will bring about a change in their policies. No longer will it be necessary, as it was for example in 1955, for the Ford Foundation to aid universities and colleges by a grant of $260 million to increase faculty salaries and to meet other pressing needs.

Rather will it be possible for them to undertake projects for which public money is unlikely to be available — namely, those which have an obvious element of risk, which give no promise of quick returns, which question the status quo, and which launch an attack on a single problem by different methods. Edward J. Meade, of the Ford Foundation, believes that one of the major new roles for the foundations will be to assist in the identification and development of educational leaders. 'American education,' he states[36] 'unfortunately, has no surplus of able, enlightened, creative, knowledgeable, and effective leaders.' In his view foundations can be more active in leadership development than the government, which must be more prudent when it comes to spending tax dollars. The government can afford to support the training of leaders only after their leadership qualities have been demonstrated.

Whether leaders of tomorrow who are at present 'insignificant people in insignificant places' (to use Meade's phrase), or 'mute inglorious Miltons' (to use Gray's), can be discovered by spending foundation money is a question that we need not pursue here. The important point is that responsible leaders of influential foundations seem prepared to divert their funds to such purposes. If they do so, it is certainly likely that they will play an important part in educational innovation in the future.

One foundation project of special interest to the writer is the Institute for Development of Educational Activities,* which is sponsored by the Charles F. Kettering Foundation. At a time when a great deal of attention is being given to ways of effecting improvement, the creation of a new institute designed specially to do this is of particular interest.

The initial conception embodies a three-pronged attack on the problem:

(i) the introduction of new ideas into schools under controlled conditions, and the study of the change occurring;

(ii) the dissemination of ideas by means of a consortium of demonstration schools;

(iii) the wider dissemination of information throughout the country.

The research programme of the Institute is facilitated by the creation of a League of Cooperating Schools in Southern California. The League of eighteen schools, together with the university Elementary School of the University of California at Los Angeles, provide a vast laboratory for educational research.

---

* Or /I/D/E/A/ as it is by initials. The Americans have a flair for coining interesting words from initial letters.

One of the major hypotheses proposed by Professor Goodlad, who is in charge of this research programme, is that the most fruitful approach to reform is to work with the individual school as a unit. The design of the project also allows for the preparation of a carefully selected group of young teachers who will join the staff of the University Elementary School, and after this experience assume teaching posts in cooperating public schools; for the development of doctoral programmes based on problems and processes of educational change in progress in the cooperating schools; and for the provision of post-doctoral experiences for professors of education,* directors of curriculum, and others desiring refreshment through on-the-scene involvement in educational change.

A bold enterprise of this kind, with such promise for practical as well as theoretical proofs of educational hypotheses, is a matter for admiration and envy by an Australian to whom the funds for such an enterprise are in the same category as manna from heaven.

The educational business houses

Education has become something of an industry in America. There is now so much more that can be sold to schools. No article on modern schooling is complete without a picture of a child attached to some sort of machine, his face glowing with the pure joy of a love of learning.

The publishing houses have always played an important supportive role to education, but now they have joined forces with the engineers to produce equipment that relieves the teacher of almost every obligation except that of paying for it. Peter Schrag[37] in the following paragraph describes recent moves made by some of the giants of the industry:

' . . . some, eyeing the growing educational market and the prospect of the federal dowry, acquired publishing houses; Random House was bought by RCA; Science Research Associates, the biggest publisher of tests, was aquired by IBM; Xerox bought American Education Publications; Raytheon purchased D.C. Heath; CBS picked up Holt, Rinehart and Winston; and General Electric combined with Time, Inc., and its affiliated textbook publishing house (Silver Burdett) to form General Learning. The publishers would, so the expectation went, provide the software (curricular materials); the electronics firm would put it into the machines.'

Combining the hardware with the software makes the whole operation efficient. Schrag[38] quotes T. L. Phillips, Raytheon's president, as follows: 'Busy educators should not have to assemble the various components and fragments of

---

* It was in this category that the writer spent some months in 1967 with the organization.

learning equipment from a multitude of sources. We will now be able to build an integrated capability – a systems approach.' And he comments himself, 'Phillips' statement carries the rhetoric of the engineer, – and of the cult of efficiency. For the first time the bungling amateurs would have the help of engineers who could really help get things organized.'

Undoubtedly the fact that big business finds education profitable means that a new influence has come onto the educational scene. In one sense this influence is as neutral as the stars. All it is doing is supplying a commodity for which there is a demand from the profession, and in producing the commodity it is relying on educational experts who can ensure that it is a worthy product. But there are disquieting features.

Business has its own methods not only of meeting a demand, but of stimulating and extending it. In fact at present not a great deal is known about the value of much of the equipment being marketed, and less about possible harmful side effect. But it is not surprising, in a world in which computers and other electronic gear play so conspicuous a part in bold new ventures, that the linking of these with educational aids creates an aura of novelty and occult power. To school principals and administrators with money to be spent quickly, these machines offer the chance of a short cut to innovation, and they appear to be equally good currency for cultural deprivation, creative activities, teacher training and vocational education. When they are offered on every hand the marketing principles of the supermarket seem to apply. Teachers tend to stop asking whether they need them, and ask instead which one is best.

More serious is the possibility that the business houses have an illegitimate effect on curricula. Peyser[39] claims that it is well known that commercial producers of instructional materials have a profound effect upon the curricula of the nation's schools. These companies are frequently perceived by teachers and others as 'monolithic originators of educational media that produce their textbooks and teaching aids through some kind of spontaneous generation'. There are three features of this that are worthy of comment.

(i) It is questionable, as a matter of principle, whether the preparation of curricula for public education should ever be allowed within the framework of private profit-making organizations.

(ii) Certain subjects lend themselves to programming more readily than others, particularly mathematical and scientific subjects. When technological methods are allowed to become prominent, these subjects tend to dominate the curriculum.

(iii) More seriously the professional role of the teacher may be even further lowered by the use of this material, in that the teacher has to use a curriculum in the construction of which he had no part and in the use of which he has no responsibility. Long[40] expresses aptly in the following quotation the subtle attrition to which the teacher's professional role is subject:

The teacher never functions alone. His classroom activities are guided by a far-flung empire of educational consultants which grows larger as technology is applied to education. There are textbook publishers, testing laboratories, and survey groups all willing and able to supply the panacea curriculum in keeping with the latest educational thinking. In this configuration, the teacher is a consumer of values and the reactor to decisions developed by persons paid to think for him, yet far removed from the actual teaching situation.'

Further light is thrown on these persons 'far removed from the actual teaching situation' in a study done by Peyser,[41] in which he gathered information from a representative sample of twenty of the more senior consultants employed by ten companies producing educational materials. Ten of these occupied full-time positions in public schools, but only one of them was a classroom teacher. The others were guidance counsellors, directors of audio-visual services, principals, supervisors, and superintendents. Nine were professors, and one was a full-time tutor. Companies prefer people with status and degrees, rather than classroom teachers.

No doubt the value to education of various kinds of machine-aided teaching will be substantial, provided educationists can keep the initiative, and ensure that it is used for proper purposes and in the proper place. The elementary school is certainly not the proper place. There is too much reception learning there already, without the added formalism of prepared programmes which both teacher and pupil have to follow in servile fashion.

Teachers' organizations

Teachers form organizations for two main purposes: to confer on matters of common interest, thereby advancing and disseminating professional knowledge; and to present a stronger front in their pursuit of better working conditions and higher salaries.

Professional and industrial objectives often become confused, and the distinction blurred, at least in the public mind. A campaign conducted by a teacher's union for higher salary and better conditions of work is usually interpreted by the public simply as an attempt to exploit an employment situation for personal and selfish ends. Undoubtedly there is this element of self-interest, but it is also true that the well-being of the profession is involved. The quality of work done in school is closely related to the quality of staff recruited, and this is dependent on economic and industrial factors as well as educational ones.

The improvement of the status of the teaching profession is a cause that is rarely espoused by the public. It is a struggle that has to be initiated and carried through by the profession itself. In a defensible sense, such campaigns are undertaken for the good of the profession, and hence for the public good. Since in most countries the majority of teachers enjoy only moderate salary and status, their activities as organized groups have been slanted towards industrial rather than professional objectives. As the major industrial advances are won, the unions tend to increase their involvement in educational matters, and begin to have ideas of setting standards for entry to the profession, establishing a code of ethical behaviour, having a voice in the control of education, and, through committees, conferences, etc., acting as a spearhead for educational advance.

In most countries these two functions, the industrial and the professional, have to be attempted concurrently by the same organization, giving attention to one or the other activity according to the maturity of the profession and the circumstances of the time. As a general rule it can be said that an industrial outlook precedes a professional one, and that professional activities increase as industrial advances are made.

In the U.S.A. these two functions appear to be catered for in two separate, and competitive, organizations, the National Education Association (NEA) and the American Federation of Teachers (AFT). Both are concerned with professional and industrial aspects of teaching, but the emphasis of the N.E.A. is on the professional, and that of the AFT on the industrial.

The NEA is the largest professional association in the world, with approximately one million members. It includes 33 departments, which cater for a wide variety of specialist groups – classroom teachers, college lecturers, elementary-school principals, and so on; and it maintains major committees and commissions which devote themselves to important educational questions. As examples may be mentioned the Educational Policies Commission, the Committee on Professional Ethics, and the Teacher Education and Professional Standards Commission. State and local groups have their own organizations, but may affiliate with the NEA.

Through its study of various aspects of American education in local meetings and in state national conferences, and through its publications, it may fairly be regarded as a major force in the country, and a model of a mature professional organization. Projects such as its recent Project on Instruction, which was reported in the four volumes *Schools for the 60s*, *Education in a Changing Society*, *Deciding what to Teach*, and *Planning and Organizing for Teaching*, are a substantial contribution to educational theory and practice.

The American Federation of Teachers was established in 1916, but has a small membership by comparison with the NEA. It does not include administrators among its ranks (who it claims exert pressure on teachers to join the NEA), and it concentrates on securing local gains rather than taking the grand national view that the NEA does. Its affiliation with labour politics and unionism has made it a controversial body within the profession. In recent years it has made substantial gains by being elected to represent the teachers in salary negotiations in a number of key cities, including Chicago, New York, Detroit, and Cleveland. Its successes in this, involving strike tactics, have enhanced its standing among teachers, and brought it into sharper competition with the NEA.

In spite of the involvement of teachers in professional activities through the NEA, and their more militant attitude with regard to salary and work conditions, their professional status in the community is not high; nor are they accorded much responsibility within the profession itself. The system of state-prescribed curricula and state-adopted textbooks is probably one of the major factors preventing a fuller professional growth. Professional development ought to be furthered by the experiences provided by the teachers in their daily work. It is there, in their own school, that they should be studying educational problems, bringing to them in realistic fashion the ideas that they have gleaned from reading and other sources, and proposing and testing solutions; it is there that freedom and responsibility should be a reality.

If teachers are not allowed to express professional behaviour in their work, they tend to deflect it to peripheral activities such as attending conferences and sitting on committees. Conferences often are pleasant social functions and may be intellectually stimulating, but if they are indulged in as a substitute for professionally satisfying work, as a kind of wish-fulfilment exercise, they become an end in themselves, basically unproductive.

In a period when the accent is on change, the role of the teachers' organization is very critical. If the two directions of growth, towards better working conditions and towards higher professional involvement, can be fused, it may well be that the teachers themselves can become a major force in influencing improvement.

Concluding Comment

As in the case of England, it is clear from an examination of the forces that have been marshalled to improve American education that the three strategies – improving the rational basis for educational practice, reeducation, and the use of power – have all been used. Most apparent are the use of power through the legislation and financial assistance of the Federal Government, and the quickening in the research drive towards a more secure theoretical basis for educational practice. The task of reeducation has not been attempted in the same grand manner. Surveying the whole scene, from federal action down to that at district level, the strategy of reeducation does not seem to be featured prominently. Because of this, it is likely that many good ideas will not really come alive in primary schools. McPhee,[42] who is a school superintendent, rather pessimistically comments on the success to date of the campaign towards innovation:

'A look at the educational changes over the past few decades would not impress one with the significance of many of them. The impression of massive change sweeping the educational world is conveyed by our journals, and by our annual reports, but these aim largely at surface features. Generally our reports to the public emphasize the new gadgets or tools or groupings we are using, rather than the changes in how the student learns, what he knows, or how he acts on his knowledge.'

Featherstone,[43] an American who recently made a comparison of British and American elementary schools, brings out well the point of the discussion in the following quotation:

'It is unlikely that curriculum projects can make a difference in this country until they can find a way to involve ordinary teachers in creating materials. America should profit from the British under- standing that the really valuable and enduring part of curriculum reform is the process of creation and thought; unless you let teachers in on that, the stuff is likely to be dead.'

Even if particular projects are successfuly introduced, the situation will not be corrected on any long-term basis by action aimed only at altering attitudes of teachers and administrators towards specific innovations, or at involving them in specific projects with a view to securing their interest and cooperation, necessary as these are. Nothing less than massive professional growth will produce the morale, the continuing motivation among teachers and administrators, that is necessary to make self-renewal a reality.

REFERENCES

1.   R. F. Campbell, 'National Federalism and Education', *Administrator's Notebook*, Midwest Administration Center, University of Chicago, May 1965.
2.   'Federal Money for Education: Programs Administered by the U.S. Office of Education, Fiscal year 1967', *American Education*, Feb. 1967.
3.   U.S. Office of Education, *Education '65: a report to the profession*, U.S. Govt. Printing Office, Washington, 1966.
4.   U.S. Office of Education, Official Publication PACE, OE 200086.
5.   *Notes and Working Papers concerning the Administration of Programs Authorized under Title III of Public Law 89-10, the Elementary and Secondary Education Act of 1965 as Amended by Public Law 89-750*, U.S. G.P.O., Washington, April 1967.
6.   *Ibid.*, p. 27.

7. H. M. Brickell, 'Local organization and administration of education', in *Implications for Education of Prospective Changes in Society* (Ed. E. L. Morphet and C. O. Ryan), An Eight-State Project, Denver, Colo., 1967, Chap. 13.

8. R. F. Campbell in *Government of Public Education for Adequate Policy Making* (Ed. William B. Mclure and Van Miller), Bureau of Educational Research, College of Education, University of Illinois, Urbana, Ill., 1960. p.67.

9. U.S. Congressional Record, 87th Congress, 2nd session (CVIII 1544), 1962.

10. T. D. Bailey 'The folklore of local control', *N.E.A. Journal*, Dec. 1961.

11. T. H. James, 'The new federal programs: how to implement them creatively and efficiently', in *Governor's Conference on Education*, Los Angeles, 1965. (mimeographed).

12. *The School Administrator*, Nov. 1962, p. 3.

13. R. L. Johns, 'State organization and responsibility in education', in *Implications for Education of Prospective Changes in Society*, 1967, Chap. 14.

14. C. S. Benson, *The Cheerful Prospect*, Houghton Mifflin, Boston, 1965.

15. K. Goldhammer, Supplementary statement to chapter 13 in *Implications for Education of Prospective Changes in Society*, (Ed. E. L. Morphet, and C. O. Ryan), An Eight-State Project, Denver, Colo., 1967.

16. H. M. Brickell, 'Local organization and administration of education, in *Implications for Education of Prospective Changes in Society*, 1967, p. 220.

17. R. L. Johns, 'State organization and responsibility in education', in *Implications for Education of Prospective Changes in Society*, 1967, p. 263.

18. H. M. Bricknell 'Local organization and administration of education', in *Implications for Education of Prospective Changes in Society*, 1967, p. 235.

19. A. S. Miller, *Private Government and the Constitution*, Center for the Study of Democratic Institutions, Santa Barbara, Calif., 1959.

20. J. E. Allen, 'State vs. Federal power', in *Challenge and Change in American Education* (Ed. Seymour E. Harris), McCutchan, Berkeley, 1965, p. 41.

21. J. B. Conant, *Shaping Educational Policy*, McGraw-Hill, New York, 1964, p. 31.

22. J. B. Conant, *The Education of American Teachers*, McGraw-Hill, New York, 1963, p. 10.

23. J. B. Conant, in *Challenge and Changes in American Education*, 1965, p. 191.

24. J. Clark Davis, Supplementary statement in *Planning and Effecting Needed Changes in Education*, An Eight-State Project, Denver, Colo., 1967, p. 36.

25. R. F. McPhee, 'Planning and effecting needed changes in local school systems' in *Planning and Effecting Needed Changes in Education*, 1967, p. 190.

26. J. D. Koerner, *The Miseducation of American Teachers*, Penguin Books, London, 1965, p. 23.

27. J. B. Conant, in *Challenge and Changes in American Education*, 1965.

28. J. I. Goodlad, in *State Committee on Public Education in California*, 1967.

29. Center for Coordinated Education, *The Nurture of Teacher Growth*, University of California at Santa Barbara, Calif., May, 1966.

30. American Council on Education, *The Improvement of Teacher Education*, Report by the Commission on Teacher Education, Washington, D.C., 1946, p. 270.

31. *Encyclopedia for Educational Research*, Macmillan, New York, 3rd Ed., 1960, p. 565.

32. U.S. Senate, *Commission on Industrial Relations*, Senate Document No. 415, U.S. G.P.O., 1916.

33. U.S. House of Representatives, *Hearings before the Select Committee to Investigate Tax Exempt Foundations and Comparable Organizations*, 82nd Session, U.S. G.P.O., 1953.

34.   E. V. Hollis, 'Foundations' in *Encyclopedia for Educational Research*, Macmillan, New York, 3rd Ed., 1958, p. 569.

35.   American Association of School Administrators' Committee on Foundations, *Private Philanthropy and Public Purposes*, American Association of School Administrators, 1201 16th St., N.W., Washington 6, D.C., 1963, p. 6.

36.   E. J. Meade, Jr., *Foundations, Schools and the Public Good*, Address given to the 43rd Annual School Administrator's Conference, Pennsylvania State University, 1965..(mimeographed).

37.   P. Schrag, 'Kids, computers and corporations', *Education in America*, supplement to *Saturday Review*, New York, May 1967, p. 80.

38.   P. Schrag, in *Private Philanthropy and Public Purposes*, 1963. p. 80.

39.   J. L. Peyser, 'The educational consultant and commercially produced instructional media', *School and Society*, 2293, Summer 1967, p. 301.

40.   R. J. Long, 'The changing role of the public school teacher as a contributor to the educational journals', *Bulletin of the National Association of Secondary School Principals*, Sept. 1962, pp. 76-77.

41.   J. L. Peyser, op. cit. (37).

42.   R. F. McPhee, op. cit, (25) p. 184.

43.   J. Featherstone, 'Teaching children to think', *The New Republic*, Sept. 9, 1967.

Conclusion

One of the most damning indictments of schools is that made recently by the American, John Holt.[1] How many of these charges may be applied fairly to us?

> (i) 'We adults destroy most of the intellectual and creative capacity of children by the things we do to them, or make them do.[2]
>
> (ii) 'We destroy the disinterested (I do not mean uninterested) love of learning in children, which is so strong when they are small, by encouraging and compelling them to work for petty and contempt-ible rewards — gold stars, or papers marked 100 and tacked to the wall, or A's on report cards, or honour rolls.'[3]
>
> (iii) 'In many ways we break down children's convictions that things make sense, or their hope that things may prove to make sense. We do it, first of all, by breaking up life into arbitrary and disconnected hunks of subject matter .... Furthermore we continually confront them with what is senseless, ambiguous, and contradictory.'[4]
>
> (iv) 'We encourage children to act stupidly, not only by scaring and confusing them, but by boring them, by filling up their days with dull, repetitive tasks that make little or no claim on their attention or demands on their intelligence. Our hearts leap for joy at the sight of a roomful of children all slogging away at some imposed task.[5]
>
> (v) 'We adults are not often honest with children, least of all in school. We tell them not what to think, but what we feel they ought to think; or what other people feel or tell us they ought to think. Pressure groups find it easy to weed out of our classrooms, texts, and libraries whatever facts, truths, and ideas they happen to find unpleasant or inconvenient.[6]

And to what extent does either of his two judgments about the primary schools of the future conform to our own?

> (i) 'Since we can't know what knowledge will be most needed in the future, it is senseless to try to teach it in advance. Instead we should

201

try to turn out people who love learning so much and learn so well
that they will be able to learn whatever needs to be learned.[7]

(ii) 'The alternative — I can see no other — is to have schools and
classrooms in which each child in his own way can satisfy his
curiosity, develop his abilities and talents, pursue his interests, and
from the adults and older children around him get a glimpse of the
great variety and richness of life.[8]

Innovation in primary education is likely to be unspectacular — in spite of
some of the unusual investigations in progress involving modern technology —
and to be measured in ordinary human terms such as increased understanding
and heightened appreciation. Old objectives, inadequately realized, will come
closer to attainment as new knowledge and more effective materials are put at
the service of the teacher and administrator. Professor Goodlad,[9] in a recent
forecast of the most important tasks facing American Schools in the next few
years, and for many generations to come, claims that these are:

'... the daily practice and demonstration of those qualities of
compassion, sensitivity, sound judgment, flexibility, adaptability,
humility, self-renewal, and many more that we have long claimed to
be seeking in the human products of education.'

'In effect,' he claims, 'this task is to infuse the means of education with the
values hitherto espoused in defining the ends.'

It seems that the innovations we should seek in primary education are
familiar enough; but for us to be successful in achieving them revolutionary new
approaches are necessary.

REFERENCES

1. J. Holt, *How Children Fail*, Delta Books, New York, 1965.
2. *Ibid.*, p. 167.
3. *Ibid.*, p. 168.
4. *Ibid.*, p. 169.
5. *Ibid.*, p. 169.
6. *Ibid.*, p. 171.
7. *Ibid.*, p. 177.
8. *Ibid.*, p. 180.
9. J. I. Goodlad, 'The educational program to 1980 and beyond', in *Implications for
    Education of Prospective Changes in Society*, (Ed. E. L. Morphet and C. O. Ryan), An
    Eight-State Project, Denver, Colo., 1967, p. 47.

AUTHOR INDEX

SUBJECT INDEX